stonewall kitchen
harvest

stonewall kitchen

harvest

celebrating the bounty of the seasons

Jim Stott, Jonathan King, and Kathy Gunst

photographs by Jeff Kauck and Jim Stott

Clarkson Potter/Publishers
new york

Published by Clarkson Potter/Publishers, New York, New York
Member of the Crown Publishing Group, a division of Random House, Inc.
www.crownpublishing.com

CLARKSON N. POTTER is a trademark and POTTER and colophon are registered trademarks of Random House, Inc.

Printed in Japan

Design by Jane Treuhaft

Library of Congress Cataloging-in-Publication Data
Stott, Jim.
Stonewall Kitchen harvest : celebrating the bounty of the seasons / Jim Stott, Jonathan King, and Kathy Gunst; photography by Jeff Kauck and Jim Stott.
Includes bibliographical references.
1. Cookery, American—New England style. 2. Stonewall Kitchen (Store) I. King, Jonathan. II. Gunst, Kathy. III. Stonewall Kitchen (Store) IV. Title.
TX715.2.N48K56   2004
641.5974—dc22   2004007454

ISBN 1-4000-5077-4

10 9 8 7 6 5 4 3 2 1

First Edition

acknowledgments

Many thanks to Deborah Krasner, our agent, who worked overtime on this project. She has been a great friend and expert professional throughout the process. We appreciate all her guidance, talent, and tenacity in seeing this project through.

Heartfelt thanks to Roy Finamore for signing on this book in the first place. And to Adina Steiman for taking it under her wing and providing such energy, enthusiasm, wisdom, and great editing.

Many thanks to Jeff Kauck for the inspired photography. To William Smith for the gorgeous food styling. Thanks to Tara Rehak, photo-shoot producer, Andrea Kuhn, prop stylist, Jeanne Rondeau, assistant stylist, and Sara Littlefield and Michele Cole, assistant food stylists, for all their hard work during the photo shoot. Thanks also to Cynthia Maranhas for all her hard work at organizing the shoot. Seldom have any of us had such fun on a photo shoot.

Special thanks from Kathy:

Deep thanks to Jonathan King and Jim Stott for asking me to become involved in this wonderful project. It has been a true pleasure to work with you both. I am so inspired by your creativity and energy.

Special thanks to Jessica Thomson, who interned with me during the writing of this book. She provided so many good ideas and such wild enthusiasm that it was infectious. I couldn't have done it without you, Jess.

And finally to my family: John, thank you for always being there for me with your words of wisdom and encouragement. Thanks to Maya for her ideas, editing, and love. And to Emma for all her creative ideas, enthusiasm, and brilliant food styling tips. I love you all.

—K.G.

Special thanks from Jonathan and Jim:

Heartfelt thanks to our coauthor Kathy Gunst, whose expertise and incredible talent are reflected in the sensational recipes she provided for this book. Kathy, your skill in the kitchen, joy, and passion for everything related to food were contagious and motivated us all. Thanks to our customers for being the inspiration for this book. For twelve years we have been supported and encouraged by all of you to continue to grow Stonewall Kitchen and to branch it out into endeavors such as *Harvest*. This book truly is for you. We hope you enjoy it.

To the dedicated staff of Stonewall Kitchen we offer our humble and deep thanks. From the production staff to the retail associates and everyone in between, it takes each and every one of you to bring our products into our customers' homes. Without your hard work, it just wouldn't happen and we want to acknowledge and express our sincerest appreciation.

Finally, to both our families for all their support.

—J.K. and J.S.

contents

introduction

If you've ever snipped fresh rosemary leaves
from a plant growing on your windowsill, you know the pleasure of the harvest. You feel the tender leaves between your fingers, and inhale the plant's earthy, licorice essence. You have a sense of anticipation, knowing that the needle-shaped, dark green leaves will transform your salad, your pasta sauce, or your roast leg of lamb into a dish that tastes vibrantly alive and fresh.

If you've ever picked an apple from a tree, or a blueberry from a bush, or squatted down on the moist ground to pluck a strawberry off the vine, you know the pleasure of the harvest. Fruit, still warm and freshly picked, drips with juice. It holds the promise of the sun, of warm pies and sweet jelly. It tastes like summer in your mouth.

If you've ever caught a fish—stood by the water, rod and reel in hand, listening to the lapping of waves, feeling the solitude, and then felt the tug at the end of the line, the excitement of knowing you've caught your dinner, you know the pleasure of the harvest. You show off your catch, clean it, and fry it up in a sizzling pan over a hot fire. These simple, satisfying acts are a reminder of the special connection that is still available to all of us as we seek out food that is truly fresh.

This book is dedicated to the idea that freshly harvested food—whether from the land or the sea—is the very best food

you can eat, and that, with a bit of effort, it is accessible to virtually everyone. It's just common sense that ingredients picked locally and in season taste better and are more satisfying than food that is harvested unripe, wrapped in plastic, and shipped thousands of miles from the place it was grown.

You may be an apartment dweller and have only a single pot of herbs on your one sunny windowsill, and access to a nearby farmers market. You may plant a garden in a small suburban plot that swells with fresh vegetables, herbs, and flowers each summer. Or you may live way out in the countryside, with a big garden that supplies most of your family's needs. It doesn't matter where you live; the joys of the harvest are always within reach.

This is not a new concept, but it is too easily forgotten. We have come to expect tomatoes in December and strawberries during a snowstorm in February. We thumb through cookbooks and think, Sure I'll make a blueberry tart in March. Why not? Berries are always available. Though we live in a world where food is shipped between continents and across time zones, defying the very notion of seasons, the truth remains: Food is meant to be eaten when it's fresh and *in season*.

The recipes you'll find in this book are, for the most part, simple ones—dishes that pay respect to the seasons and the purity of taste found in freshly harvested food. Some of the recipe titles may sound sophisticated, but once you take a good look at them, you'll see that the instructions are not difficult to follow. For example, Roasted Miso-Glazed Salmon with Asparagus and Balsamic-Glazed Cipolline Onions (page 134) sounds like something you'd find in a trendy, upscale restaurant. But take a closer look: You lightly steam asparagus. Rub a salmon fillet with fresh ginger and miso paste. Sprinkle balsamic vinegar on small onions and put them in the oven. Then roast the whole dish for 15 minutes while you set the table. Difficult? No, and it can all be done ahead of time. A tribute to the harvest in less than 30 minutes, a magnificent dish that pays homage to the abundance and beauty of spring asparagus, fresh salmon, and sweet onions.

The format of this book is somewhat unusual. Instead of organizing recipes into traditional chapters on soups, appetizers, main courses, and desserts, we decided to structure the book to honor the variety of harvests through the year.

From the Garden focuses on fresh herbs, spring greens, summer lettuces, and the wide variety of crops we find at the peak of the harvest and the height of the heat—beans, tomatoes, eggplant, peppers, corn, fennel, summer squash, and much more. Many of these ingredients are foods you're probably familiar with. But you will also learn about some unique vegetables, such as ramps, which are wild leeks that only appear in the spring in some parts of the country, and fiddlehead ferns, another spring delicacy found in parts of the Northeast.

From the Sea focuses on the world of seafood and shellfish, a harvest that has special meaning for us in our home state of Maine. In addition to popular favorites like swordfish, clams, and fillet of sole, we offer recipes for regional specialties—Florida stone crab, soft-shell crabs from Maryland, and, of course, Maine lobster. We'll also introduce you to American caviar, a virtually unknown treasure.

If you shy away from cooking fish and seafood because someone has you convinced that it's messy and difficult, this chapter will quickly change your mind. When you're dealing with freshly harvested seafood, simplicity is the key. Recipes such as Pan-Fried Whole Trout with Cornmeal Crust and Lemon Butter (page 129), the World's Best Fried Clams (page 91), Mussel Chowder (page 96), and Grilled Marinated Fish Kebobs (page 120) will convince you that cooking fish is not only easy, but thoroughly satisfying.

From the Root Cellar describes the world of winter foods—all the ingredients that we grow in summer and fall, and keep in a cool, dark spot to feed us over the winter. Very few homes actually have a traditional root cellar anymore, but the practice of storing food during the winter continues. If you dry garden herbs, or put up jars of homemade tomato sauce or jam, or even if you just have a bin in your kitchen filled with onions or potatoes, you understand the idea of an old-fashioned root cellar.

Potatoes, onions, and root vegetables like carrots, beets, turnips, parsnips, and rutabagas will keep for several months if stored under the right conditions—a dark, cool place that is close to 50 degrees. In this chapter you will learn about the world of winter and cold-weather vegetables and the transformative act of taking what are essentially unglamorous vegetables and turning them into something sublime.

Our Potato Galettes Stuffed with Greens and Gruyère (page 158) come to mind. In this dish, the humble potato is transformed into two oversized potato pancakes, which are stuffed with winter greens and grated Gruyère cheese and then baked to form an outrageously flavorful potato pie. Another dish, Beet Napoleons (page 147), is one of those show-off creations that looks like it took all day to make. Beets are roasted, thinly sliced, and then stacked into a "tower" with an herb-flavored goat cheese filling. These dishes will convince you that winter foods can be every bit as exciting as those found in other seasons.

Fruits of the Earth celebrates the wonderful variety of fresh fruit available in this country—everything from apples, pears, and grapes to berries, figs, stone fruits, and citrus. You'll learn about less common varieties—blood oranges, Fuyu persimmons, pomegranates, and Meyer lemons—and find new ideas for some of your old favorites. When you try Roast Leg of Lamb with Fresh Figs and Shallots (page 220) or Roast Pork with an Apple-Herb Stuffing and Cider-Applesauce (page 216), you'll discover that fresh fruit makes as much sense in a main dish as it does in pies, tarts, jams, jellies, and desserts.

Our hope is that this book will inspire you to find harvests in your area, seek out locally grown ingredients, and eat and cook according to the seasons. Let the recipes on these pages be your guide to easy, accessible meals that make the most of the ingredients you bring into your kitchen.

Here's to discovering the joys of *Harvest*.

—Jonathan King, Jim Stott, and Kathy Gunst

from the
garden

appetizers

Corn Fritters with Herb Butter • 18

Spanish Tomato Toast • 21

Cheese and Herb Crepes • 22

soups

Lemon, Saffron, and Orzo Soup with Roasted Vegetables • 24

English Pea and Lettuce Soup with Chive Cream • 26

Vietnamese-Style Asparagus Soup with Vermicelli Noodles and Spicy Peanut Paste • 28

salads

Raw Asian-Style Asparagus and Soybean Salad • 30

Mediterranean-Style Orzo Salad with Corn • 31

Heirloom Tomato Salad with Caramelized Onions and Goat Cheese • 33

Ultimate Summer Garden Salad • 34

Warm Spring Artichoke Salad with Fava Beans • 36

Bistro-Style Frisée Salad with Spring Ramps • 40

Zucchini Salad with Mint and Lemon • 42

main courses

Grilled Marinated Chicken with Herbs • 44

Rack of Lamb with Garlic-Herb Crust and Roasted Tomatoes • 45

Lamb Chops with Rosemary-Chive Butter • 46

Grilled Steak with Garden Salsa and Warm Tortillas • 48

Rib Eye Steaks with Smothered Fennel • 50

Penne with Sweet Sausage, Roasted Tomato Sauce, and Arugula • 53

Summer Tomato, Basil, and Niçoise Olive Pizza • 54

Grilled Italian Vegetable and Prosciutto Sandwich • 56

Asparagus and Morel Risotto • 58

side dishes

Asparagus Bundles Wrapped in Prosciutto with Garlic Butter • 61

Creamy Basil Risotto • 62

Steamed Artichokes with Green Vinaigrette • 63

Stuffed Artichokes • 64

Roasted Summer Beans with Soy-Ginger-Lemongrass Glaze • 66

Pan-Fried Tomato Slices • 67

Stuffed Tomatoes Provençal • 68

Sautéed Ramps • 70

Italian-Style Broccoli Spears with Garlic • 71

Sautéed Fiddlehead Ferns with Spring Garlic • 72

Stuffed Zucchini Blossoms • 74

sauces

Chive Puree • 77

Roasted Tomato Sauce • 78

A Trio of Pestos: Lemon Thyme–Pistachio, Cilantro-Cashew, and Mint and Toasted Pine Nut • 80

in maine,
winter lasts too long. Ask anyone.

Come April, when most of the country celebrates the arrival of spring, we often still have a blanket of icy snow stubbornly clinging to the garden. But as soon as there's a thaw, we're out there tilling the soil and working fresh compost into the warming earth. We plant radishes and early lettuce, spinach, and if we're feeling optimistic, peas. And we wait. The days grow longer and warmer and we desperately search for a sign of green. And then, there it is: a blade of grass no longer brown, a new leaf budding on a tree, an asparagus stalk just beginning to shoot through the ground.

Before we know it, we're outside planting an overly ambitious garden. Vegetables, herbs, and edible flowers paint the landscape. The first tomato is a cause for celebration. We bite into it without any embellishment—as if it was an apple—and let the sweet red juice drip down our chin and the refreshing savory essence fill our soul. And then, after a long summer growing season, the corn is suddenly higher than our heads, and we go out to the fields and strip off the husk and the silky insides to expose a streaked white and yellow beauty of an ear. We take a bite from the raw corn, right there, out in the middle of nowhere, with no one watching. One simple bite makes us wonder how anything in the world can be so naturally sweet and savory and perfect all at the same time.

corn fritters with herb butter

see photograph on page 15

makes about ten to twelve 2$^1/_2$- to 3-inch fritters; serves 4

It's hard to believe that one could ever grow tired of eating freshly harvested corn on the cob. But the truth is, we sometimes crave the sweetness of fresh corn in more sophisticated dishes. Here fresh corn is stripped from the cob, mixed into a quick batter, and made into small, savory fritters, which are served with a simple Herb Butter (page 272). You can also omit the herbs and herb butter, add 1 tablespoon of sugar to the batter, and serve the fritters for breakfast, accompanied by a pitcher of warm maple syrup.

1$^1/_2$ cups fresh corn kernels, cut off the cob
   (see opposite)
1 large egg, whisked
$^1/_2$ cup all-purpose flour
$^1/_2$ teaspoon baking powder
$^1/_3$ cup half-and-half
Salt and freshly ground black pepper
   to taste

1 tablespoon chopped fresh parsley
1 tablespoon chopped fresh basil
1 tablespoon chopped fresh chives
1 tablespoon unsalted butter, melted,
   plus extra for frying
Vegetable or olive oil for frying
$^1/_2$ cup Herb Butter (page 272)

Put the corn kernels in a large bowl. Add the egg and mix well. Stir in the flour, baking powder, half-and-half, salt, pepper, parsley, basil, and chives. Add 1 tablespoon of the melted butter and beat well. The batter will be chunky, but should be uniform.

   Heat a large skillet or griddle over medium-high heat. Add the remaining melted butter (about 1$^1/_2$ teaspoons to start) and 1$^1/_2$ teaspoons of the oil and allow them to get hot, about 1 to 2 minutes. Add heaping tablespoons of the corn batter to the pan and cook the fritters for 2 minutes. Using a spatula, gently flip the fritters and cook another 2 to 3 minutes on the other side, or until golden brown. Repeat with the remaining batter, adding more butter and oil to the pan as needed. Serve hot with the herb butter.

cutting corn off the cob

Eating corn straight from the cob is one of the wonders of summer. But we also like to cut the kernels off the cob and use them to make muffins, bread, salads, sautés, soups, and stews.

The basic method for removing corn kernels from the cob is simple: Shuck the corn, removing the silky strands that line the inside of the husk. Hold the cob upright on a flat working surface. Use a large, sharp knife to cut down the side of the cob, in a kind of sawing motion, to remove the kernels from one side of the cob. Turn the cob and repeat until all the kernels have been removed, being careful not to cut into the cob. Use the corn kernels as soon as possible.

An average ear of corn will yield about $1/2$ to $3/4$ cup of kernels.

spanish tomato toast

serves 3 to 6

In small bars throughout Spain, thick slices of crusty bread are smothered with fruity local olive oil, topped with slices of sweet, juicy, ripe tomato, and grilled until the tomato just begins to soften. The toast is served with tiny cups of strong coffee. It's a great way to start the day on a hot summer morning when ripe tomatoes are plentiful. You can also serve tomato toast for lunch, accompanied by a green salad, or as an hors d'oeuvre or first course.

6 slices bread, such as a baguette or ciabatta, about ¼ to ½ inch thick
3 tablespoons extra virgin olive oil

1 large, very ripe tomato, thinly sliced
Salt and freshly ground black pepper

Preheat the broiler.

Place the bread slices on a broiler pan or cookie sheet. Drizzle with half the oil and place under the broiler for about 1 minute, or until the toast just begins to turn golden brown. Flip the bread over and place a slice or two of tomato on top, season with salt and pepper, and drizzle the remaining oil on top. Broil for 1 or 2 minutes more, until the toast begins to turn golden brown and the tomato is just softening. Serve right away.

harvest variations

- In many Spanish *tapas* bars the tomatoes are grated, rather than sliced, to create a juicy topping. Try grating the tomatoes using the large holes of a cheese grater, and then spread the gratings onto the bread.
- Tuck a fresh basil leaf under each slice of tomato.
- Spread the bread with olive puree or tapenade before adding the tomato.
- Cut the toasts into small squares and top each with a piece of anchovy fillet for hors d'oeuvres.
- Top the tomato with very thin slices of cooked Spanish or Italian sausage.
- Sprinkle 1 tablespoon of crumbled goat cheese, feta, or blue cheese on top of the tomato toasts and broil until melted and bubbling.

cheese and herb crepes

makes about 12 crepes; serves 6

Serve these savory crepes with salads, roast chicken or meat, or as a first course accompanied by the Herb Butter on page 272.

Don't be discouraged if the first crepe sticks to the bottom of the skillet; the first crepe almost never comes out well. A tip for flipping crepes: In order to keep the cheese from sticking to the bottom of the pan, slide a thin, flat, flexible spatula under the crepe periodically as it cooks, moving it from one side to the other to keep the crepe loosened.

The batter needs to sit for at least 30 minutes and up to 6 hours before cooking, so be sure to plan accordingly.

1 cup milk, whole or 2%
3 large eggs
1 cup all-purpose flour
2 tablespoons unsalted butter, melted
1/2 cup packed grated cheddar, or your favorite hard grating cheese
1 tablespoon chopped fresh thyme, or 1/2 teaspoon dried

1 tablespoon chopped fresh rosemary, or 1/2 teaspoon dried and crumbled
1/4 teaspoon salt
Freshly ground black pepper to taste
Vegetable oil for greasing the pan
Herb Butter (page 272)

Combine the milk, 1/4 cup of water, and the eggs in a large bowl and blend with a hand-held mixer for about 1 minute. Sift the flour on top and gently mix it into the batter. Add the melted butter and mix briefly on high. Fold in the cheese, herbs, salt, and pepper. Let the crepe batter sit for at least 30 minutes, and up to 6 hours, covered, in the refrigerator.

Very lightly grease a heavy 8-inch skillet or crepe pan over low heat. (The best way to grease the pan is with a pastry brush so there is only a light coating.) Add about 1/4 cup of batter to the hot pan, immediately swirling the batter around the bottom of the pan so it creates a thin, even "pancake." Cook the crepe for about 45 seconds, loosening with a thin, flexible spatula. Gently flip the crepe and cook for another 45 seconds. Use the spatula to loosen the crepe and transfer to a plate. Repeat to use up all the batter. (You can make the crepes about 1 hour ahead of time, layer them on a plate, and keep them warm in a low, 250°F. oven, or simply reheat them, one at a time, in the crepe pan just before serving.) Serve folded in half or rolled into a cigar shape, topped with a touch of the herb butter.

lemon, saffron, and orzo soup with roasted vegetables

serves 4 to 6

The recipe for this thick, soothing soup comes from Laura Brennan, the talented chef-owner of Caffè Umbra in Boston's South End. Brennan makes the soup with spinach, asparagus, and mushrooms, but we've tried it with several different vegetables and they all produce amazing results. You can try red pepper, chopped tomato, leeks, zucchini, or any thinly sliced, freshly harvested garden vegetable. Peeling celery may seem odd, but if you remove the outer layer, the celery will be much less fibrous.

for the vegetables
1 large red onion, Vidalia onion, or leek (white part only), very thinly sliced
2 tablespoons olive oil
½ teaspoon salt
Freshly ground black pepper to taste
3 large portobello mushrooms, or 6 shiitake or crimini mushrooms, stemmed and thinly sliced
1 tablespoon chopped fresh thyme
½ pound asparagus, ends trimmed, peeled, and cut on the diagonal into 1½-inch pieces (see page 30)

for the soup
6 cups chicken broth, preferably homemade (page 269), or low-sodium canned

Salt and freshly ground black pepper to taste
Pinch of saffron (optional)
2 garlic cloves, very thinly sliced
¾ cup orzo, tubettini, or other tiny soup pasta
2 celery ribs, peeled and thinly sliced on the diagonal
2 large eggs
2 tablespoons fresh lemon juice or fresh Meyer lemon juice (see page 262)
3 tablespoons grated Parmesan cheese

About 1 cup baby spinach leaves, arugula, or any other green (optional)

Preheat the oven to 450°F.

To roast the vegetables: In a large roasting pan, toss the onion with 1 tablespoon of the oil, season with salt and pepper, and roast for 5 minutes. Mix in the mushrooms, thyme, asparagus, remaining tablespoon of oil; roast for another 15 minutes.

Meanwhile, to make the soup: Heat the chicken broth in a medium pot over medium heat. Season with salt and pepper. Add the saffron and garlic and simmer for 2 minutes. Add the pasta and cook for 4 minutes. Add the celery and cook for another 4 minutes; cover and remove from the heat.

Beat the eggs in a small bowl. Add the lemon juice, Parmesan cheese, $\frac{1}{8}$ teaspoon salt, and generous grinding of pepper. Add a ladleful of the hot broth to the egg mixture and whisk. Place the pot back on the heat and add the egg mixture to the soup, whisking constantly to avoid scrambling the eggs. Do not let the soup boil; it should be at a low simmer. Taste for seasoning and add salt and pepper as needed.

For each serving, spoon half a bowlful of broth into a large soup bowl (making sure to evenly distribute the pasta). Place a generous portion of the roasted vegetables in the middle of the bowl and scatter a few spinach leaves around the edges. The heat of the soup will "melt" the leaves into the hot soup.

english pea and lettuce soup with chive cream

serves 8

This soup uses the entire pea, pod and all. The pods are used to make a delicate pea broth, though if you're short on time, 5 to 6 cups of vegetable or chicken broth (page 269) can be substituted. The peas are sautéed with tender lettuce leaves and then pureed with the broth to make a vibrant green soup that tastes like the embodiment of the word "fresh." A chive-infused cream is swirled into the soup just before it's served.

for the pea broth
2 pounds English or shelling peas,
    pods rinsed
1 large onion, coarsely chopped
6 black peppercorns
1/8 teaspoon sea salt, or to taste
1 cup chopped fresh chives

for the soup
1 tablespoon unsalted butter
1 teaspoon olive oil
1 medium onion, chopped

1/2 cup chopped fresh chives
1/8 teaspoon sea salt, or to taste
Generous grinding of black pepper
3 cups packed tender green lettuce leaves,
    such as butterhead, buttercrunch, or leaf
    lettuce (see pages 38–39 for more on
    lettuces and greens)

for the chive cream
3/4 cup heavy cream
1/2 cup packed chopped chives

To make the broth: Shell the peas and set aside. You should have about 2 cups of shelled peas. Put the pea pods in a large pot and cover with 8 cups of cold water. Add the onion, peppercorns, salt, and chives and bring to a boil over high heat. Reduce the heat to low and cover; simmer for 10 minutes. Remove the cover and simmer for another 15 to 20 minutes, or until the broth is a pale green color and flavorful. Season to taste. Strain the broth, discarding the solids; you should have 5 to 6 cups of broth. (The broth can be made a day ahead of time. Cover and refrigerate until ready to cook the soup.)

    To make the soup: In a large soup pot, heat the butter and oil over low heat. Add the onion, chives, salt, and pepper and cook, stirring frequently, for 10 minutes. Stir in the lettuce and cook for 2 minutes, or until just wilted. Add the peas and cook for 1 minute. Add 5 cups of the pea broth and simmer, covered, for 10 minutes. Remove from the heat and let cool slightly.

    Meanwhile, make the chive cream: In a small saucepan, combine the cream and chives. Place over low heat for 5 minutes to infuse the cream with the chive flavor. Remove from the heat and let cool.

Working in batches, puree the soup and return it to the soup pot. Taste for seasoning and add more salt or pepper if needed. Heat the soup on low until just simmering. Puree the cream and chives until the cream is the subtlest pale green color. Pour into a small saucepan and heat over very low heat until almost simmering. To serve, swirl 1 or 2 teaspoons of hot cream into each bowl of soup.

relax . . . and shell some peas

You meditate. You do yoga. You go to exercise class to unwind. Here's a new idea for relaxation: Grab a comfortable chair, sit down at a table (preferably one outside with a lovely view), and discover the forgotten art of shelling freshly harvested peas. Observe the beauty of the peas cloaked within their green crisp shells. Some are so perfectly round, while others are oval. They may be the size of a good pearl, or tiny like a green dot. Shelling is a slow, methodical task, one that allows you to talk and listen to good music, or simply listen to your inner voice and enjoy the sounds of nature: the chirping of birds, the high-pitched peeping of baby frogs, or the rush of wind in the trees. Smell early summer. Think of the fragrant, fresh pea flavors to come.

vietnamese-style asparagus soup with vermicelli noodles and spicy peanut paste

serves 4

The inspiration for this soup comes from the Vietnamese dish *pho*, a steaming bowl of broth piled with fresh vegetables and noodles and a dab of chile paste. Here, a spicy peanut butter–based paste slowly releases its pungent flavors and thickens the broth. All the elements for the soup can be prepared ahead of time, and the final dish can be put together at the very last minute. The Asian ingredients are available in Asian markets and specialty shops.

for the soup and noodles

6 cups chicken broth, homemade (page 269), or low-sodium canned

3 to 4 ounces vermicelli noodles (also called angel hair rice noodles)

for the spicy peanut paste

3 tablespoons grated or minced fresh ginger

About $1/2$ teaspoon Chinese chile paste, or hot pepper sauce

$1/2$ cup chunky all-natural peanut butter

About $1/2$ teaspoon hot chile oil or hot sesame oil, or hot pepper sauce

2 tablespoons soy sauce

1 teaspoon Asian sesame oil

3 scallions (white and green parts), finely chopped

for the vegetables

1 tablespoon peanut or vegetable oil

1 teaspoon Asian sesame oil

$1/2$ cup julienned fresh ginger

5 scallions (white and green parts), cut on the diagonal into $1 1/2$-inch pieces

2 pounds asparagus, ends trimmed, peeled (see page 30), and cut on the diagonal into $1 1/2$-inch pieces

$1/2$ cup fresh cilantro leaves, very coarsely chopped

1 cup mung bean sprouts

In a medium or large pot, heat the chicken broth over medium heat until it comes to a rolling boil. Reduce the heat to low and keep hot.

Meanwhile, bring a large pot of water to boil. Add the vermicelli noodles and cook for about 2 to 3 minutes, or until the noodles are tender to the bite. Immediately drain the noodles in a colander held under very cold running water to stop the cooking. Put the noodles in a large bowl of ice cold water and separate them to avoid clumping. Set aside.

To make the paste: In a small bowl, mix the ginger, chile paste, and peanut butter, stirring until smooth. Add the chile oil, soy sauce, sesame oil, and scallions; stir until smooth. The paste will be quite thick and should have a good, spicy kick.

In a large skillet or a wok, heat the peanut oil and sesame oil over medium-high heat. Add the julienned ginger and cook, stirring frequently, for 2 minutes. Add the scallions and cook for about 20 seconds. Add the asparagus and cook for 3 minutes, stirring frequently. The vegetables should still have a bite to them and should not be completely cooked or soft; set aside. (The recipe can be made ahead of time up to this point.)

To serve, drain the noodles well and make sure the chicken broth is very hot. Ladle about $1\frac{1}{2}$ cups of the simmering broth into a large soup bowl. Add about $\frac{1}{2}$ cup of noodles and 1 cup of the sautéed asparagus-ginger mixture. Sprinkle the top of the soup with some of the cilantro and bean sprouts and add a heaping table-spoon of the spicy peanut paste. Serve the remaining cilantro, sprouts, and spicy peanut paste on the side and let everyone add as much as he or she likes.

raw asian-style asparagus and soybean salad

serves 4 as a side dish

When asparagus are truly fresh, they are so tender you can eat them raw and really take advantage of their full, earthy flavors. Here they are cut into thin pieces, tossed with an Asian-flavored dressing, and sprinkled with lightly steamed edamame (soybeans). This light, refreshing salad should be made no more than 2 hours before serving or it will lose its crisp texture. Edamame are available fresh or frozen in Asian markets. If you can't find them, substitute fresh peas or fava beans.

1 bunch (about 1 pound) asparagus, green, white, or purple, ends trimmed, and peeled (see below)
2 tablespoons Asian sesame oil
2 teaspoons soy sauce

2 teaspoons rice wine vinegar or white wine vinegar
1 teaspoon grated or finely chopped fresh ginger
Fresh ground black pepper to taste
1 cup edamame (do not defrost if frozen)

Cut the asparagus in half lengthwise and then slice on the diagonal into $1\frac{1}{2}$-inch pieces. Put the asparagus in a medium bowl and add the sesame oil, soy sauce, vinegar, and ginger, season with pepper, and gently toss. Let sit for about 15 minutes, but no more than 2 hours.

Meanwhile, bring a medium pot of water to a boil over high heat. Cook the edamame beans (in their shells) for 2 minutes. Drain and place under cold running water to stop the cooking. Drain again. Pop the beans out of the pods; you should have about $\frac{1}{2}$ cup.

Place the marinated asparagus on a serving platter and sprinkle the steamed soybeans on top. Serve at room temperature or chilled.

to peel or not to peel?

It may seem like a fussy, unnecessary step, but peeling the lower half of an asparagus stalk can make the difference between a good asparagus spear and a really buttery, tender, unforgettable one.

Begin by trimming asparagus: Hold the stalk in your hand and snap off the stem end. It will naturally snap off where it starts to get tough, at the lower 1 to $1\frac{1}{2}$ inches of the stalk. You can also use a small, sharp knife. Once trimmed, use a vegetable peeler to peel the lower half of the asparagus; continue until you see a hint of pale, whitish color. The contrast between the green asparagus tip and the peeled, whitish lower half is striking. Another advantage: peeling gives the stalks a uniform thickness, so they cook evenly.

mediterranean-style orzo salad with corn

serves 6

This simple orzo dish, chock-full of sweet, fresh summer corn, peppers, and herbs, is thoroughly appealing as a light lunch or picnic dish. Look for corn on the cob that has been picked that day. The corn husks should still have a greenish tint and not appear dry or shriveled.

1 pound orzo pasta

2 cups fresh corn kernels, cut off the cob (see page 19)

1 cup finely chopped sweet red pepper

1 cup black Kalamata olives, pitted and cut in half

¼ cup thinly sliced scallions (white and green parts)

2 tablespoons shredded or coarsely chopped regular or opal (purple) basil

2 tablespoons drained capers

¼ cup packed fresh parsley leaves, finely chopped

¼ cup olive oil

3 tablespoons wine vinegar

⅛ teaspoon salt, or to taste

Fresh ground black pepper to taste

Fresh nasturtium or other edible flowers (optional)

Bring a large pot of lightly salted water to a boil. Add the orzo and cook, stirring occasionally, for about 7 minutes, or until tender. Drain well and transfer to a large serving bowl.

Add the corn, red pepper, olives, and scallions and toss well. Add the basil, capers, parsley, oil, vinegar, salt, and pepper and gently toss. (The salad can be made about 2 hours ahead of time. Cover and refrigerate until 30 minutes before serving.) Decorate the salad with the edible flowers right before serving.

heirloom tomatoes
a world of color, texture, and flavor

Like your grandmother's china, heirloom tomatoes have been passed down from generation to generation. For decades many heirloom varieties went virtually unnoticed, known only to a handful of botanists and garden enthusiasts. Now these colorful and flavorful tomatoes are being reintroduced to gardens, markets, and restaurants as alternatives to the standard, often bland-tasting tomatoes that most of us are familiar with. There are literally dozens of heirloom varieties, with names that read like characters from exotic novels: Anna Russian, Black Krim, Momo Taro, Cherokee Purple, Brandywine, Flame, Zebra, Vogliotti, and Mountain Princess.

What exactly is an heirloom tomato? There are several characteristics that distinguish an heirloom from a modern beefsteak or cherry tomato. True heirloom varieties date back to at least 1940, and are open-pollinated. This means the tomatoes have not been crossbred or hybridized like most modern varieties. Each generation of heirloom tomato plant is virtually identical to the previous generation. Heirloom tomatoes are prized for their vast range of colors, flavors, textures, and shapes. They can be round, oblong, heart shaped, or oval and usually have skin and flesh blushed with purple, green, pink, maroon, black, white, or, of course, red. Bite into an heirloom tomato and your mouth is filled with intense flavors: sweet, sour, citrus, tart, spicy, fruity, and more.

The following guide introduces you to some of the most popular heirloom varieties:

anna russian tomatoes are dark pink and heart shaped, with an unusually sweet flavor and a velvety texture.

black krim is a dark, purplish-black, round variety. Juicy and very sweet, it is unusually popular for a black tomato.

cherokee purple is said to have been cultivated originally by the Cherokee nation. This dark purple tomato with green stripes is large, juicy, and full of sweet flavor.

green zebra, a small, round tomato with dark green stripes, has a sweet, spicy, lemony flavor.

mister stripey (tigerella) is a smallish fruit with red and yellow stripes.

momo taro (peach boy), a Japanese variety, is a dark pink tomato with a sweet, tart flavor and a meaty texture.

red brandywine is a large, bright red tomato with a sweet flavor and creamy texture.

striped german is distinguished by its red and orange stripes and sweet, rich flavor.

heirloom tomato salad with caramelized onions and goat cheese

serves 4

Look for a variety of heirloom tomatoes at your local farmers market. The balance of sweet and sour tomatoes mixed with earthy, sweet caramelized onions, creamy goat cheese, and pungent greens makes this an unforgettable summer salad.

for the onions
1 tablespoon olive oil
2 large or 4 small onions, very thinly sliced (about 2 cups)
Salt and freshly ground black pepper to taste
1 tablespoon sugar

for the vinaigrette
½ teaspoon mustard
Salt and freshly ground black pepper to taste
2 tablespoons red or white wine vinegar

5 tablespoons olive oil
1 tablespoon minced fresh chives (optional)

for the salad
2 medium, ripe heirloom tomatoes, each cut into 8 wedges
1 cup golden pear tomatoes or cherry tomatoes, cut in half if large
1 cup red pear tomatoes or cherry tomatoes, cut in half if large
1 cup packed mesclun greens
2 ounces soft goat cheese, crumbled

To caramelize the onions: Heat the oil in a large, heavy skillet over very low heat. Add the onions, salt, and pepper and stir well. Cover and cook for 12 minutes, stirring occasionally until a light golden brown. Remove the cover, sprinkle the sugar over the onions, and sauté for another 5 minutes, uncovered, stirring frequently until a rich golden brown color. Let cool completely. (The onions can be made 24 hours ahead of time; cover and refrigerate until ready to use.)

To make the dressing: Mix the mustard, salt, and pepper in a small bowl. Add the vinegar, and whisk in the oil to make a smooth vinaigrette. Mix in the chives, if using, and set aside.

To assemble the salad: Arrange the tomatoes on a platter, alternating colors and shapes. Place the greens on top of, and in between, the tomatoes. Place the onions on top of the greens and sprinkle with the goat cheese. Spoon the vinaigrette on top.

ultimate summer garden salad

serves 4 to 6

There are few dishes more satisfying than a well-made green salad at the height of the growing season—using fresh-picked garden lettuces, lush herbs, and a simple, herb-filled vinaigrette.

for the vinaigrette

1 tablespoon Dijon mustard

Salt and freshly ground black pepper
    to taste

1 1/2 tablespoons chopped fresh herbs (any
    combination of chives, basil, tarragon,
    rosemary, sage, mint, and thyme)

1 scallion (white and green parts), very
    thinly sliced

2 tablespoons red wine vinegar

6 tablespoons extra virgin olive oil

for the salad

1 large head lettuce, or about 8 loosely
    packed cups assorted greens (try
    different types like buttercrunch, frisée,
    mâche, arugula, radicchio, romaine,
    and leaf lettuce)

About 1 cup whole herb leaves (basil, sage,
    tarragon, thyme, mint, or coriander)

1/2 cup edible flowers (nasturtium, pansies,
    or sage flowers; optional)

1 cup Garlic Croûtes (page 271; optional)

To make the vinaigrette: In the bottom of a large salad bowl, mix the mustard, salt, and pepper together. Stir in the chopped herbs and the scallion, and then the vinegar. Whisk in the oil slowly. Taste for seasoning.

To make the salad: Put the lettuce and herbs in a bowl of cold water to rinse and clean, then thoroughly dry them using a salad spinner or clean tea towels. Using your hands, gently tear the greens and the herbs into small pieces and scatter them on top of the vinaigrette. Add the edible flowers on top of the lettuce. Arrange the croûtes around the salad if desired, and toss just before serving.

harvest variations

* Mash 1/4 cup of crumbled blue cheese into the vinaigrette for a blue cheese vinaigrette, or sprinkle the cheese on top of the salad.
* Add 1 tablespoon of heavy cream or milk for a creamy, thick vinaigrette.
* Mix in 1 tablespoon of fresh grated or finely chopped ginger and 1 1/2 teaspoons of soy sauce for an Asian-flavored vinaigrette.
* For a creamy, tangy vinaigrette, add 1 tablespoon of buttermilk.
* Puree the vinaigrette in a blender with 1/2 ripe avocado for a thick avocado vinaigrette.
* Puree the vinaigrette in a blender with 1/4 cup of basil leaves and 1/4 cup of plain, low-fat yogurt for a Green Goddess type of dressing.

favorite salad combinations

The simplest, very best salad is an assortment of freshly harvested greens (a good combination of textures, colors, and flavors) very gently tossed with really good wine vinegar, extra virgin olive oil, sea salt, and freshly ground black pepper. If you're looking for some more unusual options, try these:

• Buttercrunch or any other tender, buttery greens tossed with candied or toasted nuts (see page 215, a sprinkling of crumbled blue cheese, crunchy croutons, and a simple, herb-infused vinaigrette

• Mâche, watercress, and arugula (all sharp, peppery greens) tossed with slivers of raw or roasted pear, shavings of Parmesan cheese, and a classic vinaigrette

• Arugula, radicchio, and endive tossed with fresh lemon juice, fruity olive oil, and a good grinding of pepper

• Frisée and Oak Leaf salad with prosciutto strips, fresh fig wedges, and toasted pumpkin seeds

• Whole, long, crunchy leaves of romaine topped with anchovy fillets, croutons, grated or shaved strips of Parmesan cheese, and a vinaigrette flavored with mashed anchovies

• Watercress with tangerine sections and paper-thin slices of red onion

• Belgian endive leaves scattered with blue cheese crumbles and caramelized walnuts (see page 215)

• Crunchy romaine leaves with chopped hard-boiled eggs, crumbled bits of bacon, steamed green beans, pitted black Niçoise olives, and an herb-flavored vinaigrette

• Radicchio with wedges of fresh figs, crumbled goat cheese, and a balsamic vinegar–and–olive oil dressing

• Paper-thin slices of fennel mixed with a collection of greens (frisée, radicchio, and/or mâche) and topped with paper-thin shavings of Parmesan cheese, pitted black olives, and a lemony vinaigrette

• Mesclun salad topped with sautéed shallots and mushrooms (see pages 178–179 for more on mushroom varieties) and toasted walnuts in a walnut oil–and–white wine vinegar dressing

• Mesclun salad tossed with a yogurt-based, creamy vinaigrette and sprinkled with fresh herbs and pumpkin or sesame seeds

• An herb salad made with parsley as the base, tossed with whole or coarsely chopped leaves of tarragon, chive, sage, sorrel, basil, borage, and an assortment of edible flowers and dressed with an olive oil vinaigrette

• Red and white cabbage, coarsely shredded, with shredded carrots, apples, and chopped nuts in a creamy dressing

warm spring artichoke salad with fava beans

serves 4 to 6

This simple Tuscan-style salad pays homage to two of the best spring ingredients—fresh artichokes and fava beans. Also called broad beans or *fave* in Italian, fava beans resemble lima beans but have a more delicate, buttery flavor and texture. Throughout Italy, fava beans are traditionally eaten steamed or, if very young and fresh, tossed raw into salads or sautés.

Unless you grow your own (or have a farmer friend who grows them for you), chances are good you won't find fava beans fresh enough to eat raw. Preparing fava beans involves a bit of work, but their appealing texture and unique bean flavor make it well worth the effort. Serve the salad hot or at room temperature, and be sure to find a good, crusty Italian bread (ciabatta would be ideal) and sweet butter to serve with it.

Juice of 2 large lemons

3 large artichokes

2 pounds fresh fava beans, or English peas, shelled (about 2 cups)

3 tablespoons olive oil, preferably a good, fruity Italian variety

¾ cup finely chopped onion, preferably a sweet onion like a Vidalia

Salt and freshly ground black pepper to taste

1 lemon, cut into thin slices or small cubes for garnish

Fill a large bowl with cold water. Add 2 tablespoons of the lemon juice.

Using a large, sharp knife, trim about ½ inch off the artichoke stems. Cut off 1 inch from the top of the artichoke and remove all the sharp pointy tops of the leaves. Using your hands, pull off at least two layers of the outer dark green leaves until you reach a layer of more tender, pale green leaves. Cut the artichokes in half. Using your hands and a small, sharp spoon, remove the purplish leaves and fuzzy center core of the choke, and any hairy growth that covers the heart. Cut each half into 4 wedges, so that you have a total of 8 wedges from each artichoke—a total of 24 wedges. Place the artichokes in the lemon water to prevent them from turning brown while you prepare the rest of the salad.

Fill another bowl with ice water. Add about 2 inches of water to a large pot and bring to a boil over high heat. Add the fava beans, cover, and cook for 3 minutes. Drain the beans and immediately transfer to the ice water to stop them from cooking further. Drain again. Remove the fava beans from their outer skin and set aside. (If using peas, simply steam them for 3 minutes and drain.)

Fill the same large pot with 3 inches of fresh water and bring to a boil over high heat. Add the artichoke wedges, cover, and simmer for about 8 to 10 minutes, or until a leaf pulled off from the outside of the choke comes off easily. Drain and refresh under cold running water to stop the cooking process; drain again. (The salad can be made up to this point 1 to 2 hours ahead of time. Cover and refrigerate the artichokes and favas until ready to proceed.)

Heat 1½ tablespoons of the oil in a large skillet over medium-low heat. Add the onions and sauté, stirring frequently, for 4 minutes. Season with salt and pepper. Add the artichokes and sauté, stirring frequently, for 4 minutes. Add the fava beans and cook for another 3 to 4 minutes, or until the vegetables are tender and just beginning to turn a very light golden brown. Place the vegetables on a large serving platter and gently toss with the remaining 1½ tablespoons of oil and the remaining lemon juice, and season with salt and pepper. Garnish with lemon and serve hot or at room temperature.

a guide to greens

Like fine wine, the best salads have a balance of flavors and aromas. A mixture of sweet, tender leaves and juicy, crispy greens, balanced by bitter and peppery lettuces, is ideal. When you see a new type of green, be sure to try it. Mix and match. Experiment.

Always look for the freshest greens you can find, with crisp leaves and dry stems. Many pre-packaged mesclun and salad mixes can turn bad in the bag, so inspect carefully before buying. Look for greens that are tightly layered, with vibrant color.

Here are some of the most popular types of greens:

arugula (rocket or roquette), with its peppery bite and sweet undertones, has become a superstar with chefs and home cooks. Many people find it positively spicy. The long, dark green, arrow-shaped leaves grow in the spring and early summer, and there is a late-fall crop as well. New to the market is micro arugula, with tiny (two- to three-inch) leaves that look like sprouts but pack a big flavor. Wild arugula, also called sylvetta, has a stronger, sharper flavor than cultivated arugula and can be found in specialty shops. Use arugula raw in salads and sandwiches; add it to soups,

stews, and pasta sauces (where it wilts and adds a peppery flavor, see page 53); or cook it in stir-fries and sauces.

bibb lettuce is exceptionally sweet, with a tender texture and a subtle, light crunch.

black seeded simpson is a spring variety of crinkly, light green lettuce that adds a juicy quality to salads.

buttercrunch or **butterhead** may sound like candy, but it's actually a dark green, fan-shaped lettuce that is exceptionally tender, with no bitterness.

chicory is a curly, bitter-tasting relative of endive that adds a crunchy texture to salads and sautés.

dandelion greens have an intensely bitter, earthy flavor. Their jagged-edged leaves can be found wild or cultivated.

endive: There are essentially two types of endive: *Belgian endive* can be tricky to grow because the crunchy, open, cigar-shaped white leaves must be cultivated in darkness. Belgian endive adds a great crunch and slightly peppery flavor to salads; its leaves also make wonderful natural containers for dips and spreads (see page 89). *Curly endive,* sometimes mistakenly referred to as chicory, is a loose head of lacy, green-rimmed leaves, which curl at the tips and have a pleasing, mildly bitter flavor.

escarole, an Italian favorite with a broad, green leaf and a mild flavor, is usually cooked before eating: braised, slowly sautéed, or added to soups.

frisée, a member of the chicory family, is pale yellow-green with frizzy, curly leaves. It is a key element in mesclun mixtures, and it's the classic green used in bistro salads (see page 40). It has a mild, bitter flavor.

green oak leaf is a tender, crispy, dark green lettuce that adds great flavor and texture to a mixed salad. Its fan-shaped leaves have no bitterness. Also look for Red Oak Leaf.

iceberg, the classic American lettuce leaf, has been overlooked recently due to the ever-expanding, new world of exotic greens. But iceberg adds a juicy crunch to salads. It can also be used as a natural wrap for sautéed vegetables and poultry.

komatsuna provides a delicate mustard flavor. The broad, rich, tender green leaves look a bit like baby spinach, and are full of flavor and calcium.

lollo rosso and **red lollo rosso** have frilly green leaves, often tinged with dark red edges, which add great texture, color, and sweet flavor to salad.

mâche (lamb's lettuce or **corn salad),** cultivated for centuries, has long been popular throughout Europe. Mâche is prized for its sweet, nutty flavor and soft, buttery texture. A favorite in mesclun salad mixes (see below), it is loaded with vitamins A and C, and iron.

mesclun is the new iceberg. Suddenly, this salad mixture is sold in every supermarket and served at the most ordinary of restaurants. Ideally, a mesclun mix combines a variety of greens, balancing color, shape, texture, and flavor. Most include arugula, mustard greens, spicy curly cress, a romaine-type lettuce, and tender butterhead lettuce.

mustard greens are robust and spicy and come in a wide assortment of colors, shapes, and flavors. They have spiny leaves with ruffled edges. Mustard greens grow best in cooler weather (some varieties are even winter hardy). They are delicious braised or sautéed. *Mizuna* is one of our favorite varieties.

purslane adds a zesty, sour, and tangy flavor and great crunch to salads. It is supposed to have the highest known plant source of omega-3 fatty acids, and it's quite high in vitamin C. You may have tasted purslane in a traditional Greek salad.

radicchio (red chicory) is a variety of Italian lettuce that adds a wonderfully bitter flavor to salads. Its colors range from pale pink to deep maroon.

romaine offers long, crisp, light green leaves with a subtly sweet flavor. It is the classic lettuce used in Caesar salads.

sorrel is frequently found growing wild in lawns or fields in spring and again in late fall. It adds a tart, intensely lemony flavor to salads, soups, and stir-fries—a little bit goes a long way.

spinach can be found in several shapes and sizes, but good spinach is always tender and delicate, with an almost melt-in-your-mouth, buttery quality. Baby spinach, increasingly popular and available in American markets, is worth seeking out because of its exceptionally tender leaves and its tendency not to absorb water the way regular, full-grown spinach leaves do.

tatsoi is a green Asian leaf with a mild flavor that makes an interesting addition to salads and stir-fries.

watercress has a deliciously peppery bite and adds a crunchy texture and lively flavor to salads, sandwiches (think tea sandwiches), and soups (many Asian soups add watercress at the very end of cooking). It is also delicious stir-fried with a touch of chopped ginger. Watercress has an edible stem and rounded green leaves. It likes a wet environment, and grows near cool ponds and stream banks, as well as in the garden.

bistro-style frisée salad with spring ramps

A classic bistro-style salad, made with frisée lettuce, bacon, poached eggs, and a little something special—ramps, or wild leeks. When you cut into the poached egg, the yolk coats the salad with its delicious, creamy richness. For more information about ramps, see page 70.

You can prepare the ramps, bacon, and vinaigrette several hours ahead of time and poach the eggs just before serving. If ramps are not available, substitute scallions or small, tender leeks.

for the salad

1 head frisée lettuce, or about 4 cups
　　mesclun greens or a mix of bitter greens
　　(see pages 38–39 for more on greens)
5 slices thick, country-style bacon
12 ramps, green leaves removed, bulb and
　　pink stem sliced in half lengthwise, or
　　scallions (white and green parts)
Freshly ground black pepper to taste

for the vinaigrette

¼ cup extra virgin olive oil
2 tablespoons fresh lemon juice
1 tablespoon minced fresh chives (optional)
Salt and freshly ground black pepper
　　to taste

for the poached eggs

4 large eggs

To make the salad: Clean the greens thoroughly and dry with paper towels or a clean tea towel and set aside.

In a large skillet, fry the bacon over medium heat until cooked and crisp, about 3 to 4 minutes on each side, depending on the thickness. Remove the bacon and drain on paper towels. Drain all but 1 teaspoon of the bacon fat from the skillet.

Heat the skillet with the remaining bacon fat over medium-low heat. Add the ramps and cook, stirring frequently, for about 6 minutes, or until the ramps are soft and golden. Remove from the heat and set aside.

To make the vinaigrette: Whisk together all the ingredients in a small bowl, and set aside. (The recipe can be made several hours ahead of time up to this point; cover and refrigerate the vinaigrette, cooked ramps, the greens, and the bacon.)

To poach the eggs and serve the salad: Fill a large saucepan or pot with cold water and bring to a boil on high heat. Meanwhile, place the greens in a large salad bowl and toss with the vinaigrette. (You can serve the salad in the bowl or divide it among four salad plates.) Place the ramps on top of the greens, and crumble the bacon into 1-inch pieces and scatter on top of the ramps.

Reduce the heat under the saucepan to medium. Carefully crack the eggs over the water, one at a time, and cook for 2 minutes. (This will give you poached eggs with a soft, slightly runny yolk; if you want firmer yolks, cook for another minute or two.) Using a slotted spoon, remove the eggs and drain for a few seconds before gently placing them on top of the salad. Add a grinding of black pepper and serve the salad immediately.

zucchini salad with mint and lemon

serves 4 as a salad or side dish

Serve this salad at room temperature to best appreciate the full flavors of the grilled zucchini mixed with olive oil, lemon juice, and fresh chopped mint. Warm pita bread is a delicious accompaniment.

When making this recipe, look for small (about 6 inches long), tender zucchini. Avoid using enormous overgrown zucchini in this dish; they are best saved for breads, cakes, and relish.

5 small, tender zucchini (about 1 1/2 pounds)
About 3 tablespoons olive oil
3 garlic cloves, chopped
Salt and freshly ground black pepper
   to taste

4 1/2 tablespoons coarsely chopped fresh
   mint
Juice of 1 large lemon

Trim the ends off the zucchini. Cut each zucchini into long, thin slices by halving it lengthwise, placing the flat end of each half down on a cutting board, and then cutting it lengthwise into long, 1/3-inch-thick strips.

In a large skillet, heat half the oil over medium heat until almost smoking. Add half the zucchini in one layer (try not to overlap them) and scatter half the garlic on top. Cook for about 4 minutes and then, using tongs, flip over the zucchini. Sprinkle with salt, pepper, and 1 1/2 tablespoons of the mint. Cook on the other side for 3 to 4 minutes, depending on the thickness of the slices. Each slice should be

golden brown and just tender, but not falling apart. Transfer the zucchini to a large serving platter. Repeat with the remaining zucchini, oil, and garlic, and add another 1 1/2 tablespoons of the mint. Place the next batch of cooked zucchini on the serving platter, overlapping the slices if need be. Sprinkle the top of the zucchini with the lemon juice, salt, pepper, and remaining 1 1/2 tablespoons of the mint. Serve at room temperature.

zucchini

the orphan of the vegetable world

It's August and gardens are overflowing with produce. You drive down country roads and there, like homeless kittens, are baskets sitting by the side of the road pleading with those who pass by to take them away. "Free," "Take Me Please," "Zucchini," exclaim the handwritten signs. Why does such a delicious, versatile vegetable have to go begging?

Zucchini starts off life as a delicate little creature. First gorgeous yellow-orange blossoms appear, full of possibility (see pages 74–75 for a zucchini blossom recipe). Suddenly, a baby zucchini, pencil-thin, and about three inches long, hangs from the vine, calling out to be picked. You decide to wait a day; you'll cook it for dinner tomorrow night. But when you return to the plant a mere twenty-four hours later, the delicate, pencil-like squash has transformed into an overgrown, fat baseball bat of a thing. Zucchini, more than any other vegetable we know, needs to be picked when young and small because, like all good children, it grows much too fast. When it is large and overgrown, its flesh dries out and becomes fibrous, yielding a vegetable that is distinctly unappealing.

Zucchini is infinitely versatile—it can be used to make everything from soups and appetizers to cakes and breads. It's an important part of the cuisines of the Mediterranean, where zucchini are stuffed with fresh herbs and vegetables, fried into delicate fritters, and used to flavor egg dishes, pasta sauces, meat, and fish.

Dozens of heirloom varieties have been introduced (and reintroduced) in recent years, which means you can now grow and buy zucchini in myriad sizes, shapes, and colors—traditional green or yellow, black, purple, striped, white-skinned, pear-shaped, speckled, and round.

We love to grill sliced zucchini that has been marinated in a simple mixture of olive oil, lemon juice, and chopped garlic. For summer breakfasts we slice them thin and sauté them with eggs. Stuffed with herbs and vegetables, they become one of the great dishes of summer. Cooked with leeks and chives, and then pureed with vegetable or chicken stock, they make a delicate, spectacular green soup that can be served hot or chilled. We use the overgrown ones to make zucchini muffins, spreading the top with cream cheese and chopped crystallized ginger, and we often grate them into cake and quick bread batters to add moistness and flavor.

What do we do with those huge baseball bat–sized zucchini? Feed them to the chickens, of course.

grilled marinated chicken with herbs

serves 4

This simple, herb-filled marinade helps the chicken stay juicy when grilled. Plan on letting the chicken sit in the marinade for at least 2 and up to 24 hours. Cover and refrigerate until ready to grill. Serve with Lemon Thyme–Pistachio Pesto (page 80) or Cilantro-Cashew Pesto (page 81).

One 3½- pound chicken, cut into 8 pieces
½ cup dry white wine
3 garlic cloves, finely chopped
1½ tablespoons soy sauce

1 tablespoon chopped fresh thyme
1 tablespoon chopped fresh basil
Dash of Tabasco, or other hot pepper sauce

Put the chicken in a plastic bag or bowl and add the wine, garlic, soy sauce, thyme, basil, and hot pepper sauce. Coat the pieces well on all sides. Cover and refrigerate for at least 2 hours.

Preheat a charcoal or gas grill until red-hot, about 350 to 400°F. Remove the chicken from the marinade and pour the marinade into a small saucepan. Boil for 2 minutes.

Place the chicken pieces on the hot grill, cover, and cook for 8 minutes. Brush with the cooked marinade. Gently flip the chicken over and cook for another 10 to 15 minutes, or until the juices run clear, and not pink, when pierced with a small, sharp knife. The cooking time will depend on the heat of the grill. Continue basting the chicken every 5 minutes. The chicken can also be broiled. Place the chicken on a broiler pan or oven-proof skillet and broil on high for about 8 minutes on each side, brushing with the marinade once or twice. Remove and serve hot or at room temperature.

rack of lamb with garlic-herb crust and roasted tomatoes

serves 4

We can remember when rack of lamb was a cut of meat you had to order from a specialty butcher, a treat for a very special occasion. Now we can buy an exceptional rack of lamb in the local supermarket for the same price as a few lamb chops.

Here, a garlic-herb-breadcrumb mixture is pressed onto the top of the meat and then several ripe tomatoes are tucked right under the lamb bones. The meat cooks and drips juices onto the tomatoes, creating some of the most flavorful roasted tomatoes you've ever tasted. Best of all, this elegant dish can be made in less than an hour. Serve with Roasted Potatoes with Sea Salt and Herbs (page 191) or Whipped Potatoes (page 187).

3 garlic cloves, minced

2 tablespoons minced fresh rosemary, or 2 teaspoons dried, crushed

1½ tablespoons minced fresh thyme, or 1½ teaspoons dried

Salt and freshly ground black pepper to taste

¼ cup olive oil

¼ cup homemade breadcrumbs (page 270) or dried

1 rack of lamb (about 1½ pounds, 8 chops)

4 ripe, medium tomatoes, cut in half crosswise

Preheat the oven to 450°F.

In a mortar or a wooden bowl, use a pestle or the back of a spoon to mash the garlic and half the rosemary and thyme with the salt and pepper until the garlic and herbs just begin to break down. Stir in the olive oil and breadcrumbs and mix until the mixture comes together.

Place the lamb in a medium-size roasting pan or a large ovenproof skillet. Press the breadcrumb mixture onto the top of the rack (the fatty side of the meat), and press down to help it adhere to the meat. Tuck as many tomatoes as you can fit under the lamb (so the bones are just resting on or over the tomatoes) and arrange any remaining tomatoes around the meat. Sprinkle the top of the exposed tomatoes with the remaining herbs, and season with salt and pepper.

Roast the lamb for 20 minutes. Reduce the temperature to 350°F. and roast until the internal temperature is 135°F. and the meat is medium-rare, about 35 to 40 minutes more. Remove the lamb from the oven and let sit several minutes before carving into chops.

lamb chops with rosemary-chive butter

A simple grilled lamb dish that is ideal for a warm summer or autumn evening. Marinate the lamb several hours ahead of time (or overnight) and then grill the chops at the last minute. You can also broil the chops if the weather's too cold for grilling. The sauce is made by reducing the marinade and simply adding a touch of butter and additional fresh herbs.

8 lamb chops, about 1 inch thick	3 garlic cloves, minced
1 cup dry red wine	1 1/2 tablespoons balsamic vinegar
1/4 cup minced fresh rosemary	Generous grinding of black pepper
3 tablespoons minced fresh chives	2 tablespoons unsalted butter, chilled

Put the lamb chops in a plastic bag or bowl and add the wine, half the rosemary and chives, the garlic, vinegar, and pepper and seal tightly. Refrigerate and marinate for at least 2 and up to 48 hours. The longer the meat marinates, the more tender and flavorful it will be.

Preheat a charcoal or gas grill until hot, about 350 to 400°F. Place the chops on the grill and cook for 7 to 8 minutes on each side, or until slightly pink in the middle (medium-rare).

Alternately, preheat the broiler. Place chops on a broiler pan and broil, one inch from the heat, for about 4 minutes on each side, or until slightly pink in the middle (medium-rare).

Meanwhile, strain the wine marinade into a small saucepan and boil over medium heat for about 5 minutes, or until reduced and somewhat thickened. Stir in the butter and the remaining rosemary and chives and cook for 2 minutes. Serve the chops hot, drizzled with the reduced wine sauce.

grilled steak with garden salsa and warm tortillas

serves 2 to 4

Grilled or pan-fried steak, served fajita-style with warm tortillas, fresh salsa, lime wedges, and cilantro makes a quick dinner or party dish. The simple salsa is at its best at the end of the growing season, when ripe tomatoes, sweet peppers, chile peppers, and onions are plentiful and at their peak. This dish is excellent served with grilled corn on the cob (see opposite).

for the steak
1 pound London broil or top round steak
1 garlic clove, chopped
¼ cup dry red wine
Freshly ground black pepper to taste

for the salsa
2 large ripe tomatoes, chopped
1 large sweet green pepper, chopped
1 tablespoon chopped fresh jalapeño
   pepper (seeds removed), or hot pepper
   sauce to taste

2 tablespoons chopped fresh cilantro
3 tablespoons fresh lime juice
Salt and freshly ground black pepper
   to taste

1 tablespoon olive oil (if pan-frying)
4 to 6 fresh flour or corn tortillas
1 cup sour cream
1 lime, cut into wedges
Sprigs of fresh cilantro

To marinate the steak: Put the meat in a casserole dish or a plastic bag, and cover with the garlic, wine, and pepper. Refrigerate, covered, for at least 30 minutes and up to several hours. The longer you let it marinate the more flavor the steak will absorb. When the steak has marinated, remove it from the dish and pour the marinade into a small saucepan. Boil the marinade for 2 minutes and set aside.

To make the salsa: Mix the tomatoes, peppers, cilantro, lime juice, salt, and pepper. (The salsa can be made up to 4 hours ahead of time; cover and refrigerate until ready to serve.)

To cook the steak: Preheat a charcoal or gas grill until hot, about 350 to 400°F. Grill the steak for about 4 minutes on each side, or until charred on the outside and medium-rare inside. Brush with the marinade during the last few minutes of cooking. Alternately, heat a large, heavy skillet over high heat. Add 1 tablespoon of oil. Add the steak and cook for 4 minutes. Gently flip the steak over and cook for another 3 minutes. Add the marinade from the pan and reduce it for 1 minute.

Remove the meat and sprinkle with salt. Let sit for 1 minute before thinly slicing on the bias. Heat the tortillas on the grill for about 30 seconds on each side, or wrap them in foil and place them in a 300°F. oven until warm.

To serve: Put out serving plates with all the ingredients—the thinly sliced steak, warm tortillas, salsa, sour cream, lime wedges, and cilantro sprigs—and let everyone assemble their own fajitas.

grilled summer corn

Corn season is so short and so good it's hard to think you'd ever grow tired of steamed corn on the cob. But this is a great alternative, particularly when grilling season is under way.

Here's the basic recipe: Shuck the corn, keeping the husks attached at the base end of the corn. Remove and discard the silks (the fine, stringy, filamentlike stuff between the corn and the husk) and push the husks back around the ears of corn. Put the corn in a bowl or pan and cover with cold water for about 15 minutes. Meanwhile, light a fire (wood, charcoal, or gas) until hot, about 350°F. Drain the corn (it's fine if there's still a bit of water clinging to the husks) and place on the hot fire. Grill, covered, for 3 minutes. Remove the cover, flip the corn over, and grill, uncovered, for another 3 to 5 minutes, depending on how well done you like your corn. Serve hot from the grill with Herb Butter (page 272), or wedges of lime and sea salt.

rib eye steaks with smothered fennel

serves 4

The sweet, anise flavor of fennel is a fabulous complement to pan-fried steaks—it turns simple, ordinary beef into something special. Serve this dish with baked potatoes, Whipped Potatoes (page 187), Parmesan Potato Gratin (page 188), Mashed Celery Root (page 184), or sautéed spinach or escarole.

3½ teaspoons olive oil

1 teaspoon unsalted butter

2 medium fennel bulbs, fronds and core removed, and bulbs cut into ¼-inch-thick rounds

Salt and freshly ground black pepper to taste

Two 1-pound rib eye steaks, about ½ inch thick, or four ½- to ¾-pound steaks

In a large skillet, heat 1½ teaspoons of the oil and the butter over low heat. Add the fennel, salt, and pepper and cook, stirring frequently, for 20 minutes. The fennel's texture should be soft, but with a slight bite. Remove from the pan and set aside, covered, to keep warm.

Heat 1 teaspoon of the oil in the same skillet over high heat. Add the remaining teaspoon of oil to another large, heavy skillet. Let the oil get hot for about 1 minute. Add 2 steaks (or 1 large steak) to each pan and season with salt and a generous grinding of coarsely ground black pepper. Cook for 4 minutes. Using tongs, gently flip the steaks over, season with salt and pepper, and cook for another 4 minutes for medium-rare. Let the meat sit on a platter for about 2 minutes before thinly slicing it on the bias. (If the fennel isn't hot, heat it in the skillet over medium heat for a few minutes.) Serve the steak topped with the fennel.

penne with sweet sausage, roasted tomato sauce, and arugula

serves 4

The combination of sweet, meaty sausage with roasted tomatoes and the bracing, pleasingly bitter bite of fresh arugula mixes beautifully with penne.

1 1/2 pounds sweet Italian-style sausage, cut into 1-inch pieces

1 tablespoon olive oil

1/4 cup coarsely chopped fresh basil (if fresh is not available, simply omit)

1/2 cup dry red wine

4 cups Roasted Tomato Sauce (see page 78), or your favorite tomato sauce

Salt and freshly ground black pepper to taste

1 pound penne pasta

3 cups packed fresh arugula

About 1/2 cup freshly grated Parmesan cheese

Rosemary sprigs for garnish (optional)

Put the sausage in a large skillet and pour 1 cup of cold water on top. Bring to a boil over high heat, reduce the heat to medium, and cook for about 12 to 15 minutes. (If the water has not evaporated, drain it from the pan.) Remove from the heat and add the oil to the pan (being careful to avoid splatter) and place over medium heat. Let the sausages brown for 1 or 2 minutes and then add the basil and cook for 30 seconds. Add the wine and simmer for 3 minutes. Add the tomato sauce, salt, and pepper. Reduce the heat to low and simmer for 15 minutes, stirring occasionally.

Meanwhile, bring a large pot of lightly salted water to boil. Add the penne, stir well, and cook for about 12 minutes, or until the pasta is just cooked, or *al dente*.

Add the arugula to the sauce about 5 minutes before the pasta is done, stirring well. It should wilt and just begin to get soft.

Before you drain the pasta, add 3 tablespoons of the pasta water to the sausage and tomato sauce and stir well. Drain the pasta and transfer to a large serving platter or bowl. Top with the hot sauce and toss well. Sprinkle with a few tablespoons of the grated cheese and serve the remaining cheese on the side. Garnish with the rosemary, if desired.

summer tomato, basil, and niçoise olive pizza

serves 6 to 8

A pizza to celebrate summer tomatoes, fresh basil, and salty black olives. This recipe makes enough topping for two 12-inch pizzas.

1 batch Cornmeal and White Flour Pizza Dough (page 276)

4 teaspoons fruity olive oil

6 tablespoons julienned fresh basil

1/2 cup plus 6 tablespoons freshly grated Parmesan cheese

6 medium-size ripe tomatoes, very thinly sliced

Salt and freshly ground black pepper to taste

1 cup pitted Niçoise or black olives, coarsely chopped

1 1/2 pounds fresh mozzarella cheese, very thinly sliced

Position racks in the middle of the oven. Preheat the oven to 425°F.

Roll out the pizza dough on a lightly floured board to form two 12-inch rounds. Place on two large cookie sheets. Using a pastry brush or the back of a spoon, brush 1 teaspoon of the oil over each pizza. Scatter 2 tablespoons of the basil on top of each pizza and sprinkle 3 tablespoons of Parmesan cheese on top of each. Arrange the tomatoes on the dough in a circular pattern, overlapping them slightly. Sprinkle lightly with salt and pepper and the remaining 2 tablespoons of basil. Scatter the olives over the tomatoes. Place the mozzarella slices in between and on top of the tomatoes (it doesn't matter—it all depends whether or not you like the cheese melted on top of, or alongside, the tomatoes), and sprinkle the top with the remaining 1/2 cup of Parmesan cheese. Drizzle the top of the pizza with the remaining 2 teaspoons of oil.

Bake for about 15 minutes, or until the edges of the pizza just begin to turn golden brown and the cheese is melted and bubbling. Switch the positions of the cookie sheets midway through the baking time if needed so that each pizza cooks evenly.

grilled italian vegetable and prosciutto sandwich

makes 4 hearty sandwiches

This dish transcends the word "sandwich." Thin strips of eggplant and zucchini and wedges of radicchio are grilled until charred and tender, layered on long slices of crusty bread, topped with prosciutto and fresh mozzarella, and then doused with fruity olive oil and sweet balsamic vinegar.

Serve these sandwiches on a hot summer day, since everything can be prepared ahead of time and the sandwiches can be assembled just before serving. Serve the sandwiches as is, or grill them outside on a charcoal or gas fire until the cheese just begins to melt.

for the grilled vegetables

1 medium-large eggplant (about 1 pound), ends trimmed, cut lengthwise into very thin slices

1/8 teaspoon salt, plus extra for seasoning

1 head radicchio (about 6 ounces), trimmed

1 medium zucchini, ends trimmed, cut lengthwise into very thin strips

1/4 cup fruity olive oil

Generous grinding of black pepper

for the vinaigrette

2 tablespoons olive oil

2 tablespoons balsamic vinegar

Pinch of salt, or to taste

A few grindings of black pepper

1 tablespoon fresh lemon juice

to assemble the sandwiches

1 large crusty loaf ciabatta, or a thick baguette or sourdough loaf (about 1 to 1 3/4 pounds)

1/2 pound fresh mozzarella, thinly sliced

1/2 pound imported prosciutto, very thinly sliced

Salt and freshly ground black pepper to taste

1 tablespoon fruity olive oil (if reheating)

To roast the vegetables: Put the eggplant slices in a large colander and sprinkle with the 1/8 teaspoon of salt. Let sit for 20 minutes. (The salt will leech out any bitter juices from the eggplant.)

Meanwhile, light a charcoal fire or heat a gas grill to 300 to 350°F.

Rinse the eggplant under cold running water to remove the salt and pat dry with paper towels or a tea towel. Separate the leaves of the radicchio, discarding any that are wilted or bruised.

Place the eggplant, zucchini, and radicchio in a bowl and gently toss with the olive oil, some salt, and the pepper.

When the fire is hot, grill the eggplant strips for 3 minutes on each side, for a total of 5 to 6 minutes, or until they are charred and tender. Grill the zucchini for 2 minutes on each side, or until charred and tender. Grill the radicchio for 1 minute on each side, or until wilted and *almost* soft. Place the grilled vegetables on a plate and set aside. (You can grill the vegetables several hours before serving. Cover and refrigerate. Bring to room temperature before assembling the sandwiches.)

To make the vinaigrette: In a small bowl, mix the oil, vinegar, salt, pepper, and lemon juice.

To assemble the sandwiches: Cut the bread crosswise into 4 equal pieces. Cut each piece of bread in half lengthwise to yield 8 slices. Using a pastry brush or a spoon, lightly spread the vinaigrette onto all 8 slices of bread. Divide the grilled vegetables among 4 slices of the bread. Top with equal portions of the cheese. Mound the prosciutto on top of the cheese and sprinkle lightly with salt and pepper. Top each piece of bread with another piece of bread to create a sandwich.

The sandwiches can be eaten as is, or, if you want to grill them (a step that is strongly suggested), relight the charcoal grill or heat the gas grill to around 300 to 350°F. Brush the outside of the sandwiches with the tablespoon of oil and grill for about 1½ minutes on each side, or until the bread is very lightly charred and the cheese is beginning to melt. Alternately, you can heat a large, heavy skillet, add some oil, and cook the sandwiches for about 1½ minutes on each side. You will need two skillets to cook all the sandwiches at the same time.

asparagus and morel risotto

serves 4 as a main course or 6 as a first course or side dish

Two spring favorites—wild morel mushrooms and freshly harvested asparagus—combine to create this creamy, bursting-with-flavor risotto. The risotto is hearty enough to serve as a main course, accompanied by a salad of tender greens. Begin your spring feast with the English Pea and Lettuce Soup with Chive Cream on page 26. Look for good risotto-quality rice. Arborio rice (from Italy) and Calasparra rice (from Spain) are both short-grained varieties that are prized for their ability to absorb liquid without overcooking or becoming sticky.

4 cups homemade chicken (page 269) or
    vegetable broth, or canned broth
1 tablespoon plus 1 teaspoon butter
2 teaspoons olive oil
1 medium onion, finely chopped
2 tablespoons minced fresh thyme
2 tablespoons minced fresh chives
Salt and freshly ground black pepper
    to taste
1/4 pound fresh asparagus, ends trimmed,
    peeled (see page 30), and cut on the
    diagonal into 1-inch pieces

6 ounces fresh morels, stems trimmed, caps
    left whole if very small or cut into thick
    slices if large, or another variety of wild
    or cultivated mushroom, thickly sliced
    (see pages 178–179 for more about
    wild mushrooms)
1 1/2 cups Arborio or Calasparra rice
1/4 cup dry white wine
2 tablespoons heavy cream (optional)
1 1/2 cups freshly grated Parmesan cheese

Pour the broth into a saucepan and warm over low heat.

In a medium saucepan, heat 1 tablespoon of the butter and 1 teaspoon of the oil over medium-low heat. Add the onion and cook, stirring occasionally, for about 5 minutes, or until pale gold and just tender. Add half the thyme and chives and a good dash of salt and pepper, and cook for just 10 seconds. Add the asparagus and a little more than half the morels and cook, stirring frequently, for 5 minutes. Add the rice and cook for about 2 minutes, stirring to coat each grain. Raise the heat to high and add the wine; simmer 1 minute. Reduce the heat to low and gradually add the warm stock, 1 cup at a time, stirring frequently. Do not add more stock until the rice has already absorbed the stock in the pan.

After you've added the fourth, and final, cup of stock, let the risotto simmer, stirring occasionally. Meanwhile, in a small skillet, heat the remaining teaspoon of butter and of oil over medium heat. Add the remaining morels, thyme, and chives and a generous dash of salt and pepper, and sauté, stirring occasionally, for 2 minutes. Raise the heat to high and add the cream, if using. Simmer for about 2 minutes, or until the cream is almost thick enough to coat a spoon. Add the sautéed mushroom mixture to the risotto and cook, stirring, until the rice has absorbed almost all the stock and is tender. Remove from the heat (the risotto should still be a bit moist and will continue to absorb the liquid) and taste for seasoning. Gently stir in 1 cup of the grated cheese and serve hot, with the remaining cheese on the side.

asparagus pointers

thick or thin?

Ultimately, the most desirable thickness of one asparagus stalk is really a matter of taste. Many chefs believe that thicker stalks contain more flavor than thinner ones. In fact, in many parts of Europe and Japan, there is a grading system assigned to asparagus that gives thicker stalks the highest marking.

white or green?

White and green asparagus are biologically identical. White asparagus keep their pale color by spending their life buried in sand, away from direct sunlight. But, according to Kay Rentschler, writing in the *New York Times,* white asparagus taste different: "With no chlorophyll, cooked white asparagus releases no green flavor notes. . . . In white asparagus subtle flavors preside, like a buttery sweetness or a mild mushroomy woodiness."

the best way to cook asparagus?

When you find freshly harvested asparagus, try them **raw.** They are tender and bursting with flavor; the Raw Asian-Style Asparagus and Soybean Salad on page 30 is a great example. **Roasting** is another great method for preparing fresh asparagus. Tightly wrap the asparagus in aluminum foil or place in a small roasting pan or ovenproof skillet and roast for about 20 minutes (depending on the thickness) in a preheated 400°F. oven, or until the asparagus are just tender, or *al dente.* They will continue to cook once you remove them from the oven, so you don't want to overcook them. Roasting intensifies the natural asparagus flavors, without leeching any vitamins. **Steaming** is the most common method for cooking asparagus, simple to do, and delicious, particularly when you're looking for a pure, uncomplicated flavor. Steam asparagus over an inch or two of boiling water until they are *just soft,* and not limp. Asparagus can also be **stir-fried,** or **sautéed,** alone or with a variety of other vegetables, herbs, and spices.

shopping for asparagus

When asparagus are freshly harvested, straight from the just-warmed spring or early summer earth, they are exceptionally fresh and tender and need very little attention. But after they sit around for a few days (and get shipped, often across the country, to your local market), they toughen up and can dry out. Always check the stem ends of the asparagus; they should be moist—never dry looking or shriveled. And the tips shouldn't look dry or appear to be unfurling.

asparagus bundles wrapped in prosciutto with garlic butter

serves 6

This is one of those dishes that looks as if it took hours to produce, but is actually quite simple—the whole thing can be made ahead of time and popped in the oven just before serving. This is an adaptation of a recipe from Kathy's book *Relax, Company's Coming!* These asparagus bundles make a wonderful first course (with crusty bread or breadsticks) or side dish to accompany meat, fish, poultry, or pasta.

1 to 1½ pounds asparagus (about 40 spears), ends trimmed, and peeled (see page 30)

About 8 thin slices imported prosciutto (about ¼ pound, including extra for great snacking)

2 tablespoons unsalted butter

1 tablespoon olive oil

3 garlic cloves, minced

Freshly ground black pepper to taste

¼ cup freshly grated Parmesan cheese

1 lemon, cut into wedges

Bring a large skillet of water to boil over high heat. Add the asparagus and cook, covered, for 2 minutes. Immediately drain and rinse under very cold running water until the asparagus are cold. Drain again.

Position a rack in the middle of the oven and preheat the oven to 400°F.

Gather 4 to 5 asparagus spears that are of about the same thickness and line them up; trim the ends so they are the same length. Place a strip of prosciutto on a clean work surface and fold it over lengthwise to make a long, thin strip. Arrange the asparagus bundle (the 4 to 5 spears) in the middle of the prosciutto and roll the meat around it so that it envelops the middle. Put the asparagus bundle in the bottom of a large, ovenproof skillet or a large gratin dish. Repeat with the remaining asparagus and prosciutto.

In a small skillet, heat the butter and oil over medium heat. Add the garlic and cook for 3 minutes, stirring frequently, until the garlic is soft but not brown. Remove from the heat and add the pepper.

Sprinkle the cheese over the asparagus spears and drizzle the butter over all the bundles. (The dish can be made several hours ahead of time up to this point; cover and refrigerate until ready to bake.)

Bake the asparagus for about 13 to 15 minutes; the cheese should be melted and the asparagus should be tender, but not soft. Serve hot with the lemon wedges on the side.

creamy basil risotto

serves 4 to 6

This risotto is long, slow cooking at its finest. Don't rush it—plan on being near the stove for a good half hour. Settle in with a friend for a relaxing 30 minutes of intoxicating aromas. The risotto makes an ideal accompaniment to any roasted or grilled foods and to Pancetta-Wrapped Scallops on page 108.

6 cups homemade chicken broth (page 269), or 4 cups canned broth mixed with 2 cups water
1 tablespoon olive oil
1 large shallot, finely chopped
²/₃ cup packed julienned fresh basil, plus several leaves for garnish
¼ cup packed finely chopped fresh parsley

Salt and freshly ground black pepper to taste
1 cup Arborio or Bomba rice, or any good short-grain risotto rice
½ cup dry white wine
1 cup packed freshly grated Parmesan cheese

Pour the homemade broth or canned broth and water into a saucepan and warm over low heat.

In a medium, heavy saucepan, heat the oil over a low flame. Add the chopped shallot and cook for 10 minutes, stirring frequently, until pale gold. Add the basil, parsley, salt, and pepper and cook for 1 minute. Add the rice, stirring to coat each grain, and cook for about 30 seconds. Add the wine and simmer. Stir frequently and let the rice absorb all the wine before adding about 1 cup of the hot broth. The idea is to add liquid, then stir and stir and stir until just about all the liquid has been absorbed, and then add additional warm liquid. By the time you add the sixth cup of broth the rice should be quite creamy and tender. Don't worry if the risotto seems loose—that's exactly what you want.

Remove from the heat and gently stir the cheese into the rice. Taste for seasoning and add more salt and pepper if needed. Serve hot with the basil leaves on top.

steamed artichokes with green vinaigrette

serves 4

Spring artichokes, steamed until buttery-tender, taste extraordinarily good when served with this thick vinaigrette. The recipe makes about $1/2$ cup of vinaigrette; it can easily be doubled to serve more. The artichokes can be enjoyed hot, room temperature, or chilled. The vinaigrette is also delicious drizzled over other classic spring vegetables like steamed asparagus, fava beans, or fiddlehead ferns.

4 large artichokes

for the green vinaigrette
$1\frac{1}{2}$ teaspoons Dijon-style mustard
Salt and freshly ground black pepper
   to taste

3 tablespoons fresh lemon juice
$5\frac{1}{2}$ tablespoons fruity olive oil
$2\frac{1}{2}$ tablespoons drained capers
3 scallions, thinly sliced
2 tablespoons julienned fresh basil leaves,
   or 2 tablespoons minced fresh parsley

To trim the artichokes: Cut about $1/2$ to 1 inch off the tops. Use a kitchen scissors or a small, sharp knife to trim any leaves that still have sharp points. Place the trimmed artichokes in a large pot of boiling water. Cover and cook over medium-high heat for 15 to 25 minutes, depending on the size and freshness, or until the leaves pull off easily. Use a slotted spoon to flip the artichokes over from side to side once or twice to make sure all the artichoke leaves are properly cooked and tender. Drain and let cool.

To make the vinaigrette: Mix the mustard with the salt and pepper in a medium bowl. Using a whisk or a fork, mix in the lemon juice and then the olive oil. Add the capers, scallions, and basil and stir well. (The vinaigrette can be made 2 hours ahead of time; cover and refrigerate until ready to serve. Bring to room temperature before serving.)

Arrange the artichokes, warm or at room temperature, on a large platter and place the bowl of vinaigrette in the center to serve.

stuffed artichokes

serves 4

One of the great harbingers of spring, fresh artichokes, with their multilayered leaves, are ideal for stuffing. Here they are stuffed and then steamed and can be served hot or at room temperature.

When choosing fresh artichokes, always look for bright green leaves that are tightly furled and crisp (not limp); avoid any leaves with blemishes. The artichoke should feel heavy in your hand, indicating freshness.

You can omit the anchovy in this recipe if you like, though once cooked, its flavor is very subtle.

4 large artichokes
3 1/2 tablespoons olive oil
1 small onion, finely chopped
3 garlic cloves, minced
2 anchovy fillets (optional)
3 tablespoons oil from the anchovy bottle
     or can (optional)
1/4 cup minced fresh Italian parsley

1/4 cup minced fresh basil
1/2 cup freshly grated Parmesan cheese
1 1/4 cups homemade breadcrumbs (page
     270), or 1 cup store-bought
Salt and freshly ground black pepper
     to taste
1 lemon, cut into wedges (optional)

To trim the artichokes, cut about 1/2 to 1 inch off the tops. Use kitchen scissors or a small, sharp knife to trim any leaves that still have sharp points. Trim the bottom of each artichoke so it sits flat on a work surface without tumbling over. Use your fingers to loosen and separate the leaves and create spaces between them.

To make the filling, heat 1 tablespoon of the olive oil in a small skillet over low heat. Add the onion and garlic and cook, stirring frequently, for 5 minutes, being careful not to let them brown or burn. Add the anchovy fillets and 1 tablespoon of the anchovy oil, if using, and cook for another 1 or 2 minutes, or until the anchovy fillets "melt" into the sauce.

In a large bowl, mix the parsley, basil, cheese, breadcrumbs, salt (go lightly if you are adding the salty anchovies), pepper, 1 tablespoon of the olive oil, and the cooked onion-garlic-anchovy mixture. Divide the filling among the 4 artichokes. Press some of the filling between each leaf and its neighbor, and press a good portion into the center of each leaf and push down.

Place the artichokes in a large pot (not too large, though; they should be snug inside the pot so they don't wobble around). In a separate pot or a teakettle, boil 3 cups of water. Pour the water into the pot, *around but not over* the artichokes. Drizzle the remaining 1 $\frac{1}{2}$ tablespoons of olive oil over the artichokes, directly on the filling. Place the pot over high heat and bring to a boil again. Reduce the heat to low, cover, and cook the artichokes for about 35 minutes, or until a leaf pulls off easily and is tender. Use tongs and wear an oven mitt (the artichokes will be very hot) to remove the artichokes from the pot. Place them on a serving platter and serve hot or at room temperature, surrounded by the lemon wedges.

roasted summer beans with soy-ginger-lemongrass glaze

serves 8

Fresh garden green beans take on a whole new exotic twist when they're tossed with ginger, soy sauce, and fresh lemongrass. The dish can be served hot from the oven, or at room temperature. This salad makes a great addition to a picnic, and goes exceptionally well with grilled fresh tuna.

Note: If you can't find fresh lemongrass at a specialty food store or Asian grocery, you can use 1 teaspoon of grated lemon zest and 2 tablespoons of fresh lemon juice instead.

1 pound green beans, trimmed
1 pound yellow wax beans, trimmed
¼ cup soy sauce or tamari

2 tablespoons minced fresh lemongrass
 (see Note)
1½ tablespoons chopped fresh ginger
1 teaspoon Asian sesame oil

Position a rack in the middle of the oven. Preheat the oven to 400°F.

Put the green and yellow wax beans in a medium roasting pan or ovenproof skillet. Add the soy, lemongrass, ginger, and sesame oil, and toss well. Roast for 15 to 22 minutes, depending on the thickness of the beans, or until just cooked and still slightly crunchy, tossing the beans once or twice during the roasting time. Remove from the oven, transfer to a serving platter, and serve hot or at room temperature.

pan-fried tomato slices

serves 6 to 8

This is a favorite treat for a weekend breakfast. The tomatoes are cut into thick slices, coated in panko flakes or seasoned flour, and fried in a hot pan with olive oil and a touch of butter. Panko flakes are flat Japanese breadcrumbs, which are coarser than American dried breadcrunbs. They're found in the Asian section of many supermarkets and also in Asian food markets. They add an especially crunchy texture.

The tomatoes can be coated and seasoned several hours ahead of time and fried just before serving. This dish is particularly beautiful if you use a variety of heirloom tomatoes. Serve the tomatoes with fried eggs, toast, and home fries.

1 cup panko flakes, breadcrumbs, or flour
1½ teaspoons chopped fresh thyme
1 tablespoon chopped fresh chives (optional)
Salt and freshly ground black pepper to taste

5 medium, ripe summer tomatoes, sliced crosswise into ½-inch-thick rounds
2 tablespoons butter
2 tablespoons olive oil
Whole chives or nasturtium flowers or other edible flowers, for garnish (optional)

Preheat the oven to 250°F.

Put the panko, breadcrumbs, or flour in a large shallow bowl or plate. Stir in the thyme and chives, if using, and add the salt and pepper. Dip each tomato slice into the breadcrumbs, coating each side evenly. Set aside until ready to cook.

Heat a cast-iron skillet (10 inches or larger) over medium-high heat. Add 1 tablespoon of the butter and 1 tablespoon of the olive oil. When the butter has melted and begins to foam, add half the tomatoes to the pan, laying them out in a single layer so that the sides do not touch. Cook for about 4 minutes, or until the underside of each tomato begins to turn golden brown. Using a thin, flat spatula, carefully flip each slice and cook for another 3 to 4 minutes. When the tomatoes are soft, transfer them to a serving plate. Sprinkle with more salt and pepper, if desired. Keep them warm in the oven while you cook the rest. Repeat with the remaining tablespoon of butter and of olive oil, and the remaining tomatoes. Serve warm, garnished with the flowers and chives, if desired.

stuffed tomatoes provençal

serves 6

Stuffed summer tomatoes make a truly elegant dish. Use the very ripest, juiciest tomatoes you can find, and be sure to offer crusty bread to sop up all the juices. Serve hot, cold, or at room temperature as a first course, salad dish, or side dish to any roasted or grilled fish, meat, or poultry.

4 tablespoons olive oil

1 medium onion, finely chopped

2 garlic cloves, minced

Salt and freshly ground black pepper
   to taste

3 tablespoons chopped fresh basil

2 tablespoons chopped fresh chives

1 tablespoon chopped fresh thyme

6 medium tomatoes (about 4 pounds)

1/3 cup plus 2 tablespoons tapenade or
   olive puree

1/4 cup homemade breadcrumbs (page
   270), or store-bought

Position a rack in the middle of the oven. Preheat the oven to 350°F.

In a medium skillet, heat 2 tablespoons of the oil over medium-low heat. Add the onion and garlic and cook, stirring frequently, until pale gold, for 10 minutes. Season with salt and pepper and add the herbs.

Meanwhile, cut the tomatoes in half crosswise. When the onions have cooked for 10 minutes, use a melon scooper or a small spoon to very carefully scoop the flesh out of each tomato half and into the pan with the onions, being careful not to cut into the "shell." Set the hollowed-out tomato halves aside. Reduce the heat to low and let the tomato-onion-garlic mixture cook for another 10 minutes, or until tomato juices have thickened slightly. Place the tomato halves in a large gratin dish, broiler pan, or ovenproof skillet. Using a spoon, divide the 1/3 cup of tapenade equally among them, spreading it inside each.

When the onion-tomato mixture is done cooking, remove from the heat and stir in the breadcrumbs. Taste the mixture for seasoning, adding more salt and pepper if needed. Very carefully, put an equal amount of the stuffing in each tomato shell, pressing down lightly so you get as much stuffing as possible into each one. Top each stuffed tomato with an equal amount of the remaining 2 tablespoons of tapenade. Drizzle the tomatoes with the remaining 2 tablespoons of oil. (The dish can be made several hours ahead of time up to this point. Cover and refrigerate until ready to bake.)

Bake the tomatoes for 1 hour, or until the tomatoes look soft. Serve hot, at room temperature, or chilled.

sautéed ramps

Ramps, or wild leeks, are delicious sautéed with a touch of oil, salt, and pepper. Serve them as a side dish to any roasted meat, fish, or poultry dishes, or on top of polenta, rice, or pasta.

1 pound ramps (see belpw for more
    on ramps), or scallions or very thin,
    fresh leeks

1 1/2 tablespoons olive oil
Salt and freshly ground black pepper
    to taste

Cut off and discard the greens from the ramps. Trim off the root ends; you should be left with a bulb and about 3 inches of the pinkish stem. Remove any brownish skin that covers the outside of the bulbs.

In a large skillet, heat the oil over medium heat. Add the ramps and cook, stirring frequently, until almost tender, 5 minutes. Season with salt and pepper and serve hot.

ramp up the flavor

The discovery of ramps in early April is a true rite of spring, a sign that winter is over and fresh, wild foods have once again arrived.

Your first encounter with the wild leek, or ramp, will assault your nose. Ramps scream, "I am here and you can't ignore me." They look like small red scallions, their whitish, rounded, and petite bulbs attached to long, wide, bright green leaves. The leaves are removed before cooking, revealing the ramps' startlingly beautiful pale pink stems. When raw, the plants' odor can be over-whelming—a cross between wild onions and dirty socks. The flavor of ramps makes us think of a vegetable a mad scientist might concoct: a leek, a clove of garlic, a sweet Vidalia-type onion, a scallion, and a shallot, all mixed up, with the single best element extracted from each. Although the taste may at first seem delicate and subtle, within seconds the flavor expands—suddenly there is a pleasingly peppery bite towards the back of your mouth.

Found in dense hardwood forests in the eastern part of North America, ramps are hand dug, which explains why they can cost a small fortune.

Ramps can be substituted for regular leeks, but because they have a stronger flavor you need far fewer to make an impact.

italian-style broccoli spears with garlic

serves 4

This is one of our favorite ways to cook fresh broccoli: We slice it lengthwise into thin strips, lightly steam it in a large, heavy skillet, then fry it in the same pan with just a touch of olive oil and garlic until golden brown and crisp. The broccoli can be served as a side dish, or as a topping for pasta.

1 1/2 pounds broccoli
3 garlic cloves, very thinly sliced
About 1 1/2 tablespoons olive oil

Salt and freshly ground black pepper
to taste

Trim the tough ends off the broccoli stalks. Cut the broccoli lengthwise into 1/2-inch-thick strips. The strips should include the stalks as well as the florets. Place them in a large skillet and pour 1 cup of water on top. Place over high heat, cover, and cook for about 10 to 12 minutes, or until the broccoli is *almost* soft. Check the broccoli after about 8 minutes to see if the water is evaporating. If not, partially remove the cover. The idea is to cook the broccoli until it is *just tender,* but not falling apart. Since you will continue to cook it, you don't want it to be overdone at this point. If the broccoli feels almost tender but there is still water in the pan, simply pour the water out.

When the broccoli is ready, add the garlic, olive oil, salt, and pepper to the pan. Reduce the heat to medium and sauté the broccoli, adding more oil if needed, until golden brown and crisp, but tender to the bite. Season to taste and serve hot.

sautéed fiddlehead ferns with spring garlic

serves 3 to 4

This is a simple but delicious technique that highlights the fresh, wild flavors of the fiddlehead fern. The fiddleheads are blanched in boiling water and then sautéed in olive oil with lots of garlic. If you can find spring garlic (the new growth from a garlic plant that shoots up in late spring and has a deliciously subtle garlic-and-onion flavor), this dish will be even better.

Serve the fiddleheads with pasta, rice, or potatoes, or alongside any poultry or seafood dish. If you like, cool the fiddleheads to room temperature, toss with a vinaigrette, and serve as a salad.

¾ pound fresh fiddlehead ferns
2 tablespoons olive oil
1 tablespoon minced garlic or spring garlic

Salt and freshly ground black pepper
to taste

Clean and trim the fiddleheads (see opposite for tips on cleaning).

Bring a medium pot of water to a boil over high heat. Add the fiddleheads and cook for 20 seconds. Immediately drain the fiddleheads and place under very cold running water, to stop the cooking and retain the green color, until they are cool. Drain again.

In a large skillet, heat the oil over medium-high heat. Add the garlic and cook, stirring constantly, for about 10 seconds, or until golden brown, but not burnt. Add the fiddleheads and cook, stirring frequently, for about 5 minutes. Season liberally with salt and pepper. The fiddleheads are done when they are softened but still crisp, with a bite.

fiddleheads

a wild taste of spring

If it's spring and you're out walking alongside a marsh, riverbed, or stream and see a person stooped over, looking suspicious, don't fear. It's probably just someone foraging for fiddleheads. From April through the beginning of June, fiddlehead lovers along the East Coast (from Virginia through eastern Canada) forage for this unique spring vegetable.

The fresh taste of fiddlehead ferns can drive a normally sane person to put on mud boots and muck about marsh water looking for them on a damp spring day. Some compare their flavor to asparagus, okra, or green beans. A wild asparagus is what describes it best, but like most wild foods, their taste is unique and not fully comparable to anything else.

Named for its resemblance to the scroll of a violin (or fiddle), fiddleheads are the young, edible, tightly coiled frond of the ostrich (also called pohole) fern. There are thousands of varieties of ferns, but few are edible. The trick is to find the ostrich fern and eat the fronds only when they are very tightly coiled.

Whether you find your fiddleheads in a grocery store, vegetable market, or by a river, choose ones that are firm, bright green, and compact. The usually brown scale or skin, called the "chaff," which covers the outside of the fern, is a gauge of freshness. When the ferns are really fresh (as in just harvested), the scale or skin will be a green color, not brown. You need to remove the skin by rubbing it briskly with your hands. Sam Hayward, the chef of Fore Street restaurant in Portland, Maine, says he places his freshly foraged fiddleheads in a vat of cold water to keep them fresh longer. He claims the cold water makes it easier to remove the skin and prevents the fiddleheads from drying out.

Fiddleheads should be cooked within 2 to 3 days of purchase. Avoid fiddleheads that are limp, unfurled, or a pale yellow color.

stuffed zucchini blossoms

Finding orange-colored blossoms attached to zucchini plants (or pumpkin, or any other variety of squash) is one of the great joys of gardening. Squash blossoms are best picked early in the morning, while they are still open to the sun. Male blossoms will be slighter smaller, about 3 inches long, while female blossoms are around 4 to 5 inches long; see page 76 for more on blossoms.

Once you try this basic recipe for stuffing zucchini blossoms with tomatoes, breadcrumbs, and goat cheese, see the Harvest Variations on the next page for a vast array of other possibilities. This mixture also makes a delicious stuffing for zucchini or tomatoes.

Serve these delicate, savory blossoms as an hors d'oeuvre, a first course, or a side dish with poultry, beef, or fish. They also make an extravagant breakfast treat alongside fried eggs, toast, and fresh fruit. You will notice the use of the word "gentle" throughout this recipe; zucchini blossoms are very fragile and need to be treated with great care.

for the blossoms and stuffing
10 large zucchini blossoms, or blossoms from pumpkin or other squash, stems trimmed to 1 inch
3 tablespoons olive oil
1 cup chopped onion
3 garlic cloves, minced
Salt and freshly ground black pepper to taste
1/3 cup lightly packed chopped fresh basil
1/3 cup lightly packed chopped fresh parsley
1 cup finely chopped tomato

1 cup breadcrumbs, preferably homemade (page 270); or dried, store-bought can be substituted
1/2 cup crumbled soft goat cheese (1/4 pound)
10 chives, at least 6 inches long

for the batter
1/3 cup flour
1/8 teaspoon salt
Freshly ground black pepper to taste
2 tablespoons olive oil

1/4 cup olive oil for frying

To clean the blossoms: *Very gently* pry them open and rinse with cold water to remove any bugs or dirt. Clean the inside of the blossoms with a damp paper towel. Dry thoroughly on paper towels.

To make the stuffing: In a medium skillet, heat the oil over low heat. Add the onion, garlic, salt, and pepper and cook for 8 minutes, stirring frequently, until pale gold. Add the basil, parsley, and tomato and cook for another 5 minutes until the mixture is slightly thickened. Remove from the heat and gently stir in the bread-crumbs and goat cheese until well blended. Set aside; the stuffing can be made several hours ahead of time. Cover and refrigerate.

Using your fingers, very gently pry open the blossoms. Add 2 to 3 tablespoons of the stuffing, depending on the size of the blossom, gently patting it down into the blossom. Tie the top of the blossom closed with a fresh chive stem, using it like a piece of string or ribbon; see photo on page 76. (The stuffed blossoms can be made up to 2 hours ahead of time. Cover and refrigerate until ready to cook.)

To make the batter: In a small bowl, whisk the flour and $1/2$ cup of water together until smooth. Add salt, pepper, and oil. Let the batter sit for about 5 minutes. Holding the stem, coat each stuffed blossom with the batter, making sure to coat it on all sides. It's fine if some batter drips into the blossom.

In a large skillet, heat the $1/4$ cup of the olive oil over medium heat. When the oil is starting to get hot, add the blossoms, a few at a time. (To test the oil, drop in a breadcrumb; if it sizzles, it's hot enough.) Cook for about 4 minutes on each side, or until golden brown. Drain the blossoms on paper towels and sprinkle very lightly with salt. Repeat with the remaining blossoms, and serve warm.

harvest variations

- Use grated Parmesan cheese instead of goat cheese.
- Add $1/2$ to 1 cup of finely chopped cooked lamb to the stuffing.
- Add $1/4$ cup of chopped pitted black olives to the stuffing when the herbs are added.
- Add 2 teaspoons of tapenade or olive puree to the stuffing at the end.
- Add 1 tablespoon of chopped fresh ginger to the stuffing with the herbs.
- Add 1 to 2 tablespoons of chopped fresh herbs to the batter.
- Add $1/4$ cup of chopped roasted red pepper to the stuffing with the breadcrumbs and goat cheese.
- Add $1/4$ cup of pine nuts to the stuffing with the breadcrumbs.

stuff me!

the possibilities of squash blossoms

We appreciate zucchini and all manner of squash. But when it comes to our favorite part of the squash plant, the honors go to the blossom, the pale orange-yellow flower that appears before the squash forms. These delicate, subtly flavored flowers are the biggest reason to grow zucchini or other squash varieties in your garden. When they are stuffed and gently sautéed, they are an extraordinary treat—a tender flower with a delicate, appealing texture, bursting with flavor. (See Stuffed Zucchini Blossoms on pages 74–75.)

Squash blossoms are relatively new to most of us, but Native Americans have used them for many years. And throughout Mexico, squash blossoms are scrambled into eggs, stuffed and fried, and added to soups and stews.

When choosing squash blossoms—from your own garden, a farmers market, or a vegetable stand—select flowers that are brightly colored and fresh looking. They are best when picked in the early morning, when they are open to the sun and easier to clean and stuff.

According to Elizabeth Schneider, in her book *Uncommon Fruits and Vegetables,* "If you are picking the flowers from a garden, you will want to collect the male flowers only (leaving a few to continue the good work), so that your squash (the females) will develop." How do you tell a male blossom from a female? The male flowers, which blossom earlier in the season, have a narrower stem, while the female blossoms tend to be wider and look like baby squash (which, in fact, they are).

Like all flowers, squash blossoms are fragile and perishable. Plan on cooking them the same day that you buy or pick them. Don't keep them in plastic or any other container where they can get smashed; store them in a large basket with enough room for air to circulate around them and place the basket in a cool, dark spot. If it's a particularly hot or humid day, you can keep them in the refrigerator for just a few hours so they remain fresh.

To clean blossoms—whether they come from zucchini, summer squash, pumpkin, or any variety of winter squash—very gently pry them open and rinse with cold water to remove any bugs or dirt. Hold open the petals and use a damp paper towel to clean the inside of the petals. Many cooks like to dunk them in a bowl of cold water, but you have to be quick or they can become water logged. The blossom must be thoroughly dry before stuffing and cooking it.

chive puree

makes 1 cup

This brilliant green aromatic oil will keep for several days, covered and refrigerated. Drizzle it over pasta, potatoes, or rice dishes; add it to soups, stews, or vinaigrettes; or serve it as a dip for grilled shrimp, chicken, or cooked vegetables.

¾ cup chopped fresh chives
¾ cup extra virgin olive oil

Sea salt and freshly ground black pepper
   to taste

Combine the chives, oil, salt, and pepper in a food processor or blender and puree until well blended. Taste for seasoning. Transfer to a small bowl, cover, and refrigerate until ready to serve. Bring to room temperature before using.

roasted tomato sauce

makes about 10 cups

Every August, when the tomato harvest comes in, we make a rich sauce and then put up glass jars filled with it so we can enjoy the flavors of summer during the deepest winter months. We used to make sauce the traditional way—peeling the tomatoes, removing the seeds, then simmering the sauce on the stove for hours. The results were always excellent, but the work was exhausting.

One year there were so many tomatoes that it seemed we would never be able to deal with them all. So we developed a short cut. We chopped the tomatoes coarsely, forgetting about all that tedious peeling and seeding, and tossed them in a large roasting pan with onions, garlic, olive oil, and herbs. Then we placed the mixture in a *very hot* oven to make a roasted tomato sauce. The result was one of the best sauces ever. Roasting at a high temperature gives tomatoes a rich, slightly smoky flavor, and the onions and garlic become sweet as they caramelize.

The sauce can be refrigerated for 3 to 5 days, or it can be frozen in a tightly sealed plastic bag for several months. The sauce can also be processed in sterilized mason jars (25 minutes in a boiling water bath); it will keep for up to 10 months.

Toss the sauce with pasta, or serve it over grilled chicken or fish, or in any dish that calls for regular tomato sauce. You can cut the recipe in half or make a huge batch, all depending on how many tomatoes you have.

15 cloves garlic

About 8 pounds ripe tomatoes (any variety), cored and quartered

10 medium onions, quartered

1 cup chopped fresh herbs (rosemary, basil, thyme, oregano, parsley, and/or chives)

About ¼ cup olive oil

½ teaspoon salt, or to taste

Generous grinding of black pepper

3 or 4 tablespoons sugar (optional)

Preheat the oven to 450°F.

Peel the garlic and chop 5 of the cloves. Leave the remaining 10 cloves whole. In a large roasting pan, gently toss together the tomatoes, whole and chopped garlic, onions, herbs, oil, salt, and pepper. Roast for 25 minutes. Gently stir the vegetables. Roast for another 25 minutes and gently toss. Roast for another 45 minutes, or until the tomatoes are softened and somewhat broken down into a sauce, with a golden brown crust on top. Remove from the oven and taste for seasoning. If the sauce tastes bitter, add a few tablespoons of the sugar.

Pour the sauce into clean, sterile jars or freezer bags and refrigerate, can, or freeze.

harvest variations

Add any of the following ingredients to the sauce after it has roasted for about 50 minutes:

- ¼ cup drained capers
- ½ cup pitted black and/or green olives
- 2 to 3 tablespoons olive puree or tapenade
- 1 cup sautéed or raw mushrooms (See pages 178–179 for more about different mushroom varieties.)
- About 1 cup of any chopped raw or cooked vegetable
- 3 anchovy fillets, minced, or 1 tablespoon anchovy puree
- A good dash of red chile flakes or hot pepper sauce
- If you like a smoother sauce, pour the finished sauce into a blender or food processor and blend until it reaches the desired consistency.

a trio of pestos

lemon thyme–pistachio pesto

makes about ½ cup

Look for lemon thyme (or any variety of fresh thyme) at your local farmers market or check the Resources section (page 279) for a mail-order source for seeds or plants. If you can't find lemon thyme, an equal amount of fresh regular thyme plus a teaspoon of grated lemon zest makes a good substitute.

This pesto goes well with grilled chicken, lamb, or beef and can be tossed with noodles, rice dishes, couscous, or grilled vegetables. It can also be served as a dip with taco chips or flatbreads.

²/₃ cup chopped fresh lemon thyme
¼ cup salted pistachio nuts, shelled

½ cup olive oil
Freshly ground black pepper to taste

In a food processor, puree the thyme and pistachios, then, with the motor running, gradually add the oil. Season with pepper. Cover and refrigerate until ready to use. The pesto will keep for at least a day or two. Serve at room temperature.

cilantro-cashew pesto

Even those who claim to dislike cilantro (also known as coriander or Chinese parsley) fall in love with this full-flavored pesto. Serve it with grilled poultry, fish (particularly shrimp or salmon), or as a dip with taco chips or flatbread.

⅔ cup chopped fresh cilantro
¼ cup salted cashews
1 small garlic clove, chopped

½ cup olive oil
Freshly ground black pepper to taste

In a food processor, puree the cilantro, cashews, and garlic. Slowly add the oil and blend until almost smooth. Season with pepper. Cover and refrigerate until ready to use. The pesto will keep for at least a day or two. Serve at room temperature.

mint and toasted pine nut pesto

makes about 1½ cups

This is the ultimate accompaniment to grilled butterflied lamb or roasted leg of lamb, and it can also be used as a dip with shrimp, vegetables, and toasted pita bread.

½ cup pine nuts
2 cups packed fresh mint leaves
1 cup olive oil

⅛ teaspoon salt, or to taste
A few grindings of black pepper

Preheat the oven to 400°F. Place the nuts on a cookie sheet and bake for 10 minutes, or until golden brown, making sure they don't burn. Remove from the oven.

In a blender or food processor, whirl the mint until coarsely chopped. Add the toasted nuts, the oil, salt, and pepper and process until all the nuts are chopped and the pesto has a coarse texture. The pesto can be made several hours ahead of time and will keep for a day or two. Cover and refrigerate until ready to use. Serve at room temperature.

from the
sea

sometimes

it takes a visit from friends to remind us

of why we love living in Maine. We take our guests and head out to the beach to our favorite lobster shack, and grab a picnic table overlooking the water. We take in the pungent, briny scent of the lobsters steaming, and watch as their shells turn a bright scarlet red. Fat steamer clams, corn on the cob, and local potatoes baked inside their skin will be served alongside the crustaceans, making this the perfect meal. Our friends marvel at the beauty of the rocky shore, the way the temperature feels just right (not too hot or too cold), and the excitement of waiting to eat a lobster fresh from local water. One bite of that sweet, satisfying lobster meat and it's hard not to feel a rush of pride to be part of this remarkable coastal landscape.

crab and watercress dumplings with a cilantro dipping sauce

makes 24 dumplings; serves 6 to 8

If you've never made dumplings at home because you think they're too difficult, think again. By using premade dumpling wrappers (also called "wonton wrappers") from the grocery store or an Asian market, you can put together these dumplings in very little time. They can be made several hours ahead and steamed just before serving. For a more luxurious version, substitute cooked lobster meat for the crab.

for the dumplings

1/2 pound coarsely chopped fresh crabmeat
1 cup packed coarsely chopped, stemmed watercress (try to find small, tender leaves)
2 tablespoons minced fresh ginger
3 tablespoons chopped scallion (white and green parts)
1 tablespoon finely chopped fresh cilantro
2 teaspoons Asian sesame oil
24 wonton wrappers, defrosted if frozen

for the dipping sauce

1/3 cup soy sauce or tamari
2 tablespoons rice vinegar
1 tablespoon minced fresh ginger
1 tablespoon Asian sesame oil
2 tablespoons chopped fresh cilantro
2 tablespoons chopped scallion (white and green parts)

About 8 to 10 lettuce leaves (iceberg or romaine)

To make the filling: In a bowl, gently mix the crabmeat, watercress, ginger, scallion, cilantro, and sesame oil and set aside.

To form the dumplings: Fill a small bowl with water. Keep the wonton wrappers covered as you work so they don't dry out. Place a wonton wrapper on a clean work surface and place about 1 tablespoon of filling in the center. Lightly dab the edges of the wrapper with water and bring together two opposite corners to make a triangle, with the filling inside. Press together the edges to seal. Pull together the two corners at the base of the triangle to meet in the middle and press together, using water to help the dough stick together. Pinch all the edges so that a sealed pocket is formed. If using round wrappers, pinch the opposite sides together to make a pouch. Repeat with the remaining wrappers and filling, making about 24 dumplings.

To make the dipping sauce: Mix the soy sauce, rice vinegar, ginger, sesame oil, cilantro, and scallions; set aside.

To steam the dumplings: Bring about 2 to 3 inches of water to a boil in a steamer or in a large wok. Line the bottom of a steamer basket or a Chinese bamboo steamer

recipe continues

tray with lettuce leaves (this keeps the dumplings from sticking) and place the dumplings on top, making sure they don't touch each other. Place the steamer basket on top of the water (making sure it's not touching the water), cover, and steam the dumplings for 6 minutes, or until tender. (The filling is already cooked, so you are simply heating it up and making the wrapper tender and hot.) Serve hot, with the dipping sauce.

stone crabs
the prized shellfish of florida

Most hard-shell crabs require a great deal of work: Cracking the shells to extract tiny morsels of meat is often a frustrating process. The first time we tasted stone crabs—which, by Florida law, are harvested only from October 15 to May 15—we discovered a variety of hard-shell crabs where the satisfaction far outweighed the frustration.

As we cracked open the huge claws of the creature, and found that a regular fork (not a minuscule little tong) could extract huge bite fulls of meat, we launched into a lengthy discussion about the merits of Maine lobster versus Florida stone crab. And while some at the table (the true New Englanders) insisted that lobster was the winning crustacean, others felt that the meat from the stone crabs, with its outstanding flavor and satisfying meaty texture, might just be better. Or maybe as good.

Talking to the folks at Moore's Stone Crab in Longboat Key, Florida (see Resources on page 281), we learned about the unusual techniques used to harvest stone crabs, so named because their shells are hard as stone. The crabs are harvested from Texas, on the Gulf of Mexico, as far north as North Carolina, on the Atlantic. But the majority of stone crabs come from Florida's West Coast and the Florida Keys. The boxes or traps, made from either wood or plastic, are weighed down with cement and contain one hole so the crab walks in, but can't get out. Water temperature is crucial to the quality of stone crab—if the water gets too cold it causes the meat to stick to the inside of the shell. (This explains why stone crabs are never frozen raw inside the shell. When you mail-order stone crabs, they always arrive fresh and fully cooked in the shell.)

Unlike lobster, stone crabs are not killed. Fishermen force the claws off the live crabs and then toss the crabs back into the water, where the limbs regenerate. One reason why stone crab is so expensive is that it takes great skill to rip the claw off a live creature and not lose one of your own fingers in the process.

There are generally three sizes of stone crab: *Jumbo,* or large crabs, are about five claws to the pound, *large* or *selects* are seven claws to the pound, and *medium* are eight claws to the pound.

The crabs are cooked in plain water (without seasonings) and are served hot, room temperature, or cold, accompanied by lemon slices, melted butter, or a mustard sauce. We don't think they need much more than a squirt of fresh lemon juice.

endive spears with lobster salad and lime

serves 4 to 6

Cooked lobster meat (or crabmeat) is transformed into an elegant hors d'oeuvre when mixed with fresh lime juice and a touch of mayonnaise and spooned onto crunchy endive spears. The whole thing takes about 5 minutes!

$1/2$ pound cooked fresh lobster meat,
    coarsely chopped, or cooked crabmeat,
    thawed if frozen
Juice of $1 1/2$ limes (about 2 to 3 tablespoons)
2 tablespoons Homemade Mayonnaise
    (page 273), or store-bought

Freshly ground black pepper to taste
14 endive spears
2 tablespoons drained capers
Sweet Hungarian paprika

Gently mix together the lobster or crab, lime juice, mayonnaise, and pepper in a medium bowl. Place a heaping tablespoon of the mixture onto each endive spear and arrange the spears on a small plate. Scatter the capers on top and sprinkle with paprika.

world's best fried clams

Don't be afraid to deep-fry at home—once you try these fried clams you'll see it's well worth the effort. Soft-shell (or steamer) clams are marinated in milk and then dipped in a fabulous buttermilk and cornmeal batter. The clams fry until golden brown—crispy on the outside and tender, soft, and briny on the inside. Serve hot with lemon wedges, Tartar Sauce (page 275), and Buttermilk Onion Rings (page 197).

About 5 to 6 cups good-quality canola or peanut oil

1 pound frying clams (also called shucked soft-shell or steamer clams; about 2 cups)

1 cup milk, whole or 2%

1 large egg

½ cup buttermilk

¾ cup good-quality cornmeal

¼ cup all-purpose flour

⅛ teaspoon salt

Freshly ground black pepper to taste

Tabasco or other hot pepper sauce

1 lemon, cut into small wedges

Tartar Sauce (page 275)

Pour 2 to 3 inches of oil in a large, deep, heavy skillet (cast iron or a wok is ideal). Heat over high heat until the oil is very hot, but not burning, about 350°F. when tested on a deep-frying thermometer. (If you don't have a thermometer, you can test the heat by dropping a tiny bit of cornmeal into the oil; it should sizzle immediately.)

Meanwhile, "marinate" the clams by placing them in a bowl with the 1 cup of milk.

To make the batter, beat the egg in a large bowl. Stir in the buttermilk and cornmeal. Add the flour, salt, pepper, and several dashes of the hot pepper sauce, and stir until smooth.

When the oil is hot, remove the clams from the milk, a few at a time, and drop in the batter bowl. Coat well. Add about 8 clams at a time to the hot oil, making sure not to crowd the pan, and fry for about 1 to 2 minutes, or until golden brown and puffed on both sides. Remove with a slotted spoon and drain on paper towels. Repeat with the remaining clams.

Serve immediately, or keep warm in a 200°F. oven until all the clams are cooked. Don't let the clams sit around too long, or they will get soggy. Serve with lemon wedges and Tartar Sauce.

shrimp, corn, and ginger pancakes

makes about ten 2- to 3-inch pancakes; serves 4 to 5

Look for the freshest shrimp you can find for these irresistible pancakes. In the dead of winter, we like to make these with tiny, pink Maine shrimp (see page 107), which are delicate and exceedingly sweet.

There are many ways to serve these simple, savory pancakes—try them with a dollop of Lemon-Ginger Mayonnaise (page 275), or topped with Herb Butter (page 272), or as a first course or hors d'oeuvre accompanied by Fresh Mango Winter Salsa (page 261).

2 eggs
1/2 pound Maine shrimp or other small
    shrimp, peeled, deveined, and coarsely
    chopped
1/4 cup chopped scallion (white and green
    parts) plus (optional) 2 tablespoons
    minced for garnish
2 teaspoons lemon juice or Meyer lemon
    juice (see page 262)
1/2 cup coarse cornmeal

1/2 teaspoon baking powder
2 tablespoons minced fresh ginger
1 1/2 tablespoons melted butter
Salt and freshly ground black pepper
    to taste
Vegetable oil for frying
Lemon-Ginger Mayonnaise (page 275),
    melted Herb Butter (page 272), or
    Fresh Mango Winter Salsa (page 261)
    for serving.

In a large bowl, whisk the eggs. Add the shrimp, 1/4 cup of scallion, the lemon juice, cornmeal, baking powder, ginger, and melted butter and mix well. Season with salt and pepper.

In a large skillet, heat a tablespoon of the oil over medium heat. Add heaping tablespoons of batter to the hot pan and, using the back of a spatula, flatten the pancakes; they will be around 2 to 3 inches in diameter. Cook for 2 minutes, gently flip, and cook for another 2 minutes on the other side. Repeat with the remaining batter. Serve hot, sprinkled with 2 tablespoons of minced scallions, if desired, and accompanied by the mayonnaise, herb butter, or salsa.

new england–style fish stew

serves 4 to 6

Lobster, clams, mussels, and thick chunks of haddock are simmered with tomatoes, herbs, and garlic to create this rich, seductive fish stew. If you prepare the broth ahead of time, the whole dish comes together very quickly. If you'd rather not cut up a lobster into 16 pieces, you can have the fishmonger do it for you, but the lobster needs to be cooked no more than an hour after it is cut up. You can buy fish stock for the broth at the fishmonger's or in the freezer section of some specialty shops. Serve the stew with Garlic Croûtes (page 271) and a big green salad.

for the broth

2 tablespoons olive oil
1 medium onion, very thinly sliced
1 medium leek (white part only), cut into
    thin rounds
Freshly ground black pepper to taste
3 tablespoons julienned fresh basil
4 garlic cloves, very thinly sliced
$\frac{1}{2}$ cup minced fresh parsley
1 teaspoon saffron threads
1 tablespoon chopped fresh thyme
One 28-ounce can whole peeled tomatoes
2 cups fish stock or clam juice
1 cup dry white wine

for finishing the stew

12 cherrystone clams or 16 littleneck clams
1$\frac{1}{2}$ pounds mussels
2 tablespoons cornmeal
One 1$\frac{1}{2}$-pound lobster
1$\frac{1}{2}$ tablespoons olive oil
2 garlic cloves, minced
1 pound haddock, thickly sliced, or any
    firm-fleshed fish, skinned and cut into
    2-inch pieces
8 to 10 Garlic Croûtes (page 271)
$\frac{1}{2}$ cup minced fresh parsley for garnish

To make the broth: In a large pot, heat the oil over low heat. Add the onions and leek and cook, stirring frequently, for 10 minutes, until a pale golden color. Season with pepper. Add the basil, garlic, parsley, saffron, and thyme, and cook 30 seconds. Add the tomatoes, squeezing them apart with your hands to "chop" them as you add them to the pot. Add the fish stock and wine and raise the heat to high. Bring the liquid to a boil, reduce the heat to low, cover, and simmer for 30 minutes. (The broth can be made a day ahead of time; cover and refrigerate until ready to prepare the stew.)

    To finish the stew: Heat the broth over medium heat until simmering. Meanwhile, scrub the clams and mussels with a brush to remove any sand, grit, or dirt from the shells. If necessary, remove the beards from the mussels (see page 97;

recipe continues

cultivated mussels don't have beards). Put the shellfish in a large bowl and cover with cold water. Sprinkle the cornmeal on top and let sit for about 15 minutes. The clams and mussels will open their shells to "eat" the cornmeal and release any sand trapped inside. Drain the clams and mussels and rinse well under cold running water.

If you've brought home a live lobster, place it on a work surface, shell side down. Using a large, sharp knife, make an incision where the tail and body connect, with the blade facing the head of the lobster. Push down on the knife, cutting the body in two. (This will kill the lobster.) Using your hands, twist the tail off and pull off the claws. Separate the body into halves, then cut into quarters, slicing across the body. Remove and discard the sac at the top of the head. Remove the green tomalley and set aside.

Cut the tail across into four pieces. Separate the knuckle from each claw. With a quick movement, use the back of the knife to crack the top of the claw. Remove any rubber bands. Turn the knife over and cut the claw in half at the joint. Make a small incision in the soft bottom part of the knuckle and cut in half. At the end of this process, you should have 16 pieces of lobster. Put the pieces in a large bowl and set aside.

In a large skillet, heat the oil over medium heat. Add the minced garlic and cook 10 seconds. Add the haddock pieces, cook for 30 seconds, and gently flip; cook for another 30 seconds. Remove the skillet from the heat.

When the broth is simmering, add the lobster pieces, cover, and cook for 2 minutes. Add the clams and cook for 2 minutes. Add the mussels and haddock and cook until the clams and mussels are open, the lobster is pink and cooked through, and the haddock is cooked (the haddock may fall apart, which is fine; it will thicken and flavor the stew).

Serve the stew piping hot in large bowls, accompanied by Garlic Croûtes and a sprinkling of chopped parsley.

mussel chowder

serves 4 as a main course, and 6 as a soup course

Mussels add a delicate texture and flavor to this traditional creamy soup, which is far more subtle than clam chowder. The base of the chowder is mussel broth, made by simply steaming open mussels. This impressive dish can be made from start to finish in about an hour. It is elegant enough to serve as a first course at a dinner party, but also hearty enough to sip out of a mug on a cold winter's night.

2 pounds cultivated or wild mussels, cleaned and debearded (see opposite)

3 ounces salt pork or thick country-style bacon, cut into very small cubes

1 medium onion, finely chopped

3 small russet or Yukon gold potatoes (about $1/2$ pound), peeled and cubed

Salt and freshly ground black pepper to taste

$1\,1/2$ teaspoons chopped fresh thyme, or $1/2$ teaspoon dried thyme

1 cup dry white wine

1 cup heavy cream

In a large pot, boil $1\,1/3$ cups of water over high heat. Add the mussels, stir well, cover, and steam for about 5 minutes. The mussels should be *just barely open*. Using a slotted spoon, transfer the mussels to a bowl and let cool. Pour the mussel broth remaining in the pot into a small bowl and set aside. There should be about 2 cups of broth. Remove the mussels from their shells and discard the shells. Set the mussel meat aside. (If you are making this ahead of time, cover the broth and the mussels and refrigerate.)

Clean out the large pot and add the salt pork. Cook over low heat for about 4 minutes; raise the heat to medium and cook for another 5 to 6 minutes, stirring occasionally, until the salt pork is crisp and golden brown. Remove the crisp cubes with a slotted spoon and drain on paper towels; leave the fat in the bottom of the pot. Add the onion and cook over low heat, stirring frequently, for 4 minutes. Add the potatoes, salt, pepper, and thyme and cook for 1 minute, stirring. Raise the heat to high and add the wine and then the mussel broth, being careful to leave out any debris or sand that has settled in the bottom of the bowl.

Once the broth has come to a boil, reduce the heat to low, cover, and cook for 6 minutes. Remove the cover and cook for another 6 minutes; the potatoes should be just about tender. Reduce the heat to very low and add the cream; simmer for 5 minutes. Add the reserved mussels and cook just to warm them through, another 5 minutes. Taste for seasoning and add more salt or pepper as needed. Serve piping hot with a sprinkling of the crispy salt pork cubes on top.

more on mussels . . .

Not long ago, people turned up their noses at mussels—they were very low on the shellfish totem pole. Aside from cooks familiar with Mediterranean cuisine, most people never thought about mussels, or cared for them. These days, thankfully, things have changed: You can find them on menus in the most highbrow restaurants, where chefs steam them open to make soups, chowders, pasta sauces, salads, and sophisticated stews.

bearded or clean shaven?

Many wild mussels arrive at fish stores still wearing a beard—the hairy-looking stuff that mussels use to cling to rocks, ropes, and docks. Buying mussels with the beard still attached means more work, but the beard can actually keep a mussel alive longer after harvesting, ensuring its freshness. To remove the beard, simply pull it off with your fingers, working close to the shell.

culling

It is essential to cull shellfish—that is, to sort the live ones from the dead. Since dead shellfish deteriorate rapidly, they are not safe to eat. If a mussel or clam is gaping open, you should squeeze it together with your fingers. If it is alive, it will immediately close up. If it doesn't remain closed, it should be discarded. Conversely, if a clam or mussel remains closed after cooking, it should also be discarded.

wild or cultured

There are three general types of mussels: The first is the **wild mussel,** which grows in seawater and attaches itself to ledges, poles, boats, and rocks offshore. These are the least expensive type of mussel on the market and have the strongest flavor. Real mussel lovers adore the wild, almost gamy flavor of wild mussels, while others find it too strong. Fishermen scrape them off rocks and ledges, and place them in a tumbling machine to remove the barnacles and beards. The downside to wild mussels: They sometimes contain pearls, which can be an unfortunate surprise when you're biting on one, and they tend to be full of grit and sand, which makes cleaning them labor-intensive.

The second variety is the **cultivated mussel,** which has quickly become the most common mussel in fish markets. These mussels are found in the wild, dredged off the bottoms of rocks and ledges, and brought to shore. They are then depurated, a cleaning process whereby the mussels are hung and washed in fresh (not salt) water, and the beards and barnacles are removed mechanically.

The third, and possibly most appealing, mussel is the **rope-cultured mussel.** These are seed mussels placed in biodegradable bags, which are suspended from rafts and placed in clear seawater. Because they are suspended, they grow like wild mussels, feeding on nutrient-rich waters. They tend to grow quickly and their shells are thin. Although the shells can be fragile during cooking, rope-cultured mussels offer a mild, very sweet flavor. They are the most expensive variety of mussel, but many chefs feel they have a superior flavor and texture.

steamer clam pan roast

serves 4 as a first course

We first discovered shellfish pan roasts at the famed Grand Central Oyster Bar restaurant in New York City's Grand Central Terminal. There chefs use fresh oysters, clams, or lobster and add cream and a few simple seasonings to make a chowderlike stew that is outrageously delicious. In this supremely simple rendition, a shallot is sautéed, clams are added, hot milk and cream are poured on top, and the whole stew is seasoned with a dash of Worcestershire sauce. Serve as a first or main course with hot biscuits or crusty bread.

2 cups milk, whole or 2%
1/2 cup heavy cream
1 tablespoon unsalted butter
2 tablespoons minced shallots
1 pound frying clams (also called shucked
   soft-shell or steamer clams; about 2 cups)

Dash of Worcestershire sauce
Salt and freshly ground black pepper
   to taste
Sweet Hungarian paprika

In a medium pot, heat the milk and cream over medium-low heat for about 5 minutes, or until hot but *not boiling*.

In a large, deep skillet, heat the butter over medium heat. Add the shallots and sauté for about 1 minute, stirring, until softened and translucent. Add the clams and season with Worcestershire, salt, and pepper. Cook for 1 minute, stirring frequently. Pour the hot milk mixture on top and cook for 2 to 3 minutes, or until piping hot. Taste for seasoning, sprinkle with paprika, and serve immediately.

harvest variations
Instead of clams, substitute one of the following:
* 1 pound fresh oysters
* 1 pound raw or cooked lobster meat, coarsely chopped. If raw, cook for 5 minutes; if cooked, cook only for 2 to 3 minutes.
* 1/2 pound shelled and deveined shrimp and 1/2 pound diver scallops (see page 106), cooked for 3 to 4 minutes

new england winter salad of watercress, sautéed scallops, oranges, and almonds

serves 4 as a main course or 6 as a salad course

A bed of crunchy, peppery watercress is topped with sweet scallops, tangy orange sections, and sautéed slivered almonds. Serve the salad warm with crusty bread.

2 oranges or tangerines or clementines

1½ cups watercress leaves

2 tablespoons unsalted butter

½ cup slivered almonds

Salt and freshly ground black pepper
   to taste

About 1 cup all-purpose flour

1 pound fresh sea scallops or diver scallops
   (see page 106)

1 tablespoon olive oil

Juice of 1 large orange (about ½ cup)

⅓ cup dry vermouth or dry white wine

Cut the oranges crosswise into 8 thin slices, remove the rind, and cut each slice into quarters. Or peel the tangerines or clementines, separate into segments, and cut each in half.

Place the watercress in the center of a large serving platter. Surround it with the orange segments, scattering a few pieces of orange on top of the watercress as well as around it.

In a small skillet, heat 1 tablespoon of the butter. Add the almonds and sauté for about 5 minutes, stirring frequently, until golden brown. Season with salt and pepper, and set aside.

Put the flour in a bowl or plastic bag, and season it liberally with salt and pepper. Dredge the scallops in the seasoned flour, making sure to coat them on all sides.

Combine the remaining tablespoon of butter and the oil in a large, heavy skillet over high heat. When the fat is quite hot, add the scallops, being careful not to crowd them. Cook for 2 minutes and, using tongs, flip the scallops over. They should be a golden brown color on one side. Cook for another 2 to 3 minutes, until the scallops are just cooked through (you can test one by removing it from the pan and cutting it in half). Place the scallops on top of the watercress. Add the orange juice and vermouth to the hot skillet and boil down over high heat for 2 minutes, or until thickened and slightly reduced. Scatter the warm almonds on top of the scallops and drizzle the pan juices over the whole platter. Serve immediately.

portuguese roasted clams with chorizo, tomatoes, and onions

serves 3 as a main course or 4 as an appetizer

Based on an old Portuguese recipe called *Porco à Alentejana*, this dish combines fresh clams with slices of onion, spicy chorizo sausage, fresh tomatoes, garlic, and white wine, all roasted in a hot oven. Spoon the juicy clam stew over Whipped Potatoes (page 187) or linguine, accompanied by warm, crusty bread and a bottle of crisp white wine, such as a Portuguese Vinho Verde or a sparkling Italian Prosecco.

1 tablespoon olive oil

½ pound chorizo, linguica, or a fairly spicy Italian sausage, cut into ½- to 1-inch-thick pieces

1 large onion, thinly sliced

Dash of cayenne pepper or hot pepper sauce

24 littleneck clams, 16 cherrystone clams, or 2 pounds debearded mussels (see page 97), cleaned

1 large, ripe tomato (or 2 medium), coarsely chopped (about 2 cups)

4 garlic cloves, chopped

½ cup coarsely chopped or julienned fresh basil, or finely chopped parsley

1 cup dry white wine

Preheat the oven to 450°F.

In a large, ovenproof skillet or shallow casserole, heat the oil over medium heat. Add the sausage slices and onion, and cook for about 5 minutes, until golden brown. (Reduce the heat to low if the sausage begins to burn.) Add the cayenne or hot pepper sauce and stir well.

Remove the skillet from the heat and carefully pour off any excess oil from the bottom of the pan. Arrange the clams on top of the sausage and onions. Scatter the tomato, garlic, and basil on top of the clams and add the wine. Roast, uncovered, for 8 minutes. Remove from oven, stir well, and roast another 5 to 15 minutes, or until the clams *just open*. (Don't wait until the clam shells are wide open. As soon as they open enough for you to see the clams, it's time to remove them from the oven, or the clams will overcook and become tough.) Serve immediately.

clam primer

There are six major varieties of clams you should know about, each type treated differently in the kitchen.

quahogs (pronounced CO-hog or KWO-hog) are the largest East Coast clams, generally used for making chowder, clam cakes, and clam pies. Their hard shells can be as large as 4 to 5 inches across. Quahogs are almost never eaten raw; they're just too big and tough.

cherrystones, generally about 2 to 3 inches wide, are eaten raw or cooked. Their fresh and briny flavor and tender texture make them ideal for pasta sauces, roasting, or adding to fish stews.

littlenecks, ranging in size from 1 to 2½ inches, tend to be the most expensive clams. They are small, delicately flavored, and just the right size for eating raw—a touch of fresh lemon juice or a squirt of hot pepper sauce is ideal. When cooking with littlenecks, you need to be extra careful not to let them overcook, or they will become rubbery. To play it safe, as soon as the shell begins to open, take the clams off the heat.

mahogany clams are a real delicacy. Small, and almost round, with a gorgeous mahogany hued shell, these delicate creatures should only be cooked briefly. They add fabulous flavor to paellas, fish soups, and stews.

soft-shell clams (steamer clams or **frying clams)** have a shell that is softer and more oblong than the hard-shell varieties, and the "neck" (siphon) of the clam sticks out of the shell. Steamers are incredibly tender, and are always cooked before eating. They are prized for their sweet, nutty flavor. They can be steamed, or used to make fried clams (see page 91), pan roasts (see page 98), or chowders.

razor clams, also a soft-shell clam variety, have a long, narrow, brown-colored shell that looks like the handle of an old-fashioned barber's straight razor. They are delicious steamed, braised, stir-fried, or sautéed.

shopping tips

When buying hard-shell clams, look for shells that are tightly closed. If a shell is gaping, squeeze it shut with your fingers. If it doesn't stay shut, discard it. For soft-shell clams, squeeze the neck (the part outside the shell). If it has any movement at all, it's alive.

bucatini with mahogany clams

serves 4

This classic Italian dish is always a favorite, and we try to make it whenever we find freshly harvested clams. Small mahogany clams (see page 102) are sautéed with olive oil, copious amounts of garlic, a dash of red chile flakes, and some wine to produce one of the great pasta sauces of all time. Bucatini is a thick type of spaghetti that's hollow in the middle—perfect for soaking up sauces.

Pinch of salt

1 pound bucatini, linguine, or spaghetti

3 tablespoons olive oil

2 garlic cloves, very thinly sliced

Pinch of red chile flakes

Freshly ground black pepper to taste

¾ cup minced fresh parsley

2 pounds mahogany clams, littlenecks, or cherrystones, scrubbed clean

1½ cups dry white wine

Bring a large pot of water to boil over high heat for the pasta. Sprinkle with the salt. Add the bucatini and cook about 8 to 10 minutes, or until just cooked, or *al dente*. Drain and transfer to a large serving plate or bowl.

While the pasta cooks, heat the oil over medium heat in a large skillet. Add the garlic and cook for about 2 minutes. Sprinkle with the chile flakes (a little bit goes a long way, so don't overdo it unless you want a really spicy sauce) and stir. Add the pepper and half the parsley and cook for 5 seconds. Add the clams, stir well to coat them well, and raise the heat to high. Add the wine and cover. Cook for 3 minutes. Remove the cover, stir well, and let the clam sauce cook for another 5 to 7 minutes, or until all the clams are *just open*. Littlenecks and cherrystones will take longer than mahogany clams—about 8 to 10 minutes.

Pour the clams and the sauce over the pasta and sprinkle with the remaining parsley.

scallops, shrimp, and clams in a cream sauce over linguine

serves 4 to 6

Though it sounds complex, this sophisticated seafood sauce can be partially prepared ahead of time and then finished off in the time it takes to boil the pasta. Finding really fresh scallops, shrimp, and clams is crucial for this dish. Serve it with a mixed green salad, a crusty loaf of bread, and a good dry white wine.

2 tablespoons olive oil
1 cup finely chopped Vidalia onion
3 garlic cloves, very thinly sliced
Salt and freshly ground black pepper
 to taste
2 cups dry white wine
½ cup heavy cream
½ cup julienned fresh basil
About ½ cup all-purpose flour

1 pound sea scallops or diver scallops
 (see page 106)
1 pound thin spaghetti or linguine
1 teaspoon unsalted butter
1 pound large shrimp, peeled and
 deveined, with tails intact
1½ pounds mahogany, littleneck, or
 cherrystone clams, or debearded mussels
 (see page 97), scrubbed clean

In a large pot, heat 1 tablespoon of the oil over low heat. Add the onion and garlic, season with salt and pepper, and cook for 10 minutes, stirring occasionally; the onions should become golden brown. Raise the heat to medium-high and add 1½ cups of the wine; simmer for about 8 to 10 minutes, or until reduced by almost half. Add the cream and half the basil, reduce the heat to low, and cook for about 8 minutes, until the sauce is thickened and somewhat reduced. It should look creamy and be thick enough to coat the back of a spoon. (The sauce can be made a day ahead of time up to this point. Cover and refrigerate.)

On a large plate, mix the flour with a generous dash of salt and pepper. Dredge the scallops in the seasoned flour to coat lightly on all sides. Meanwhile, boil a large pot of water for the pasta. Cook the spaghetti for about 10 minutes, or until *al dente,* or just tender, and drain.

In a large skillet, heat the butter with the remaining tablespoon of oil over medium-high heat. When the fat is hot, add the scallops in a single layer and sprinkle with pepper. Cook for 2 minutes. Gently flip the scallops and cook for another minute on the other side; they should be golden brown, but not totally cooked through. Transfer to a plate and set aside. Add the shrimp to the pan and cook for 1½ minutes on each side. Transfer the shrimp to the plate with the scallops. Raise

recipe continues

the heat to high and deglaze the skillet with the remaining $^1/_2$ cup of wine. Simmer for about 4 minutes, scraping any browned bits remaining on the bottom of the pan.

Heat the cream sauce in a large pot over medium heat. Add the reduced wine from the skillet. When the liquid is simmering, add the scallops, shrimp, and clams, stir well to coat all the seafood, and cover. Cook for about 5 minutes, or until all the clams are open.

Place the cooked pasta on a very large, warm serving plate or bowl and top with the seafood sauce. Garnish with the remaining basil.

sweet scallops

diver scallops

Whenever we visited upscale restaurants and saw diver scallops on the menu, we wondered why these scallops warranted such hefty prices. Our friend Jamie Wright, of Browne Trading Company, a top-of-the-line seafood and specialty food shop in Portland, Maine, had the answer.

Diver scallops, Wright informs us, are just what they sound like: scallops that have been harvested by hand by scuba divers. Ordinary scallops are harvested by large fishing boats that drag a forklike contraption along the bottom of the ocean and grab scallops. Unfortunately, they also disturb much of the sea life that lives around the scallops, making it an environmentally unfriendly harvesting technique. When the forks drag along the bottom of the sea, Wright explains, "it disturbs the delicate ecosystem and can disrupt sea life. When scallops are hand picked by divers, there is no harm to the surrounding environment."

But, Wright points out, the biggest difference between diver scallops and those dragged along the bottom of the sea is found in the taste of the scallops themselves. "When a fork drags through muck, it brings up the scallops and frequently breaks the scallop shell," Wright explains. "The meat can be bruised, which deteriorates the quality of the scallop quickly. When scallops are picked by hand, they arrive alive and squirming!"

Be forewarned, all this freshness and hand picking will cost you; diver scallops sell for around twenty dollars per pound. Look for diver scallops from Maine (where Wright claims they are the best; see Resources on pages 280–281) from December through April. In more southerly parts of New England, diver scallops are harvested throughout the summer in limited supply.

wet or dry? the scallop deception

When you're shopping for fresh scallops, avoid ones that look wet or milky, or are soaking in any kind of watery liquid. Many supermarkets and not-too-classy fish vendors soak the scallops in a watery solution to plump them up and make them look wet, glossy, and fresh. In fact, the scallops soak up this chemically treated water and lose a good deal of their taste, ending up washed out and watery. (Not to mention the fact that the plumped-up scallops weigh more and can bring in a higher price.)

Go against your instincts, and look for "dry" scallops—not dried-out ones, but clear, unmuddled, fresh scallops that are not soaked or plumped up with water.

stir-fried shrimp with
fresh pomegranate juice and ginger

serves 2 as a main course or 4 as a first course

In this vibrant dish, fresh pomegranate juice gives the shrimp a sweet-and-sour flavor that is further enhanced by fresh ginger. Serve with rice or couscous, or as a first course on top of a bed of spicy watercress, sprinkled with a few pomegranate seeds.

1 tablespoon olive oil
1 garlic clove, very thinly sliced
2 scallions (white and green parts), chopped
3 tablespoons chopped fresh chives or parsley

1 pound medium to large shrimp or 1½ pounds Maine shrimp, peeled and deveined, with tails intact
Freshly ground black pepper to taste
⅓ to ⅔ cup fresh pomegranate juice (see page 225)
1 tablespoon unsalted butter

In a wok or a large, heavy skillet, heat the oil over medium-high heat. Add the garlic and cook for 30 seconds, stirring constantly. Add half the scallions and chives and cook for another 30 seconds. Add the shrimp and cook for 2 minutes, stirring frequently. Add the pepper and cook for another 2 minutes. Add the pomegranate juice and cook for 1 minute more. Remove the shrimp with a slotted spoon. Raise the heat to high and cook down the juices for another 2 minutes, or until thick enough to coat the back of a spoon. Add the butter, remove the dish from the heat, and let the butter melt into the smooth sauce. Pour the pomegranate sauce over the shrimp with the remaining scallions and chives and serve hot.

maine shrimp
a delicacy in the dead of winter

Picture a tiny pink morsel, the size of a child's thumb, full of briny juice and ocean freshness. Meet Maine shrimp—harvested from mid-January until the end of February.

Although sold primarily throughout New England, Maine shrimp can often be found (or requested) at fish stores around the country. These tiny shrimp are usually sold with the heads and tails attached, which means they can be a lot of work to clean before you can cook and eat them (there are about seventy shrimp to a pound). If you can find them shelled and headless, it's worth paying the extra money because it will save you a good deal of time. Use these soft, pink nuggets in stir-fries, chowders, or fish stews, or sauté them in olive oil with plenty of garlic and served over pasta or rice.

pancetta-wrapped scallops
on creamy basil risotto

serves 4 as a main course or 8 as an appetizer

This is a new approach to the classic dish "angels on horseback," in which oysters (or scallops) are wrapped in bacon and broiled. Here each tender scallop is wrapped in a thin strip of peppery pancetta and sautéed in garlicky oil. The pan juices are then reduced with vermouth and a touch of butter. The scallops are sophisticated on their own, but even more delicious served over Creamy Basil Risotto (page 62).

Creamy Basil Risotto (page 62)
1/2 cup all-purpose flour
Salt and freshly ground black pepper
   to taste
1 pound fresh sea scallops or diver scallops
   (about 30 scallops; see page 106)
4 to 6 ounces very thinly sliced pancetta
   (see page 109)

2 tablespoons olive oil
2 garlic cloves, minced
2 tablespoons unsalted butter
1/3 cup minced fresh parsley
1 cup dry vermouth or dry white wine

Make the risotto and keep warm.

Put the flour on a plate or into a plastic bag and season liberally with salt and pepper.

Rinse the scallops under cold water, drain, and pat dry with paper towels.

To prepare the pancetta, you want to make a slit in it so it can be laid out in long, thin strips, unraveling the meat. (The natural shape of pancetta is like a pinwheel.) Wrap a strip of pancetta around a scallop so that the middle of the scallop is enclosed by the meat. When you look at the top of the scallop, there should be a little bit of white scallop showing on either side of the pink meat. Use your fingers to press the pancetta down into the scallop to help it adhere. Repeat with the remaining scallops. Next, dredge them in the seasoned flour, and set them aside on a clean plate. (This can be done several hours ahead of time; wrap in plastic and refrigerate until ready to cook.)

In a large, heavy skillet, heat the oil over high heat. Add half the garlic, stir briefly, and immediately begin adding the scallops to the hot pan. Cook for 2 minutes, or until golden brown on one side. Carefully flip the scallops over using tongs and scatter the remaining garlic into the pan with 1 tablespoon of the butter. Cook for another 2 minutes. Add the parsley and vermouth and simmer for 1 to 2 minutes. Use a slotted spoon to transfer the scallops to a warm serving plate and continue to reduce the vermouth for 1 minute. Add the remaining tablespoon of butter and whisk into the sauce; cook down for another 1 to 2 minutes, or until the butter is melted and the sauce is thickened.

To serve, spoon warm risotto on a serving plate and top with the scallops. Drizzle the sauce from the skillet on top. (If not serving with risotto, serve 7 or 8 scallops per person, drizzled with the warm pan juices.)

pancetta pointers

Pancetta is a type of Italian bacon that offers a completely different flavor from that of traditional American bacon. Unlike regular bacon, which is smoked, pancetta is salted, lightly spiced, cured, and then rolled up like salami. It provides a full, rich flavor of salt and pepper, and a little bit goes a long way when flavoring dishes— from risottos and pasta sauces to sautéed fish and chicken. You can find pancetta in butcher shops and Italian specialty stores. Pancetta, lightly cooked, makes a great topping for salads.

stonewall mussels

serves 4

This simple recipe is one of Jonathan and Jim's favorite ways to cook mussels: steaming them open with garlic and a splash of wine. Serve the mussels on top of pasta as a main course, or as a first course accompanied by the Garlic Croûtes on page 271.

2 tablespoons olive oil

2 to 3 garlic cloves, very thinly sliced

2 pounds debearded mussels (see page 97), scrubbed clean

1½ cups dry white wine

Tiny pinch of salt

Generous grinding of black pepper

¼ cup minced fresh parsley

Put the oil in a large pot and place over moderate heat. Add the garlic and cook for 1 minute, stirring constantly. Add the mussels to the pan and cook, stirring, for 1 to 2 minutes. Raise the heat to high, add the wine, and bring to a boil. Cook for 4 to 5 minutes, or until the mussels *just open*. Remove the mussels with a slotted spoon and place in a serving bowl. Reduce the liquid in the pan over a high heat, add the salt and pepper and parsley, and cook for another 2 to 3 minutes, until slightly thickened. Taste for seasoning. Pour the hot broth over the mussels and serve immediately.

harvest variations

You can also add any or all of the following to the broth:

- ¼ cup julienned fresh basil
- 1 cup chopped fresh tomatoes
- 1 cup pitted black olives
- 1 cup toasted chopped almonds or walnuts
- ½ cup pesto (see pages 80–81)

eugenia camelio's stuffed lobster bodies in red sauce

serves 4 to 8

Several times a month Kathy travels to WBUR in Boston to talk about food and to cook on the award-winning public radio show *Here and Now*. WBUR also happens to be the radio home of Ray and Tom Magliozzi, the hosts of the enormously popular public radio show *Car Talk*. Ray, it turns out, loves to cook and frequently shares recipes with Kathy—old Italian favorites like this pasta sauce, which comes from his grandmother, Eugenia.

What we love about this dish is that it uses lobster bodies—the often neglected part of the lobster that's left after the tail and the claws have been removed. Lobster bodies can be found at any good fish market that sells live lobster or cooked lobster meat. In Maine you can still buy a dozen bodies for about three dollars! Considering that cooked lobster meat sells for around thirty dollars per pound, this is one of the last great seafood deals around! The bodies are stuffed with a wonderfully aromatic mixture of breadcrumbs, garlic, pitted black olives, red chile flakes, and olive oil and then simmered for several hours in a simple homemade tomato sauce. The result is a thick, lobster-infused red sauce that, to quote Ray, "is to die for." You eat the stuffing out of the bodies and slurp up the rich sauce with the pasta. Like so many other great sauces, this one needs to simmer for several hours and is best made a day ahead of time. Serve on top of linguine, bucatini, or spaghetti.

for the tomato sauce

6 garlic cloves

3 tablespoons olive oil

1 large onion, coarsely chopped

1 cup very coarsely chopped fresh basil

1/2 teaspoon red chile flakes, or to taste

1 cup good dry red wine, preferably Italian

Three 28-ounce cans whole Italian tomatoes

1 bay leaf

1/8 teaspoon sea salt, or to taste

3 black peppercorns

for stuffing the lobster bodies

2 cups seasoned Italian breadcrumbs

2 to 3 garlic cloves, chopped

1 cup coarsely chopped pitted black olives, preferably Italian or Greek

Dash of red chile flakes, or to taste

Freshly ground black pepper to taste

1/3 cup olive oil

8 cooked lobster bodies

1 to 1 1/2 pounds linguine, bucatini, or spaghetti

To make the sauce: Peel the garlic cloves, chop 3, and leave the remaining 3 whole. In a large pot, heat the oil over low heat. Add the onion and cook, stirring frequently, for 5 minutes. Add the chopped garlic and cook for 1 minute. Add half the basil and the chile flakes (add a little less than 1/2 teaspoon, and add more later if you want a spicier sauce) and cook for 30 seconds, stirring well. Raise the heat to high and add the wine. Boil gently for about 3 minutes. Reduce the heat, and stir in the tomatoes, whole garlic cloves, the remaining basil, the bay leaf, salt, and peppercorns. Cover and simmer, stirring occasionally, for about 1 hour. The sauce should be thick and full of flavor; season to taste. (The tomato sauce can be made 1 or 2 days ahead of time. Refrigerate until ready to finish off the dish.)

To stuff the lobster bodies: In a medium bowl, mix the breadcrumbs, garlic, olives, chile flakes, pepper, and oil. There should be enough oil to moisten all the breadcrumbs. (The breadcrumb stuffing can be prepared several hours ahead of time.) Hold a lobster body in your hand. The end that was connected to the tail will have an opening. Stuff about 1/3 to almost 1/2 cup of the breadcrumb mixture (depending on the size of the lobster body) into that hollow, pressing down to stuff the body completely. Repeat with the remaining bodies.

Bring the tomato sauce to a gentle simmer over low heat. Place the stuffed lobster bodies into the simmering sauce, spoon sauce over them, cover, and simmer for about 2 to 3 hours. The dish is done when the sauce is thick and bursting with flavor. (The finished sauce can also be made 1 day ahead of time.)

About 15 minutes before serving, bring a large pot of water to boil. Add the pasta and cook until *al dente,* about 8 to 14 minutes, depending on the thickness of the pasta you use. Drain and place the pasta on a large platter. Carefully pour the sauce on top and arrange the lobster bodies over the hot sauce.

homarus americanus
sweet, sweet lobster

In Maine, where we live, lobster isn't just a type of shellfish, it's a way of life. Maine fishing villages wouldn't be nearly as picturesque without lobster boats moored in the harbor and lobster traps stacked on the docks. The rugged Maine lobsterman (and, more recently, lobsterwoman) is a fixture in state lore and politics. The lobster logo is everywhere—on t-shirts, hats, flags, handbags. It even used to be the symbol on Maine license plates.

Our philosophy about cooking lobster is this: the more simply prepared, the better. Stay away from fancy sauces and lobsters flamed with alcohol or stuffed with shrimp, scallops, and other unnecessary ingredients. That's like putting ketchup on your caviar.

shopping for lobster
Look for very lively lobsters from a good fish market. When the lobsters are picked up out of the tank, they should be squirming and kicking—not lethargic or droopy.

lobster terminology
Like every other special food, there is special terminology for lobster sizes. We spoke with Michael Goflin, owner of Finestkind Fish Market in York, Maine, to help us make sense of some of the vocabulary and learn what type of lobster is best for what dish:

A **cull** is any sized lobster that has lost a claw—a one-clawed creature. Culls can be used like any other type of lobster, there will just be less claw meat.

A **chicken** is a 1- to 1¼-pound lobster. Chickens are best steamed or boiled as they aren't quite big enough for broiling. Chickens can also be chopped and used in stir-fries and pan roasts.

Then there are **quarters** and **halves** (1¼-pound to 1½-pound or 1½-pound to 1¾-pound lobsters, respectively). These larger lobsters are excellent for steaming, boiling, or broiling. Many cooks feel this is the best weight for a lobster—just enough meat to really satisfy.

Selects are lobsters between 2 and 4 pounds. These large lobsters can be steamed or boiled, but, because of all the meat, they are excellent broiled.

A **jumbo** is just what it sounds like—generally any lobster over 4 pounds. Some cooks feel these enormous lobsters are tough and are best used for chowders, pan roasts, and other dishes for which the meat is cooked and then used outside the shell.

X-halves or **Philadelphia halves** are lobsters between 1.4 and 1.45 pounds.

Our favorite term, the **Popeye Lobster,** refers to a male lobster with a tiny body and big claws.

color
Lobsters can be red, orange, green, spotted black, brown, blue-tinged, green-striped, or an orangey rust color (lobsters found near shipwrecks seem to take on this rust color). The color doesn't affect the flavor of the meat—and they all turn bright red when cooked.

telling the boys from the girls

How do you tell the difference between a male and a female lobster? You guessed it! Look between the lobster's legs, and find the two feelers located at the base of the tail. If they're hard, it's a male; if they feel soft, feathery, and flexible, you've got yourself a lady. Female lobsters also have a small rectangular piece of shell between their second pair of walking legs and tend to have a wider tail so they can carry a small sac filled with thousands of rich, tiny, coral-colored eggs, their roe. Many people prefer female lobsters because they can be sweeter and meatier than their male counterparts.

hard-shell versus soft-shell

Depending on the season, you will find lobsters with either a *hard* or *soft shell.* Lobsters molt frequently (twenty-five times during their first five years of life). When a lobster molts, its flesh shrivels (as much as 40 to 50 percent) so it can free itself from its shell. There is a general consensus that soft-shell lobsters are not nearly as good as hard-shells because they offer less meat and more water. But, according to Sam Hayward, chef of Fore Street, the highly acclaimed Portland, Maine, restaurant, "soft-shell lobsters are sweeter, and have a far more tender texture. The myth that soft-shells provide less meat than hard-shells is simply untrue." When you crack open a soft-shell lobster, lots of water spills out. But, Chef Hayward points out, the shells of a hard-shell lobster weigh much

more than that of a soft-shell, so you are getting the same amount of meat in a 1½-pound soft-shell lobster as you do in a 1½-pound hard-shell variety. Many cooks feel that soft-shell lobsters are also better than hard-shells for summer grilling because the heat from the fire can permeate the lobster shell and cook the meat without toughening it. Soft-shells are generally found after the Fourth of July for just a short season.

steaming——the best cooking method

Steaming produces the juiciest, most tender lobster meat. To steam a lobster: Fill the bottom of a large pot with about 2 inches of water and sprinkle with sea salt. (If you have access to fresh seawater use it—you'll have the best lobster. You can also add a few strips of dried seaweed instead of the salt.) Bring the water to a rolling boil and add the lobsters to the pot *back first* (shell side down), so that all the juices get caught in the shell and are not lost in the pot. Cover and steam for about 12 minutes for a 1-pound lobster and about 20 minutes for a 2-pounder. To test for doneness, simply pull off one of the small legs; if it comes off easily, the lobster is ready. Drain and serve with melted butter, lemon wedges, and plenty of oversized paper napkins. A baked potato, a few ears of corn on the cob, and an ice-cold beer or two wouldn't hurt!

grilled lobster with tarragon-chive butter

serves 4

If you've never grilled lobster outdoors over an open fire, you're in for a treat. In many ways this preparation is a lot easier than boiling or steaming lobster indoors. All you need to do is split the lobsters down the middle, season them with an herb butter, and throw them on a hot grill.

The lobster is cooked over indirect heat—the coals are pushed off to one side, allowing the lobster to cook slowly and become moist, slightly smoky, and herb infused. If you are squeamish about the idea of cutting a live lobster, ask your fish store to do it for you, but be sure to cook the lobsters within about an hour after they have been cut.

Serve with Grilled Summer Corn (page 49), Sweet Potato Fries with Aioli (page 194), a tomato salad, and lots of ice-cold beer or a somewhat fruity white wine.

6 tablespoons unsalted butter at room temperature	Pinch of sea salt, or to taste
¼ cup chopped fresh chives	Freshly ground black pepper to taste
2 tablespoons chopped fresh thyme	Four 1¼- to 1½-pound lobsters, preferably
1½ tablespoons chopped fresh tarragon	soft-shell (see page 115)
	1 lemon, cut into wedges

To make the herb butter: In a small bowl, mix together the butter, chives, thyme, tarragon, salt, and pepper. The herbs should be fully incorporated into the butter. The herb butter can be made several hours ahead of time; cover and refrigerate until ready to cook the lobsters.

Light a fire—either charcoal, wood, or gas—and heat until the embers are quite hot. If your grill has a built-in thermometer, you should aim for 400°F.

Meanwhile, prepare the lobsters: Place them on a clean work surface, shell side down. Place a tea towel over a lobster's head and plunge a knife into the body, directly below the head, and split the lobster open, cutting it down the middle, *almost* all the way through. The lobster shell should remain attached, not separated into two halves. (This technique may seem gruesome, but many experts claim it's more humane than plunging the poor things into a pot of boiling water.) Remove and discard the sac at the top of the head. Alternately, have your fish store cut the lobster for you.

Put a quarter of the herb butter in the body and throughout the tail of each lobster, pushing the butter into the lobster meat.

Rake all the charcoal or wood to one side of the barbecue. If using a gas barbecue, heat only one side. Place the lobsters on the side *without* the coals or heat, shell side down, so that you don't lose any juices. Cover the grill and cook for about 15 minutes. Remove the cover and cook for another 2 to 6 minutes, depending on the size of your lobster. The butter will baste the lobster meat. The lobster is done as soon as the tail meat feels firm, and not soft and raw. Remove from the hot grill, place on a platter, and scatter with the lemon wedges.

soft-shell crabs with brown lemon butter and slivered almonds

serves 2 to 4

We like soft-shell crabs served simply, without a lot of fancy embellishment. Here they are very lightly coated with a seasoned cornmeal mixture and sautéed for just a few minutes in a very hot skillet. Most soft-shell crabs are now sold already cleaned. If you find live soft-shell crabs, ask your fish store to clean them for you.

2 lemons

About ¹/₂ cup coarse cornmeal

¹/₄ cup all-purpose flour

¹/₈ teaspoon salt

Freshly ground black pepper to taste

4 large soft-shell crabs, cleaned

2 teaspoons olive oil

2 tablespoons butter

¹/₂ cup slivered almonds

Juice 1 lemon and cut the second into wedges or thinly slice crosswise.

On a large plate, mix the cornmeal, flour, salt, and pepper. Lightly dredge the crabs in the mixture, making sure to coat them on both sides.

In a large skillet, heat the oil and 1 tablespoon of the butter over medium-high heat. When the oil is hot (it will barely sizzle), add the crabs, making sure not to crowd the pan. Cook the crabs for 3 minutes and gently flip them over with a spatula or tongs. Cook for 3 minutes on the other side and gently transfer the crabs to a warm serving platter.

Heat the remaining tablespoon of butter in the skillet until it sizzles, but do not let it burn. Add the almonds and cook, stirring constantly, for 2 to 3 minutes, or until golden brown. Add the lemon juice and cook for about 30 seconds. Pour the almonds and juices from the pan on top of the crabs and garnish with the lemon wedges.

where's your shell?
the story of the soft-shell crab

This is a story about nature and moon phases and seasons. It is the story of the soft-shell crab, a spring delicacy that crab lovers look forward to like kids counting down to Christmas Day.

There are over four hundred varieties of crab in the world, but nothing quite like the soft-shell crab. A specialty of the eastern seaboard, soft-shell crabs are blue crabs that have shed their old hard shells at the end of the long winter. Blue crabs are said to be influenced by the phases of the moon. These newly molted crabs, sometimes referred to as "peelers," begin to shed their outgrown shells on the first full moon of May.

The season for soft-shells is short. Harvesting begins in late spring and lasts for just a few months, making them a truly seasonal food. The crabs need to be caught while they are still entirely soft, just after the molting has occurred, and before the hard shell begins to grow back.

What makes soft-shell crabs so extraordinary is that, unlike other crabs, which require work to break through the hard shell and extract tiny bits of meat, the entire soft-shell crab is edible—they are exceedingly juicy crustaceans with a fresh taste of the sea.

Many restaurants deep-fry soft-shell crabs, which is a shame. There is no need to add excessive fat to these delicious morsels. We prefer to grill or sauté them in just a tiny bit of olive oil or butter, and let the natural flavors of the crab come through.

Look for very fresh crabs. Many companies now flash-freeze soft-shell crabs in season, and they are far better than you might think, but nothing really compares to the fresh ones. Soft-shells should have a fresh odor, not a fishy one. Ask your fish store to clean the crabs for you, and be sure to cook them the same day you buy them. They do not last long, even under refrigeration.

Soft-shell crabs are best when accompanied by other seasonal foods: roasted new potatoes, steamed or roasted asparagus or fiddlehead ferns, or a salad of delicate spring greens.

grilled marinated fish kebobs

serves 6 to 12

For these delicious and colorful kebobs, chunks of fish are interspersed with cherry tomatoes, onions, whole basil leaves, thin slices of lemon and lime, and colorful sweet peppers. You can use any variety of firm-fleshed, thickly cut fish that can hold up to the heat of the hot grill. The important thing is that everything on the skewer be about the same size.

The kebobs can be marinated and arranged on skewers several hours before serving, making this an ideal dish for entertaining. Serve with lemon and lime wedges, a rice dish, warm pita bread, and a mixed green salad. The kebobs are also delicious served with a yogurt and grated cucumber sauce, Fresh Mango Winter Salsa (page 261), or Aioli (Garlic Mayonnaise, page 274).

¾ pound fresh tuna steak, cut into 1- to 1½-inch chunks	1 teaspoon chopped fresh thyme and/or basil
1 pound swordfish steak, cut into 1- to 1½-inch chunks	Freshly ground black pepper to taste
1 pound medium or large shrimp, deveined, with the shell on	2 large lemons, washed
½ pound sea scallops (see page 106)	2 limes, washed
2 tablespoons olive oil	About 1 cup cherry tomatoes
2 garlic cloves, chopped	1 sweet green pepper, cut into small chunks
¾ cup dry white wine	1 sweet red pepper, cut into small chunks
1 tablespoon chopped fresh chives	1 sweet yellow pepper, cut into small chunks
	2 red onions, cut into small wedges
	About 1 cup fresh basil leaves

Place the tuna, swordfish, shrimp, and scallops in a large bowl and add the oil, garlic, wine, chives, thyme, and pepper and toss well. Cover and refrigerate and marinate for at least 15 minutes and up to several hours.

Cut 1 lemon and 1 lime into paper-thin slices. Cut the remaining lemon and lime into wedges. If using bamboo skewers for the kebobs, soak them in cold water for at least 10 minutes before using. This will make them less likely to catch fire on the grill.

Working with metal or bamboo skewers, thread alternating pieces of swordfish, tuna, scallop, and shrimp with the tomatoes, peppers, onions, lemon and lime slices, and basil leaves. You want each skewer to have a combination of each type of fish and vegetable—repeat until each skewer is filled. Although there is no specific order for these kebobs, the lemon and lime slices are particularly good placed directly next to the fish, so the citrus juices can drip on the fish as it cooks. A tip: Place a wedge from the end of the lemon or lime on the ends of the skewers to keep the more delicate fish from falling off.

Set the skewers in a broiler pan. Pour the marinade on top. (The kebobs can be prepared about 6 to 8 hours ahead of time. Cover and refrigerate until ready to grill.)

Light a charcoal, gas, or wood fire and heat until red hot, about 350 to 400°F. Place the skewers on the grill and cook the kebobs for 4 minutes. Using tongs, gently flip the skewers over and cook the kebobs another 4 to 6 minutes, or until the fish is cooked through and the vegetables are tender. The cooking time will depend greatly on the heat of your fire. Serve hot, straight from the grill, on a large platter surrounded by the lemon and lime wedges.

harvest variations

- Add thin slices of summer squash, eggplant, or any other favorite fresh vegetable.
- Add 1 or 2 bay leaves to each skewer.

grilled swordfish provençal-style

serves 6

Meaty swordfish steaks are marinated in olive oil, lemon juice, thyme, and white wine and cooked under the broiler or over a fire until just tender. For a pungent Mediterranean touch, spoon a stripe of tapenade (or olive puree) down the center of each steak as it cooks. Tapenade, a puree of olives, anchovies, and herbs, can be found in specialty food shops. Serve this with pasta and a salad of fresh greens tossed with a light vinaigrette.

Two 1-pound swordfish steaks, about 1 inch thick
3 tablespoons olive oil
2 tablespoons fresh lemon juice
¼ cup dry white wine

2 garlic cloves, very thinly sliced
2 tablespoons chopped fresh thyme
Freshly ground black pepper to taste
¼ cup tapenade, olive puree, or olive pesto
1 lemon, cut into wedges

Place the swordfish steaks in a broiler pan or shallow casserole. Pour the oil, lemon juice, and wine on top of both steaks. Scatter the garlic and thyme between the two steaks and add a generous grinding of pepper. Turn the steaks so both sides are well coated in the marinade. Marinate for at least 15 minutes and up to several hours. Cover and refrigerate if marinating for longer than 15 minutes.

Preheat the broiler or light a charcoal or gas grill and heat until it reaches 350 to 400°F.

If broiling, keep the swordfish in the pan with the marinade and broil for 4 minutes on each side, about 1 inch from the heat. Remove from the broiler and spoon a stripe of tapenade down the middle of each swordfish steak and spoon some of the marinade from the bottom of the pan on top. Broil for another 2 minutes. If grilling, remove the swordfish from the marinade and grill for 4 minutes on each side. Baste the fish with the marinade every few minutes. Spoon the tapenade down the middle of each swordfish steak and grill for another 2 minutes, basting with the marinade. Serve hot with lemon wedges.

tuna tacos with avocado cream

serves 8

In Mexico, fresh fish is often grilled with lime juice, peppers, and cilantro and served on warm flour or corn tortillas, accompanied by fresh salsa and avocado slices or guacamole. You can use virtually any type of fish for these tacos, but a dense, meaty fish like tuna or bluefish is ideal. Shrimp and lobster are also popular throughout the Baja peninsula, and you can substitute either of these for the fish.

If you prepare the salsa and avocado cream ahead, you can put these tacos together in no time. This is a great dish for a summer barbecue or any outdoor event.

for the fresh summer salsa
1 cup finely chopped sweet green pepper
2 scallions (white and green parts), thinly
   sliced
2 cups chopped ripe tomatoes
2 to 3 tablespoons chopped fresh cilantro
Juice of 1 large or 2 small limes
2 tablespoons olive oil
1 tablespoon finely chopped jalapeño
   pepper, or splash of hot pepper sauce
Salt and freshly ground black pepper
   to taste

for the avocado cream
3 just-ripe avocados, pitted
$1/2$ cup plus 1 tablespoon heavy cream
Salt and freshly ground black pepper
   to taste

for the fish and tortillas
Two 1-pound tuna steaks or bluefish fillets,
   about $3/4$ inch thick, or 2 pounds large
   shrimp, peeled and deveined
2 teaspoons olive oil
Juice of 2 limes
Freshly ground black pepper to taste
   (it should be coarse)
8 large fresh flour tortillas (7 inches wide)
   or 8 to 16 small fresh corn tortillas
   (about $4^1/2$ inches wide)

for serving
8 romaine lettuce leaves, whole or coarsely
   chopped
1 lime, cut into 8 wedges
1 cup chopped ripe tomatoes
About $1/2$ cup chopped fresh cilantro

To make the salsa: Gently mix all the ingredients together and taste for seasoning; add more salt, pepper, and jalapeño if needed. (The salsa should be made no more than 2 hours before serving. Cover and refrigerate until ready to serve.)

To make the avocado cream: Put the avocados in the container of a food processor or blender and blend. Add the cream, salt, and pepper and puree until smooth. (The avocado cream should be made no more than 2 hours ahead of time. Cover and refrigerate until ready to serve.)

To prepare the fish and tortillas: Light a gas or charcoal fire and heat until red hot, about 350 to 400°F. Alternately, preheat the oven broiler with a rack set about 4 inches from the heat.

Put the tuna in a nonreactive bowl and add the oil, lime juice, and coarsely ground pepper. Turn over the fish to coat all sides. Don't let the tuna marinate for more than 15 minutes or the citrus will "cook" it.

Grill or broil the tuna for 3 minutes. Turn the tuna over and grill for another 3 to 4 minutes, until medium-rare, and still pinkish inside. (If you like tuna well done, grill it for a total of 9 to 10 minutes. If you are using shrimp, you only need to grill them 2 to 3 minutes.) Remove from heat. Add the tortillas to the hot grill and grill for about 30 seconds to 1 minute on each side, until hot.

To serve: Slice the tuna and place on a serving plate. Accompany with the warm tortillas and bowls of the avocado cream, the salsa, lettuce leaves, lime wedges, chopped tomatoes, and cilantro. Let everyone assemble the tacos at the table. Alternately, spread the warm tortillas with avocado cream and a spoonful of salsa. Add the lettuce leaves. Top with tuna slices, cilantro, chopped tomatoes, and a squirt of lime juice. Roll up the tortillas and serve.

cedar plank–grilled halibut steaks

serves 2 to 4

Halibut can be very bland and dull, but we found that when you marinate it, and cook it on an open fire on a cedar plank, it can become a thoroughly enticing, full-flavored fish. You can also try this marinade and grilling technique on salmon, cod, bluefish, or any other firm-fleshed fish fillet or steak. We've also tried adding a few scallops to the marinade and grilling them alongside the halibut as a garnish.

If you've never worked with a cedar plank before, it's quite easy. The trick is to find an untreated piece of cedar (they are now sold in gourmet food shops and specialty grocery stores; see Resources on page 279). The cedar plank, soaked in cold water for a few minutes and then placed directly on a hot grill, infuses the fish with a delicious, subtly smoky, cedar flavor.

1 untreated cedar plank, about 15 inches
   long and 7 inches wide
2 lemons
Two 1-pound boneless halibut steaks, about
   1½ inches thick

2 tablespoons olive oil
Freshly ground black pepper to taste
¼ cup sake, vermouth, or dry white wine

Put the cedar plank in a sink and cover with cold water.

Grate 1 tablespoon of zest from 1 lemon and juice the lemon to obtain 2 to 3 tablespoons of juice. Cut the second lemon into wedges. Place the fish steaks in a nonreactive pan or bowl and cover with the oil, lemon juice and zest, pepper, and sake. Turn the steaks once or twice to make sure the marinade coats both sides.

Light a charcoal, gas, or wood fire and heat until the embers are hot, about 300 to 350°F. Put the plank directly on the grill and place the fish steaks on top. Cover the grill and cook for 10 minutes. Remove the cover, baste the fish with the marinade, and let the fish cook for another 8 to 12 minutes, depending on the thickness, or until the fish is opaque in the center. Serve with lemon wedges.

flounder fillets with spinach-parmesan stuffing

serves 4

Many restaurants serve rolled, stuffed fish fillets, but they never appeal because the stuffing is always so rich and overwhelms the delicate flavor of the fish. Here, fillets of flounder or sole are rolled around a quick sauté of baby spinach with garlic and then dusted very lightly with Parmesan cheese. Serve with rice, a simple pasta dish, or your favorite potatoes. Note: Fish fillets vary in size; choose fillets of uniform size so that all the fish will cook evenly.

1 tablespoon olive oil
1 garlic clove, very thinly sliced
¾ pound baby or regular spinach, thick
    stems removed
Salt and freshly ground black pepper
    to taste

8 fillets of flounder or sole (about 1 to
    1½ pounds; see Note)
About ¼ cup grated Parmesan cheese
½ to ¾ cup dry white wine
2 tablespoons unsalted butter
About ¼ cup homemade breadcrumbs
    (page 270), or store-bought

Heat the oil in a large skillet over medium-high heat. Add the garlic and cook for about 10 seconds, stirring constantly. Add the spinach in batches and cook, stirring frequently, until it is just soft, about 5 minutes. Season with salt and pepper. Place the spinach on a plate. Drain any excess water or liquid out of the spinach by taking another plate of the same size and pressing down on the spinach and discarding the liquid. Finely chop the drained spinach and set aside.

Lay out a fillet of fish on a clean surface and sprinkle very lightly with salt and pepper. Place 1 to 2 tablespoons of the cooked spinach mixture on the fish fillet, spreading it out evenly. Sprinkle about 1½ teaspoons of the cheese on top of the spinach. Roll up the fillet, working from the thinner end, and place in a broiler pan, roasting pan, or ovenproof skillet with the seam of the roll down. Repeat with the remaining fish, spinach, and cheese. (The dish can be made several hours ahead of time; cover and refrigerate until ready to cook the fish.)

Position a rack in the middle of the oven. Preheat the oven to 400°F.

Pour ½ cup of the wine on top of the fish and bake for 12 minutes. Remove from the oven and preheat the broiler. If the pan is dry, add another ¼ cup wine to the bottom of the pan. Add the butter to the wine in the bottom of the pan and broil the fish for 2 minutes. Remove from the oven and sprinkle the fillets lightly with the breadcrumbs. Spoon a tablespoon of the liquid from the bottom of the pan on top of the fish to moisten the breadcrumbs, and broil for another 3 to 4 minutes.

pan-fried whole trout with cornmeal crust and lemon butter

serves 2

The trick to pan-frying whole fish is to use a very heavy good skillet and to heat the oil to a high temperature without its smoking. The high heat sears the skin of the fish, sealing in the natural juices. You will need boned and gutted trout for this dish. If you prefer not to do the work yourself, your fishmonger can do it for you. To create a more sophisticated flavor, add a few tablespoons of chopped caperberries (olive-sized capers) or slivered almonds to the lemon butter.

Try the trout for dinner with rice pilaf or couscous and sautéed greens, or as a special treat for breakfast, served with home fries and fried eggs.

2 large lemons

About 1 cup coarse cornmeal

2 whole, deboned trout (with heads and tails intact), gutted, rinsed, and patted dry

Salt and freshly ground black pepper to taste

About 4$\frac{1}{2}$ tablespoons unsalted butter

$\frac{1}{2}$ cup chopped caperberries, capers, or slivered almonds (optional)

Juice 1 lemon and cut the other into wedges.

Put the cornmeal on a large plate or in a plastic bag. Dredge the trout on both sides, making sure the cornmeal sticks to the skin. Season with the salt and pepper.

In a large, heavy skillet heat 1$\frac{1}{2}$ tablespoons of the butter over medium-high heat. (To test the heat of the pan, drop a speck of cornmeal into the oil; if it sizzles, the pan is perfectly hot.) Add both trout, and cook for 5 minutes. Using a spatula, carefully flip the trout over and add another tablespoon of the butter. Cook for 5 minutes, gently pressing down on the fish with a spatula. Cook for another 2 to 3 minutes, until the skin is crisp and golden brown on both sides and the flesh inside is cooked through. (Flip up the skin and peek at the flesh; it should be opaque in the center.)

Transfer the cooked trout to a plate. Add the remaining 2 tablespoons of butter to the hot pan. Add the lemon juice and the caperberries or almonds if using, and cook for about 1 minute, until the butter is melted. Pour the hot lemon butter on top of the trout and serve immediately with the lemon wedges.

roasted shallot, chive, and buttermilk pancakes with lemon crème fraîche and a trio of american caviars

makes about 16 pancakes; serves 4 to 6 as an appetizer

These light, fluffy, chive-flecked pancakes make a great foil for the intense richness and pop-in-your-mouth texture of fresh caviar. Open the Champagne and start celebrating!

You can serve the pancakes with as much or as little caviar as your budget allows. A small amount of red salmon, black American sturgeon, and golden whitefish caviar side by side on the pancakes makes for a gorgeous presentation. See page 132 for more on American caviar, which can be found in the refrigerated section of many grocery stores and specialty food shops (see Resources on pages 280–281). Truth be told, the pancakes are pretty special, even without the caviar!

for the lemon-cream topping
1 cup crème fraîche, or sour cream (see opposite)
1 teaspoon minced chives, or very finely chopped scallions
½ teaspoon grated lemon zest

for the pancakes
1 large shallot
½ teaspoon olive oil
Freshly ground black pepper to taste
2 tablespoons unsalted butter, plus 2 teaspoons for greasing the pan

1 cup all-purpose flour
1 cup buttermilk
2 large eggs
4 tablespoons minced fresh chives, or very finely chopped scallions (green part only)
1 teaspoon baking powder
½ teaspoon baking soda
⅛ teaspoon salt

1 ounce black, red, and/or golden American caviar for serving

To make the lemon-cream topping, mix the crème fraîche, chives, and lemon zest in a small bowl and set aside.

To make the pancakes, begin by roasting the shallot: Preheat the oven to 400°F. Put the shallot in a small, ovenproof skillet (or small roasting pan) and coat with the oil and some pepper. Roast for 20 minutes or until softened. Remove from the oven and let cool. Remove the outer, browned layer and discard. Chop the shallot and set aside. (The shallot can be roasted a day ahead of time.)

Reduce the oven to 200°F. so that you can keep the pancakes warm as you cook them. Melt 2 tablespoons of the butter in a small pot.

In a large bowl, mix the melted butter with the flour, buttermilk, eggs, chives, chopped shallots, baking powder, baking soda, salt, and a good grinding of pepper and whisk until smooth.

Heat a large skillet over medium heat. Add $^1/_2$ teaspoon of the remaining butter and let it get hot. Add heaping tablespoons of batter to the skillet to make 2-inch pancakes, and cook them for about 1 to $1^1/_2$ minutes; gently flip and cook for another minute. Repeat with the remaining batter, adding more butter as needed.

Keep the pancakes warm on an ovenproof plate in the oven until all of them have been cooked. Serve hot, topped with a dollop of the crème fraîche mixture and a spoonful of caviar.

making crème fraîche

Tangy, thick, creamy crème fraîche is now sold in many supermarkets and specialty food shops across the country. But you can also make a fairly acceptable substitute by mixing heavy cream and buttermilk and letting it sit overnight. To make your own crème fraîche: Mix 1 cup of heavy cream with 1 tablespoon of buttermilk or plain yogurt in a bowl, plastic container, or a resealable plastic bag and let sit, unrefrigerated, in a warm spot overnight. Stir the mixture together and refrigerate. It will thicken and take on a pleasingly tangy, sour flavor. Keep, covered, in the refrigerator for up to 2 weeks.

Use crème fraîche in virtually any dish to which you might add sour cream, including soups, stews, vinaigrettes, and salads. Serve a dollop on roasted vegetables, sweet or savory pancakes, tarts, pound cake, mixed fresh berries, slices of ripe melon, or a mixed fruit salad.

american caviar
three cheers for the red, gold, and black

American caviar has an image problem. When most people think of caviar, they imagine fancy tins from Russia and Iran—luxury, big bucks, and fancy dinners. Choosing American caviar can seem like trading in a fine imported wine for a Budweiser. But nothing could be further from the truth.

The American caviar industry has come a long way. There are now several types of domestic caviar that are well worth seeking out. In general, American caviar is *much* less expensive than imported (way less than half the price), far fresher (it doesn't have to travel nearly as far), and, in some cases, every bit as good.

We like to serve an assortment of American caviars with pancakes (pages 130–131), on thin slices of roasted potatoes, as a garnish for sautéed or grilled fish, or the traditional way—with crackers, sour cream, chopped boiled egg, chopped onion, and a good bottle of bubbly. Give it a try; you're in for a pleasant surprise.

red caviar (**salmon caviar**)
This type of roe is prized for its firm texture, large, round size, and excellent bursts of flavor. Although it is referred to as red caviar, the roe actually has an orange-red color. This is the roe frequently served on top of sushi, and it makes a delicious dip mixed with sour cream and chopped fresh scallions or chives. Plan on paying about seven to eight dollars per ounce.

Chinook and **coho salmon roe** are also worth looking for. These salmon, transplanted from the Pacific Northwest to the Great Lakes, are hatchery-raised fish, and they have a stunning orange-colored roe. The cost is around eight dollars an ounce.

Sea trout roe is a delicate caviar that many feel is superior to salmon roe. The roe is found in trout indigenous to the Great Lakes, with orange-yellow eggs that are slightly smaller than salmon roe. It sells for around six to seven dollars per ounce.

golden caviar (**whitefish roe**)
These caviars come from whitefish found in the northern lakes. Their yellow-gold color and mild, creamy, almost delicate flavor make them a delicious topping or garnish for other fish dishes, or to top a baked potato. This is the least expensive type of caviar (around four to six dollars per ounce), and we think it's one of the most underrated foods around.

black caviar (**spoonbill** *or* **paddlefish caviar**)
This roe is harvested from a prehistoric fish species found primarily in the South, where it swims in many Mississippi and Tennessee rivers. Its flesh has a smooth, creamy texture, and the small, silvery roe are bursting with a rich, complex saltiness.

American Black Pearl caviar (White Sturgeon Caviar) are from white sturgeon from the Pacific and sturgeon raised in artesian well water in California. This black roe rivals Caspian caviar most closely, and while it costs more than any other variety of American caviar, at about thirty-five dollars an ounce, it is still far less expensive than the imported stuff.

fillet of sole with slivered almonds, capers, and whole lemon slices

serves 4

Why is it that so many people find cooking fish intimidating? This dish should be taught in Fish Cookery 101 for its utter simplicity, and surprisingly complex flavors.

Tender, buttery fillets of sole or flounder are dredged in flour, sautéed over a high heat, and cooked until just done. The pan is then deglazed with almonds, capers, lemon slices, and a touch of white wine or vermouth. (Organic lemons are preferable in this dish because the entire lemon, rind and all, can be eaten.) Serve with pasta, rice, or potatoes.

1 cup all-purpose flour
Salt and freshly ground black pepper
   to taste
1 pound fillet of sole, flounder, or yellowtail
   flounder
About 2 tablespoons unsalted butter
About 1 tablespoon olive oil
1/2 cup slivered almonds

1/4 cup capers, drained
3 tablespoons fresh lemon juice
1 lemon or Meyer lemon, preferably
   organic, washed, dried, and cut into
   paper-thin slices (see page 262)
About 1/4 cup dry white vermouth
   or dry white wine
1/4 cup minced fresh parsley

Put the flour on a plate or in a plastic bag and season with the salt and pepper. Lightly dredge the fish fillets in the seasoned flour.

In a large skillet, heat half the butter and oil over high heat. Add a few fillets of fish, being careful not to crowd the skillet, and cook for about 3 to 4 minutes. Gently flip the fish over and cook for another 2 to 3 minutes, or until the fish is just cooked through and golden brown. Place the fish on a warm serving plate and cover loosely with aluminum foil. Repeat with the remaining fish, adding butter and oil to the pan as needed.

When all the fish is on the serving plate, add 1 tablespoon of butter to the skillet. Reduce the heat to medium, add the almonds, and cook, stirring frequently, for 2 minutes. Add the capers, lemon juice, lemon slices, and vermouth and cook for 2 to 3 minutes, or until the wine has been reduced by about half. Pour the hot sauce over the fish, garnish with the minced parsley, and serve immediately.

roasted miso-glazed salmon with asparagus and balsamic-glazed cipolline onions

serves 3 to 4

Although there are several steps involved in this dish, it is simple enough to make for a weeknight supper. A salmon fillet is rubbed with miso paste, grated fresh ginger, sesame oil, and just a touch of soy. The asparagus are lightly steamed until *al dente,* then arranged as a bed for the salmon. Cipolline onions—small, oval-shaped onions that are prized for their mild, sweet flavor—are tossed with grated ginger and balsamic vinegar, and roasted until golden brown and caramelized. The whole dish makes for a striking presentation; serve it with roast potatoes, pasta, orzo, or couscous.

for the onions

¾ pound cipolline, or pearl onions, peeled and left whole

1 teaspoon grated fresh ginger

½ teaspoon Asian sesame oil

1½ tablespoons balsamic vinegar

1 tablespoon soy sauce

Freshly ground black pepper to taste

for the asparagus and salmon

1 pound medium asparagus, about ½ inch thick, ends trimmed, and peeled (see page 30)

1 pound salmon fillet, preferably wild

1 tablespoon miso paste, preferably white miso

1 tablespoon grated fresh ginger

½ teaspoon Asian sesame oil

1 tablespoon soy sauce

2 tablespoons fresh lemon juice

To roast the onions: Preheat the oven to 400°F. Put them in a small, ovenproof skillet or gratin dish and toss with the ginger, sesame oil, balsamic vinegar, soy sauce, and pepper. Roast for 15 minutes, tossing them once or twice. They will be firm, but should be glazed and a deep golden color. Remove from the oven and set aside. Raise the oven temperature to 450°F.

Boil about 2 inches of water in a medium-sized pot or skillet. Add the asparagus and simmer over medium heat for 4 minutes; the asparagus should not be totally cooked and tender, but should be *al dente.* Drain and place under cold running water to stop the cooking; drain again.

To finish the dish: Put half the asparagus in the bottom of an ovenproof, medium-size skillet or gratin dish and put the other half over the bottom layer to form a criss-cross pattern. Place the salmon fillet on top of the asparagus, skin side down. Rub the miso paste and ginger into the flesh of the fish. Drizzle with the sesame oil and soy sauce. Place the roasted onions around the asparagus and salmon. (The recipe can be made several hours ahead of time up to this point. Cover and refrigerate until ready to cook.)

Pour the lemon juice over the salmon and asparagus. Roast the salmon, asparagus, and onions for 12 to 16 minutes, depending on the thickness of the fillet, or until the flesh is opaque. Remove from the oven and serve immediately.

roasted salmon with olive topping and fennel salad

serves 6

The combination of buttery, full-flavored salmon, salty olives, and the anise-flavored crunch of fresh raw fennel is superb. The inspiration for this dish comes from Chez Panisse, Alice Waters' famed restaurant in Berkeley, California.

The salmon is sautéed and then roasted, but it can also be grilled outdoors on a wood, charcoal, or gas fire.

for the fennel salad
2 large fennel bulbs (about 2½ pounds)
Juice of 1 large lemon
¼ cup olive oil
½ teaspoon sea salt, or to taste
Freshly ground black pepper to taste

for the olive topping
½ cup green and/or black olives, pitted
    and thinly sliced

1½ tablespoons olive oil
Freshly ground black pepper to taste

for the salmon
1 tablespoon olive oil
2 garlic cloves, thinly sliced
3 pounds fresh salmon fillets, preferably
    wild, approximately 1 inch thick
Freshly ground black pepper to taste
Juice of 1 lemon

To make the fennel salad: Trim the fronds and stalks off the fennel bulbs and discard or save for another use. Slice off the bottoms and trim any brown spots. Cut the fennel bulbs in half lengthwise and then crosswise into thin slices. Put the fennel slices in a large bowl and toss with the lemon juice, oil, salt, and pepper. (The salad can be made up to 1 hour ahead of time; cover and refrigerate.)

To make the olive topping: In a small bowl, combine the olives, oil, and pepper and set aside. (The topping can be prepared several hours ahead of time; cover and refrigerate.)

To cook the salmon: Position a rack in the middle of the oven and preheat the oven to 400°F. In a large, ovenproof skillet, heat the oil over medium-high heat. Add the garlic and cook for about 1 minute. Add the salmon fillets, skin side down, add a grinding of pepper, and squeeze half the lemon juice on top. Cook for 2 minutes, and, using a spatula, gently flip over the salmon, skin side up. Add the remaining lemon juice, more pepper, and cook for 2 more minutes. Put the skillet in the preheated oven. Roast the salmon for approximately 8 minutes, or until cooked through, or, if you like it on the rare side (pink in the middle), for only 6 to 7 minutes.

To serve, gently flip the salmon fillets skin side down onto plates or a serving platter. Spoon the olive topping down the center of each fillet. Spoon some or all of the fennel salad next to the salmon, and serve the remaining salad in a bowl on the side. Serve hot or at room temperature.

sea salt
is there really a difference?

We are big fans of sea salt. Many people ask, is it really worth it to spend five, eight, or fifteen dollars on salt when you can buy regular iodized supermarket salt for around a buck? It's like trying to explain why we're willing to spend money on Parmigiano-Reggiano instead of buying cheap, flavorless Parmesan cheese in a plastic container from the supermarket. It's all a matter of taste, and good sea salt can add a multifaceted flavor to all kinds of food.

The sea salt industry is booming. There are now specialty salts sold from all over the world—white- and gray-colored salts from Brittany and Provence, pink salt from Hawaii, gray salt from England, and chunky white salts from various U.S. waters.

One of our favorite varieties is Maine Sea Salt, harvested from the Casco Bay in Bailey Island, Maine. We went to visit Steve Cook in Richmond, Maine, to learn more about what makes his salt so unique. Cook takes close to 8,000 gallons of saltwater from the bay every few months and transfers it to a pool-like structure set over a wood-burning fire. As he feeds the fire hardwood from local forests, the saltwater evaporates. When the water has evaporated by about 60 percent, Cook siphons the reduced seawater to shallow pools placed inside solar greenhouses. The water sits in these pools and dries out in the sun; Cook refers to the process as "solar finishing." As the water evaporates a white, salty residue sits at the bottom of the pools. It's quite amazing to see exactly how much salt there is in this pristine water.

All the work is done by hand. "This salt is chemical free," says Cook. "Morton's salt is all about being consumer friendly. They figured out how to put additives in it and make all salt look and taste the same. So I come along and break all the big plans and do the opposite. There's nothing in this salt except what you get from the ocean."

The taste of Maine Sea Salt has the full briny flavor of the ocean, a depth of flavor you won't find in regular table salt. As Cook likes to say: "You take a taste of my salt and there's the first impression in the mouth. And then a second taste comes out. And then a third. It's amazing what happens when you sprinkle some of this salt onto a slice of ripe, raw tomato." (See Resources on page 279 for mail-order information on Maine Sea Salt and other specialty sea salts.)

We like to add sea salt to vinaigrettes, salads, roasted and grilled foods, vegetable dishes, soups, stews, tarts—just about anything and everything. Sprinkle some on your dinner tonight and see what a difference it can make in your food.

spanish-style roasted cod and littleneck clams on potato slices

see photograph on page 83

serves 2 to 4

Roasting a firm-fleshed fish on top of potato slices is a popular Spanish and Portuguese technique. Here the cod is surrounded by littleneck clams; the juices from the clams and the cod baste the potatoes to create a moist, fabulously flavored dish.

4 teaspoons olive oil

1 pound potatoes, preferably Yukon gold, peeled and thinly sliced

Salt and freshly ground black pepper to taste

2 teaspoons chopped fresh thyme

1 pound fresh cod, haddock, or halibut fillets

Pinch of red chile flakes (optional)

1 tablespoon homemade breadcrumbs (page 270) or store-bought

1 tablespoon unsalted butter, cut into small cubes

1½ dozen littleneck or mahogany clams, scrubbed clean (about 2 pounds)

3 tablespoons chopped fresh parsley (optional)

Position a rack in the middle of the oven and preheat the oven to 400°F.

Grease the bottom of a large (about 14-inch) gratin dish, ovenproof skillet, or earthenware dish with 1 teaspoon of the oil. Arrange the potato slices in an overlapping pattern to create one layer. Season liberally with salt and pepper and 1 teaspoon of the thyme. Brush the top with 2 teaspoons of the oil and bake for 20 minutes.

Remove the potatoes from the oven and raise the temperature to 450°F. Place the cod fillets on top of the potatoes and brush with the remaining teaspoon of oil. Season with salt, pepper, the remaining teaspoon of thyme, and the chile flakes, if you want to give the dish a spicy bite. Sprinkle with the breadcrumbs and top with the butter cubes. Place the clams around the cod. Roast the fish for 10 minutes. Remove from the oven and carefully flip the clams over to release their juice, without disturbing any of the potatoes. Roast another 5 to 8 minutes, or until the clams have just opened and the fish is opaque. Remove from the oven; baste the top of the fish with the clam juices and serve immediately, sprinkled with the parsley.

here fishy, fishy

a guide to cooking some favorites

Fish and shellfish can be prepared using a wide variety of techniques. Is there one way that's best? It all depends on what you're in the mood for, and what kind of fish you'll be cooking. With that philosophy in mind, here is a basic guide to the best methods of preparing a wide variety of fish and shellfish.

black sea bass is a white, flaky fish with a buttery, tender, and moist skin; it is excellent sautéed, roasted, or grilled.

bluefish, an oily, full-flavored fish, is best roasted, broiled, sautéed, or, for thick fillets, grilled.

catfish is tender and full flavored, and can be pan-fried, broiled, grilled, or sautéed.

clams can be eaten raw on the half shell, roasted until they just open (see page 100), shucked and sautéed, and added to soups, stews, and chowders.

cod, fluke, halibut, and **haddock** are fairly neutral-flavored fish that adapt well to grilling, pan-searing, pan-frying, or roasting. You can also cut them into chunks for shish kebabs (see page 120), soups, stews, and chowders.

flounder, sole, and **lemon sole** fillets tend to be thin and delicate, making them a good choice for sautéing, poaching, oven steaming *en papillote* (wrapped in parchment paper), or added to soups and stews at the very end of the cooking.

lobster is generally steamed, boiled, broiled, or grilled, but it also can be pan-seared, chopped into pieces and added to stir-fries, soups, stews, and chowders.

monkfish, also called Angler's Fish, All-Mouth, and Poor Man's Lobster, has a rich flavor that some compare to lobster. Fillets can be grilled, roasted, oven-steamed *en papillote* (in parchment paper), and added to soups, stews, and chowders. The cheeks are considered a delicacy.

mussels are delicious roasted until the shell just opens, braised, steamed, poached, and added to soups, stews, and chowders (see page 96).

salmon, preferably wild as opposed to farm-raised, is full of flavor and amazingly versatile. We like to roast it (see pages 134 and 136), grill it (see page 126), poach it, sauté it, and add it to chowders.

scallops are delicious sautéed (see pages 99 and 104), grilled directly over a fire or on cedar planks (see page 126), pan-fried, roasted, and added to shish kebabs (see page 120), soups, stews, and chowders.

shad is a delicate, uniquely flavored fish that is delicious sautéed, broiled, or pan-fried. It can also be grilled directly over a fire or over cedar planks (see page 126).

shad roe is extremely fragile and holds up best when lightly coated in seasoned flour and sautéed. Bacon is a classic accompaniment.

shrimp can be grilled, roasted, pan-fried, broiled, poached, boiled, sautéed, stir-fried, steamed *en papillote,* and added to shish kebabs (see page 120), soups, stews, and chowders.

striped bass, a firm-fleshed fish, is good braised, roasted, grilled, oven-steamed *en papillote,* sautéed, broiled, or cut into chunks and added to shish kebabs (see page 120), soups, and stews.

swordfish, a thick, firm-fleshed fish, is superb grilled (see page 123), roasted, or sautéed. It can be added to shish kebabs (see page 120), soups, stews, and chowders, but it can't be cooked in liquid for long periods, or it becomes tough.

tuna is a firm, meaty fish that is excellent raw, but it's also wonderful grilled, roasted, broiled, sautéed, or added in chunks to soups, stews, and shish kebabs (see page 120).

from the
root cellar

bright

winter sunlight filters in through the basement window. It creates a shadow on baskets of onions, picked in late autumn, their brown skins now dry and crinkly, tightly wrapped around the pungent vegetables. They sit quietly next to a wooden crate overflowing with potatoes—Katahdins, Green Mountains, yellow Bintjes, and small red new potatoes. We sneak down here throughout the snowy winter season, grabbing an onion or two, a couple of potatoes, some garden garlic, or perhaps a winter squash, its bright orange and green stripes reminding us of a season gone by. Each time we head down into the cellar and grab some of our produce, we are aware of the power of the autumn harvest, and the way it sustains us. The potatoes will be sliced with some of those onions, a grating of cheese, perhaps a splash of milk, and baked until golden brown and creamy. On the coldest of winter nights, they will warm us with memories of a season gone by, another one to look forward to.

winter squash and sage ravioli

makes 40 ravioli; serves 4 to 6

Making homemade ravioli sounds time-consuming and complex, right? Well, in this case, it isn't, really. Here egg roll wrappers (available at most supermarkets) are filled with a sage-flavored squash puree. If you use packaged egg roll wrappers and prepare the squash puree ahead of time, the ravioli can be put together surprisingly quickly. The ravioli are served with a simple sage butter and dollop of crème fraîche.

Serve the ravioli with the Fried Sage Leaves on page 151.

One 16-ounce package 6-inch-square egg roll wrappers (20 egg roll wrapers)
About 1½ cups Italian-Style Winter Squash Puree (page 186)
3 tablespoons unsalted butter
1 tablespoon fresh sage, chopped, or 1 teaspoon dried
Freshly ground black pepper to taste
2 tablespoons crème fraîche
⅛ teaspoon salt, or to taste
Whole sage leaves, for garnish

Place an egg roll wrapper on a clean surface. Using a small, dull kitchen knife, score the dough into 4 equal squares. (The idea is not to cut through the dough, but simply to create lines that mark off 4 separate boxes.) Place 1 tablespoon of the squash puree in the center of each of the 4 squares.

Fill a small bowl with water and, using your finger, moisten the outer edge of the wrapper and the scoring lines. Place a second sheet of the dough on top. Using your fingers, pinch the dough together along the outside of the egg roll wrappers to seal them. Then pinch or press down the dough along the outline of each of the 4 boxes and in between them. (This seals together and creates 4 ravioli.) If there appear to be air pockets in the dough, use your fingers to seal a small circle around the filling so air will not get in. Use a pizza cutter or a knife to cut each of the 4 ravioli out of the dough. Repeat. (Don't make the ravioli more than 1 hour before cooking, or they will dry out.) Place on paper towels, without stacking them.

Bring a large pot of water to a boil.

Meanwhile, in a small saucepan, melt the butter. Add the sage and a generous grinding of pepper and cook over low heat for 1 minute.

Boil the ravioli, without crowding the pot, for 4 minutes, stirring to make sure they don't stick. Carefully drain the ravioli and place on a large serving platter in one layer. (The ravioli are delicate and will stick to one another.) Pour the sage butter over the pasta and place a dollop of the crème fraîche on top. Sprinkle with the salt, season with pepper, and place the sage leaves in the middle as a garnish.

sampling squash

Delicata. Golden Nugget. Orange Hubbard. Turks' Turban. Hopi Orange. Lady Godiva. Kabocha. Poetry? Well yes, but these are also some of the many varieties of winter squash.

Gardeners harvest winter squash in the fall and keep them for several months, enjoying fresh squash throughout the winter. The squash needs to be stored in a dry, cool, dark spot, where they can last for up to 3 to 6 months, depending on the conditions. You want to store winter squash at around 50°F.—when it's warmer the squash tends to deteriorate, and freezing temperatures can ruin its firm texture. Choose hard-shelled squash without any soft spots. The colors should be bright, vibrant, and fresh looking. And when you look for squash—whether in a farmers market or the supermarket—pick ones that feel heavy in your hand; this is a sign that there is a good deal of edible flesh. The yellow-orange flesh inside winter squash contains plenty of vitamin A, vitamin C, niacin, phosphorus, and potassium.

The following guide introduces you to some new squash varieties, and describes some old favorites:

acorn squash are acorn shaped with green to yellow-gold to white skin and deep furrows. The flesh is a pumpkin orange-yellow, with a firm, dry texture and a moderately sweet flavor. Try stuffing acorn squash with cranberries and maple syrup and baking it until tender.

australian blue or **blue hubbard** is an unusually large variety with a gray-blue exterior and a slightly sweet, pumpkin-flavored flesh. Australian Blue can be pureed and mashed, and makes excellent soup.

banana squash is long and banana shaped and grows up to 2 to 3 feet long. The skin tends to be pale orange and the flesh golden. The flavor is full, the texture somewhat dry; it's delicious stuffed and baked, or pureed.

buttercup is a round, flat-looking squash with dark green skin and grayish stripes and a crown that is generally lighter in color. The orange-colored flesh is exceptionally sweet, with a rich, buttery texture. Buttercup is delicious baked or roasted.

butternut is long with a bulbous end. This pale tan–colored squash is excellent baked, steamed, pureed, or mashed. It can be cut into thin rounds and roasted with maple syrup and chopped fresh sage.

delicata looks more like a small green-and-yellow striped, elongated watermelon than a winter squash. This is a moist, delicately flavored, sweet squash with orange flesh and, if it is not overgrown, an edible skin. Some say the flavor tastes like buttered corn. The large cavity is ideal for stuffing.

sweet dumpling is a gorgeous ivory-and-green-striped round squash with pale orange flesh that some say tastes as sweet as candy. Delicious baked, Sweet Dumplings can also be stuffed and then roasted.

beet napoleons

makes about 14 napoleons; serves 4 or 5

Don't you just love recipes that look so elegant and restaurant-worthy that people think you spent the whole day in the kitchen? This is one. Yellow and red beets are roasted until tender, then sliced and layered with a chive-flavored goat cheese. The napoleons are then drizzled with a dramatic emerald-green chive puree. The whole dish can be made ahead of time and plated just before serving, making it an ideal first course for any dinner party. It also makes a great lunch dish, served with crusty bread and an arugula salad.

1 1/2 pounds small red and/or yellow beets, no larger than 1 to 1 1/2 inches across

6 ounces soft goat cheese

1 tablespoon sour cream or heavy cream

1/4 cup packed minced fresh chives

1/8 teaspoon salt, or to taste

Freshly ground black pepper to taste

Chive Puree (page 77)

Preheat the oven to 400°F. Place 4 beets on a large piece of foil and wrap tightly. Repeat with the remaining beets. Roast for about 1 hour, or until tender. Beets can vary widely in cooking time. Small, fresh beets may be ready after only 45 minutes of roasting, while large, dense, not-quite-as-fresh beets can take up to 1 1/2 hours. To test, insert a small, sharp knife into the center; the beet should feel soft and tender all the way through. Let cool for about 5 to 10 minutes. Using your fingers or a small, sharp knife, peel off the beet skin and trim the ends. Thinly slice the beets and set aside to cool completely.

Meanwhile, place the goat cheese, sour cream, chives, salt, and pepper in a small bowl. Using the back of a spoon or a rubber spatula, cream the cheese until soft and the chives are fully incorporated. Make the Chive Puree. (The beets, cheese filling, and Chive Puree can be made a day ahead of time; cover and refrigerate until ready to assemble.)

To assemble, place a slice of red beet on a plate. Spread about 1/2 teaspoon of the cheese mixture on top and then top with a slice of yellow beet. Spread another 1/2 teaspoon of cheese on top and then top the cheese with a third slice of red beet. You can use any color combination you like: all yellow, all red, or alternating colors. You can also place 1/2 teaspoon of the cheese filling on the top beet slice. Repeat to form the remaining napoleons.

To serve, place a small pool of Chive Puree (1 to 3 tablespoons, depending on the size of the plate) on a salad plate and arrange 2 or 3 napoleons in the center of the puree. Serve at room temperature with any remaining Chive Puree on the side.

cold potato and leek soup with chive puree

see photograph on page 141

serves 8

Plan on making this cold, creamy potato and leek soup at least 8 hours before serving to give it time to chill. The soup and the Chive Puree can be made 24 hours ahead of time. Served hot, this soup is a delicious way to warm up on a winter's day.

2 1/2 pounds leeks (about 8 medium)
1 1/2 tablespoons olive oil
2 tablespoons minced fresh chives
1 tablespoon chopped fresh thyme
3 pounds medium-starch potatoes (such as russets or Yukon gold), peeled and cut into 2-inch pieces (about 5 very large potatoes)

8 cups homemade chicken (page 269) or vegetable broth, or canned broth
1/4 teaspoon salt, or to taste
Freshly ground black pepper to taste
1/2 cup plus 2 tablespoons heavy cream
Chive Puree (page 77)

Cut the leeks in two crosswise to separate the dark green portion from the white. Discard the greens or save for vegetable stock. Cut the white part of the leeks in half lengthwise, and rinse out any dirt between the layers, then cut the leek crosswise into 2-inch pieces.

In a large soup pot, heat the oil over medium-low heat. Add the leeks, chives, and thyme and stir. Reduce the heat to low, cover, and cook for 10 minutes, stirring occasionally. Add the potatoes, stir well, and cook for 2 minutes. Raise the heat to high and add the broth, salt, and pepper. (Be careful not to oversalt the soup if using canned chicken broth.) Bring to a boil, reduce the heat to low, and simmer, covered, for about 15 minutes, or until the potatoes are tender. Remove from the heat and let cool slightly.

In a food processor or blender, puree the soup in batches until smooth. Pour into a large bowl, stir in the cream, and taste for seasoning. Add salt and pepper if needed. Cover and refrigerate for at least 8 hours, or until well chilled. Serve cold with a generous teaspoon of Chive Puree swirled into each bowl.

cream of celery root and ginger soup

serves 6 to 8

This is a creamy soup infused with a deep celery flavor. Serve it piping hot with a sprinkling of chopped fresh parsley or chervil. A loaf of warm, crusty bread and a robust red wine are the perfect accompaniments for a simple dinner or hearty lunch.

2½ pounds celery root (also called
    celeriac; see page 185)
1 tablespoon olive oil
1 leek (white part only), cut in half
    lengthwise, rinsed, and finely chopped
Salt and freshly ground black pepper
    to taste

2 tablespoons chopped fresh ginger
6 cups homemade chicken (page 269) or
    vegetable broth, or canned broth
½ cup heavy cream
½ cup chopped fresh parsley or fresh
    chervil (optional)

Peel the celery root with a sharp knife, cut into 2-inch pieces, and set aside.

In a large soup pot, heat the oil over low heat. Add the chopped leek and cook, stirring frequently, for about 5 minutes, or until the leek is tender. Season with salt and pepper, add half the ginger, and cook for 30 seconds, stirring well. Add the celery root chunks and cook, stirring, for another minute. Add the chicken broth, raise the heat to high, and bring to a boil. Reduce the heat to low, cover, and simmer for about 25 to 35 minutes, or until the celery root feels tender when tested with a small, sharp knife. Remove from the heat, add the remaining ginger, and let cool for a few minutes.

Working in batches, puree the soup in a food processor or blender until smooth. Pour the pureed soup back into the pot and taste for seasoning, adding more salt and pepper as needed. (The ginger flavor will be quite pronounced at this point; but it mellows when the cream is added.) Add the cream and bring to a simmer over low heat, about 10 minutes. Serve piping hot with a sprinkling of parsley or chervil.

pumpkin soup with fried sage leaves

serves 10 to 12

The pale orange color of this creamy, soothing soup is spectacular, particularly when topped with fried green sage leaves. The soup can be made with virtually any type of winter squash and can be prepared 24 hours ahead of time; it can also be frozen.

Look for a small sugar pumpkin to make the soup. Many sugar pumpkins (Baby Bear, Jack Be Little, and Wee-B-Little) are marketed as cooking pumpkins, as opposed to carving or ornamental pumpkins. Sugar pumpkins are sweeter and a lot easier to cook with (some are stringless), but you can use any type of fresh pumpkin. The smaller the pumpkin, the easier it will be to chop into small pieces.

for the soup
2 pounds sugar pumpkin, or acorn, butternut, or any other winter squash
1 tablespoon olive oil
1 teaspoon butter
3 leeks (white part only) cut in half lengthwise, rinsed, and cut into 1-inch pieces (about 2 cups)
1 tablespoon chopped fresh thyme, or 1 teaspoon dried
1 tablespoon chopped fresh sage

Salt and freshly ground black pepper to taste
7 cups homemade chicken (page 269) or vegetable broth

for the garnish
About 1 cup heavy cream or crème fraîche (optional)
2 cups Garlic Croûtes (see page 271), optional
Fried sage leaves (optional; see page 151)

Using a large, sharp knife, cut the pumpkin in half, and remove the seeds and stringy sections and discard; or you can save the seeds for roasting. Cut the pumpkin into 2- to 3-inch chunks. Carefully cut the rind off the pumpkin chunks and cut the flesh into 1- to 2-inch pieces. You should have about 8 cups.

In a large soup pot, heat the oil and butter over medium-low heat. Add the leeks and sauté, stirring frequently, for 4 minutes. Add pumpkin chunks, thyme, sage, salt, and pepper. Cover and cook for 5 minutes. Remove the cover, add the chicken broth, and bring to a boil over high heat. Reduce the heat to low, cover, and simmer for about 25 minutes, or until the pumpkin is tender. Remove from the heat and let cool slightly.

Puree the soup in a blender or food processor, working in batches. Taste for seasoning, return the pureed soup to the pot, and warm over low heat. Drizzle the cream or crème fraîche into the soup, or swirl into each bowl, and top with a few croutons and the sage leaves, if desired.

fried sage leaves

You can use this technique—frying whole herbs in hot oil—with any type of fresh herb, but sage works particularly well. The herbs must be cleaned of any dirt and thoroughly patted dry before frying. Use as a garnish for soups, stews, pasta dishes, and salads. Fried sage leaves are also a delicious treat served alongside a martini.

To make the fried sage leaves, you'll need 2 to 3 cups of olive or safflower oil, a bunch of very fresh sage, and some good sea salt. Carefully snip off and separate small bundles of the sage (about 3 to 4 leaves attached to every small piece of stem) and set aside. Heat the oil in a medium-sized, heavy skillet over high heat until the oil just begins to smoke, and very carefully lower the sage into the hot oil. (The oil is hot enough when the sage leaves immediately begin to sizzle.) Fry for about 30 seconds. Remove the sage with a slotted spoon and drain on paper towels or a clean brown grocery bag. Don't fry the leaves more than 15 minutes ahead of time or they will wilt. Sprinkle the fried leaves with sea salt.

french lentil soup

serves 6 to 8

It was a cold January day, and there was a leftover ham bone in the refrigerator, and some lentils in the pantry. We simmered the bone with red wine, a handful of the lentils, some leeks, celery, and parsley, and served this thick, savory soup piping hot with Garlic Croûtes (page 271) and a hearty salad. Ask for a ham bone from your butcher. You can also substitute a bone from a roast leg of lamb.

One 2- to 3-pound ham bone (preferably smoked), with some meat still clinging to the bone, or the bone from a roasted leg of lamb (see page 220)

1 cup dry red wine

3 medium leeks (white parts only), cut in half lengthwise, rinsed, and cut into thin circles

3 celery stalks, finely chopped

½ cup finely chopped fresh Italian parsley

1½ cups French Puy lentils (see below for more on lentils)

1 tablespoon crushed dried rosemary

¼ teaspoon salt, or to taste

Freshly ground black pepper to taste

Garlic Croûtes (page 271), or store-bought croutons

Put the ham bone in a large soup pot. Add 10 cups of water, the wine, leeks, celery, parsley, lentils, rosemary, salt (use a light hand because the ham bone tends to be salty), and a generous grinding of pepper and bring to a boil over high heat. Reduce the heat to low, cover, and simmer for about 1½ hours, or until the lentils are tender and the broth is very flavorful. If there is meat clinging to the bone, remove the bone and cut the meat into small cubes. Add the meat to the soup and discard the bone. Taste for seasoning and serve piping hot topped with the Garlic Croûtes.

the language of lentils

Lentils are a staple of Middle Eastern and Mediterranean cooking. Unlike beans, which need to soak overnight, lentils can be cooked immediately and become tender and creamy in less than an hour. They provide calcium and vitamins A and B, and are an excellent source of iron and phosphorus.

There are three major varieties of lentil: Tiny, dark green French lentils, called *lentilles du Puy*, or **Puy lentils,** are highly prized for their ability to hold their shape when cooked. They have a smooth, creamy texture with a clean, delicious flavor. The reddish-orange **Egyptian** or **red lentils** are smaller, rounder, and widely used in Indian cooking. They tend to fall apart when cooked and form a thick, sweetly flavored puree. There's also the common **brown** or **yellow lentil,** a small lentil with a deep, rich flavor.

Lentils may be stored in a cool, dark spot for up to a year. They can be used in soups (see above), as a side dish, and in salads. Lentils go particularly well with roast duck and poultry.

roasted mushroom and leek soup
with crispy pancetta

serves 8

This soup will taste particularly complex, with an almost meaty flavor, if you find a good variety of mushrooms. To clean the mushrooms, see page 179.

You'll want to use a total of about 1½ pounds of mushrooms of any variety you like; see pages 178–179 for more information about different varieties.

3½ ounces shiitake mushrooms, stem ends trimmed

6 ounces crimini mushrooms, stem ends trimmed

½ pound button mushrooms, stem ends trimmed, cut in half if large

6 ounces portobello mushrooms, coarsely chopped to match the size of the other mushrooms

3 leeks (white part only) cut in half lengthwise, rinsed, and cut into 1-inch pieces

1 large red or Vidalia onion, chopped into 1-inch pieces

3 tablespoons olive oil

1½ tablespoons chopped fresh thyme, or ½ teaspoon dried

Salt and freshly ground black pepper to taste

¼ cup dry red or white wine

5 cups homemade chicken (page 269) or vegetable broth, or canned broth

About ¼ cup heavy cream, optional

6 thin slices pancetta (about 2 ounces; see page 109 for more on pancetta)

Preheat the oven to 400°F. Position a rack in the middle of the oven.

In a large roasting pan, toss the mushrooms, leeks, onion, two tablespoons of the oil, the thyme, salt, and pepper until well combined. Roast for 45 minutes, tossing the mushrooms once or twice as they cook. Remove from the pan and immediately deglaze the pan with the wine and then the broth.

Working in batches, puree the broth with the mushrooms in the container of a food processor or blender. Pour the pureed soup into a large soup pot and add the cream, if using. Taste for seasoning and add salt and pepper if needed. (The soup can be made 1 day ahead of time up to this point.)

To prepare the pancetta: Put the remaining tablespoon of oil in a medium skillet over low heat and add the pancetta. Cook, turning frequently, until the meat is crisp on both sides like bacon, about 5 to 10 minutes. Drain on paper towels and, using your hands, break the pancetta into 1-inch pieces.

To serve the soup: Reheat the soup until simmering. Serve sprinkled with several pieces of crisp pancetta.

baked goat cheese and caramelized onion salad with rosemary-infused honey

serves 6

Baked goat cheese salad could be considered the official dish of the "new California cuisine." It all began in the early seventies at Alice Waters's highly acclaimed restaurant, Chez Panisse in Berkeley, California. Goat cheese salad spread like mint in a wild garden patch; it can now be found, in one form or another, on restaurant menus across the country. The reason is simple: The creamy tang of baked goat cheese makes a delicious companion to bitter greens. In this rendition we've added the natural sweetness of caramelized onions, and an herb-flavored honey drizzled on top.

for the onions
1 tablespoon olive oil
3 medium-sized sweet onions, such as
    Vidalia, very thinly sliced
1½ teaspoons sugar

for the goat cheese
½ pound soft goat cheese log
½ cup breadcrumbs, preferably homemade
    (page 270)
1 tablespoon minced fresh rosemary,
    or 1 teaspoon dried
1 tablespoon minced fresh thyme, or
    1 teaspoon dried

¼ teaspoon sea salt, or to taste
Freshly ground black pepper to taste

for the salad
3 cups dark, leafy greens such as arugula,
    mizuna (a mustard green), baby
    spinach, or watercress (see pages 38–39
    for more on greens)
3 tablespoons olive oil
1½ tablespoons red wine vinegar
Salt and freshly ground black pepper
    to taste
¼ cup Rosemary-Infused Honey (see
    page 202) or honey

To caramelize the onions: Heat the oil in a large skillet over low heat. Add the onions and cook, stirring frequently, until the onions are soft and have taken on a caramel color, about 15 minutes. Sprinkle with the sugar, stir well, and cook for another 2 to 3 minutes. Remove from the heat and set aside.

To prepare the goat cheese: Preheat the oven to 400°F. Place a sheet of parchment paper or aluminum foil on a baking sheet. Using a sharp knife or a piece of string held taut, slice the goat cheese into ⅓-inch-thick rounds. You should have 12 rounds. In a small bowl, mix the breadcrumbs, rosemary, thyme, salt, and pepper. Dredge the goat cheese slices in the breadcrumb mixture, making sure to coat them well on both sides, and place on the prepared baking sheet. (The recipe can be prepared ahead of time up to this point. Cover and refrigerate the onions and goat cheese until ready to serve.)

Bake the goat cheese for 5 minutes. Using a spatula, gently flip the goat cheese over and bake for another 5 to 10 minutes, or until the cheese just begins to bubble and ooze on the sides. Remove from the pan and let cool for several minutes.

To finish the salad: While the cheese is cooling, toss the greens, oil, vinegar, salt, and pepper in a bowl. If you made the onions ahead of time, reheat them in a skillet over low heat until warm.

Heat the rosemary honey until warm by placing it in a measuring cup and placing the cup in a small saucepan of simmering water. Heat until the honey becomes fluid, about 3 to 5 minutes.

Divide the salad among six plates. Place a spoonful of the warm onions beside each salad and top with 2 goat cheese rounds. Drizzle the honey on top of the salad greens or onions.

roasted beet salad with maple-glazed walnuts and chive-ginger dressing

serves 4 to 6

Look for golden beets (or a combination of red and golden beets) for this salad to create the dramatic visual contrast of golden yellow against the glazed brown walnuts and bright green chives. Peeling cooked beets can be messy; you may want to wear rubber gloves so you don't stain your fingers, and work on a sheet of plastic wrap to avoid staining your counters or work surface.

for the beets and walnuts

9 small to medium yellow and/or red beets, preferably no bigger than 2 inches across

1 tablespoon olive oil

1 teaspoon butter

1 cup walnut halves

2 1/2 tablespoons maple syrup

Salt and freshly ground black pepper to taste

for the ginger vinaigrette

1 tablespoons finely chopped or grated fresh ginger

Salt and freshly ground black pepper to taste

1 1/2 tablespoons minced fresh chives, or minced chopped scallions (green parts only)

2 tablespoons balsamic or red wine vinegar

4 1/2 tablespoons olive oil

1 1/2 tablespoons minced fresh chives, or minced chopped scallions (green part only), for garnish

To prepare the beets and walnuts: Position a rack in the middle of the oven and preheat the oven to 400°F. Using 3 large pieces of aluminum foil, create 3 "packages," wrapping 3 beets in each. Roast for 1 hour to 1 hour and 15 minutes, or until the beets feel tender in the center when pierced with a small, sharp knife. (Some of the beets may be done after 45 minutes of roasting, while others may take closer to 1 1/2 hours, depending on their thickness and freshness. Keep checking and removing the beets as they finish cooking.) Remove from the oven and let cool for a few minutes. Unwrap each packet and, using your fingers or a small, sharp knife, peel off the beet skin.

In a medium skillet, heat the oil and butter over medium heat. Add the walnuts and cook, stirring, for 2 minutes. Add the maple syrup, salt, and pepper and cook, stirring frequently, for about 4 minutes, or until all the walnuts are glazed. Remove from the heat and set aside. (The beets and walnuts can be made 24 hours ahead of time; cover and refrigerate.)

To make the vinaigrette: Mix the ginger, salt, pepper, chives, vinegar, and oil in a small bowl.

Thinly slice the beets and arrange on a serving platter. Spoon the walnuts around the edges of the beets and pour the vinaigrette on top. Garnish the salad with the chives. Serve cold or at room temperature.

harvest variation
Serve the salad on top of well-rinsed baby greens.

potato galettes stuffed with greens and gruyère

serves 4 as a main course or 6 as a side dish

Imagine two large, crispy potato pancakes, filled with sautéed greens and grated Gruyère cheese, baked until golden brown, with cheese oozing out of the middle. Enticing, right? Making a potato galette can be tricky business— it's tough to brown the potatoes and keep them from sticking to the pan, while making sure the inside of the galette is tender and cooked through, and the outside is still crispy. But this recipe is the triumphant result of many, many attempts and is a sure-fire way to make winning galettes. The dish can be made ahead of time and heated just before serving, making it ideal party food.

for the potatoes

2 pounds high- or medium-starch potatoes like russets or Yukon golds, peeled (about 6 medium)

About 2 teaspoons unsalted butter

About 1 tablespoon plus 2 teaspoons vegetable or olive oil

Salt and freshly ground black pepper

for the stuffing

1 tablespoon olive oil

1/2 pound baby spinach, Swiss chard, kale, or assorted greens, thick stems trimmed, and coarsely chopped

Salt and freshly ground black pepper to taste

1 cup grated Gruyère cheese

To cook the potatoes: Using the large holes on a box grater, grate half the potatoes— about 3. (Do not grate them all at once, or they will discolor while you are waiting to cook them.)

Heat an 8- to 10-inch heavy, ovenproof skillet (cast iron is ideal) over medium heat. Add 1 teaspoon of the butter and 1 teaspoon of the oil and let the butter sizzle. Add the grated potatoes, pressing down with the flat side of a spatula to create one flat pancake. Season with salt and pepper. Let cook for 7 to 9 minutes on one side, or until crisp and golden brown, using a flat spatula to loosen the bottom of the potato cake and prevent it from sticking. The goal is to let the potatoes brown, cook through, and stay loosened from the bottom of the pan. While the first galette is cooking, grate the remaining potatoes.

Once the bottom of the first galette is done, use one or two spatulas to carefully flip it over, adding another teaspoon of oil to the bottom of the pan. Cook for 5 to 6 minutes on the other side, loosening the potato with the spatula as directed above. Carefully flip the galette onto a large plate. You can also use a heat-proof plate to cover the pan and invert the galette directly onto the plate.

Make another galette with the remaining potatoes, using the butter and oil as needed to keep the pan greased and help the potatoes brown. When the second galette is done, flip it out onto another plate.

Meanwhile, in another large skillet, prepare the stuffing: Heat the olive oil over medium heat. Add the greens and cook, stirring, for about 5 minutes, until wilted and just soft. Season with salt and pepper and set aside.

To assemble the dish: Position a rack in the middle of the oven and preheat the oven to 450°F. Grease the skillet in which you cooked the galette very lightly and place one of the galettes on the bottom (choose the one that looks least attractive). Spoon the cooked greens on top, pressing down to create a flat surface. Sprinkle the cheese over the greens and top with the remaining galette. (The dish can be made up to 12 hours ahead up to this point. Cover and refrigerate until ready to bake and serve.)

Place the galette in the oven and bake for 15 to 20 minutes, or until the cheese has melted and the cake is hot, crispy, and golden brown. If you want the top layer to be a darker, golden brown, place the galette under the broiler for 2 to 4 minutes just before serving.

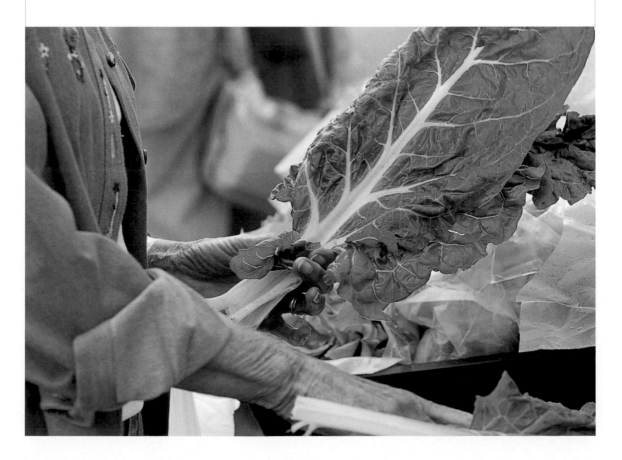

swiss chard tart with a potato crust

makes 2 tarts; each serves 4 to 6

Instead of traditional pastry, the crust for this tart is formed from very thin slices of potato. The potatoes turn out to be perfect for the job, since the outside edges turn a gorgeous golden brown and become crisp, like homemade chips. The tart makes a superb brunch dish—you could even add bacon to the filling for a tart that combines eggs, bacon, and potatoes all in one dish. Or serve the tart as an appetizer or main course.

This recipe makes two tarts; serve them both or freeze one, tightly covered with foil, for up to 3 months.

1½ pounds Swiss chard
¼ cup plus 2 tablespoons olive oil
1 large garlic clove, very thinly sliced
Salt and freshly ground black pepper
    to taste
2 large high-starch potatoes, like Idaho
    (8 to 10 ounces), unpeeled and scrubbed
    clean

3 teaspoons chopped fresh thyme
1 heaping cup freshly grated Parmesan
    cheese
2 large eggs
2 cups ricotta cheese

Trim the stems of the chard, wash the leaves thoroughly, drain, and dry. Coarsely chop the chard. In a large skillet, heat 2 tablespoons of the oil over medium heat. Add half the garlic and half the chard and cook, stirring frequently. As the chard cooks down, add the remaining chard and garlic. Season with salt and a generous grinding of pepper. Cook for about 10 minutes, stirring until the chard is just tender. Tilt the skillet to the side and blot up any excess liquid with a paper towel. Let cool.

To make the crust, slice the potatoes *very* thinly. It's fine if some of the slices are smaller than the others—the important thing is to make them fairly uniform in thickness. Create a thin layer of the potato slices on the bottom of two pie plates (preferably glass), slightly overlapping them to create a solid bottom "crust." Gently tuck potato slices along the edges to create a border up the sides of the pie plates. When you're done, you should have two solid pie "crusts." Use thin or oddly shaped potato slices to fill in any gaps. Discard the remaining slices. Drizzle 2 tablespoons of the oil over each crust, swirling the pan slightly so the oil spreads between the potato layers and drips to the bottom. Sprinkle each crust with ½ teaspoon of the thyme, some salt and pepper, and a heaping ¼ cup of Parmesan cheese.

Position a rack in the middle of the oven and preheat the oven to 400°F.

Whisk the eggs in a large bowl and whisk in the ricotta, the remaining 2 teaspoons of thyme, and the remaining ½ cup of Parmesan cheese. Season with salt and pepper. Add the cooled sautéed chard and mix well. Divide the filling between the two pie crusts and press down lightly.

Bake the tart for 20 minutes. Reduce the heat to 350°F. and bake for another 10 minutes. The potato crust should turn brown and crisp, and the filling should feel solid and firm when gently touched with your fingers. Let cool about 5 minutes before cutting into wedges.

five-onion and bacon tart with thyme crust

serves 4 to 6 as a main course or 8 to 10 as a first course or hors d'oeuvre

Leeks, onions, scallions, shallots, and garlic are slowly cooked until sweet and tender, then mixed with reduced cream, Parmesan cheese, and fresh thyme. Feel free to omit the bacon if you want to make this a vegetarian tart. Serve the tart with a winter salad of baby spinach and tiny sections of sweet tangerines.

You'll need a tart pan with a removable bottom, preferably a rectangular one that is 11 inches long by 8 inches wide and 1 inch deep. You can also use a round pan. If you're pressed for time, you can always use a premade frozen pie crust (just sprinkle it with some fresh or dried thyme before filling).

for the pastry

2 cups all-purpose flour
Pinch of salt
1 tablespoon chopped fresh thyme,
   or 1 teaspoon dried
1 cup (2 sticks) unsalted butter, cut into
   cubes
1/4 cup ice water, or as needed

for the filling

4 strips thick, country-style bacon
2 tablespoons olive oil, or 1 tablespoon
   olive oil and 1 tablespoon garlic oil
1 medium onion, very thinly sliced

1/2 pound leeks (about 3 thin leeks, or 1 to
   2 medium-large, white part only), cut in
   half lengthwise, rinsed, and thinly sliced
   (discard the green part)
1 large shallot, very thinly sliced
2 small garlic cloves, very thinly sliced
2 scallions (white and green parts), trimmed
   and chopped
1 teaspoon unsalted butter
1 tablespoon chopped fresh thyme,
   or 1/2 teaspoon dried
Salt and freshly ground black pepper
   to taste
1 cup heavy cream
1 cup freshly grated Parmesan or Gruyère
   cheese

To make the pastry: Blend the flour with the salt and thyme in the bowl of a food processor. Add the butter and pulse about 15 to 20 times, or until the mixture resembles coarse cornmeal. Add about 1/4 cup of the water, or just enough to make the pastry dough begin to come together and pull away from the sides of the bowl. Add another 1 or 2 tablespoons of water if needed. Alternately, you can make the pastry by hand. Combine the flour and salt in a bowl. Add the butter and, using two kitchen knives or a pastry blender, work the butter into the flour until it resembles coarse cornmeal. Add enough water so that the dough just begins to come together when mixed with a wooden spoon. Transfer the dough from the food processor or

recipe continues

bowl to a large sheet of aluminum foil and wrap it up into a ball. Refrigerate for at least 2 hours. (The dough can be made 1 day ahead of time, or frozen for several months.)

Meanwhile, begin the filling: In a skillet, cook the bacon over medium heat until crisp on both sides, about 5 to 8 minutes, depending on the thickness. Drain on paper towels and let cool. Gently crumble the bacon into 1/2-inch pieces and set aside.

In a clean, large skillet, heat 1 tablespoon of the oil over low heat. Add the onion and cook for 5 minutes, stirring frequently. Add the leeks, shallot, garlic, scallions, butter, and half the thyme to the skillet and season with salt and pepper. Cook over very low heat for 15 minutes, stirring frequently. Transfer the mixture to a large bowl. (The onion mixture and bacon can be made 1 day ahead of time. Cover and refrigerate until needed.)

To assemble and bake the tart: Position a rack in the middle of the oven and pre-heat the oven to 350°F. In the same large skillet in which you cooked the onions, heat the cream, remaining thyme, and a generous sprinkle of pepper over low heat. Simmer for 5 to 8 minutes, or until thickened and a thick, buttery-looking cream appears around the edges of the skillet. Let cool slightly.

Meanwhile, working on a lightly floured surface, roll out the chilled dough into a rectangle about 12 inches long by 9 or 10 inches wide. The pastry will be fairly thin—about 1/4 inch thick. Drape the dough over the tart pan and press down lightly. Trim off the overhanging dough and reserve. Press the pastry into the tart pan.

Add the cream to the onion mixture and stir well. Stir in the reserved bacon pieces and the grated cheese and pile the mixture into the prepared crust.

You can leave the tart as is, or cut thin strips out of any of the remaining scraps of dough and make a lattice pattern on top of the tart. You may only have enough for 5 to 6 long strips, so you might want to simply place horizontal strips on top of the dough, pressing down on the dough strips where they meet the crust to make sure they are attached.

Place the tart on a cookie sheet and bake for about 1 hour, or until golden brown. If the tart is browning too quickly, reduce the oven temperature to 325°F and cover loosely with aluminum foil. Let cool a few minutes and, wearing oven mitts, remove the tart from the pan by gently lifting the bottom up out of the pan. Serve hot or at room temperature.

roots below

Turnips, rutabagas, and parsnips are the poor cousins of the root vegetable family. These wintry root vegetables, in the words of Rodney Dangerfield, "don't get no respect." Let's be honest: Plain steamed turnips or rutabagas aren't the sexiest flavors in the world. Roast them, however, allowing their natural sugars to emerge, and they take on a depth of flavor and sweetness that is surprisingly good. The outside becomes crisp like a potato and the inside stays tender and full of earthy flavor. Turnips, rutabagas, and parsnips are also delicious sautéed in a hot skillet with chopped fresh rosemary, or steamed and mashed with potatoes and butter. They can be cubed and simmered in soups, or added to stews for a rich flavor.

choosing and prepping root vegetables

Select vegetables that are on the small side, as they tend to get tough and fibrous when allowed to grow past their prime. Look for turnips with the greens still attached, indicating freshness. Look for firm specimens that are not much bigger than 3 inches across. Rutabagas (or yellow turnips) are often found coated in wax—be sure to peel them entirely before cooking. They should be firm and smooth, and feel heavy for their size. Parsnips are planted in the summer and often allowed to winter over (increasing the sugar content), then harvested in early spring. They have the most delicate and buttery flavor of these root vegetables. Be sure to peel them before cooking. Look for firm parsnips that aren't too thick, without spots or roots sprouting.

cooking them up

Our favorite way to cook root vegetables is to roast them. Simply peel ½ pound each of turnips, rutabagas, and parsnips and cut them into 2-inch pieces. Toss them with a few tablespoons of good olive oil in a large roasting pan and add sea salt, pepper, and some chopped fresh (or dry) thyme and rosemary. Roast in a preheated 450°F. oven for 30 minutes. Reduce the oven temperature to 350°F. and roast for another 30 to 45 minutes, or until they are tender.

harvest variations

• For a roasted root vegetable puree, remove the vegetables from the oven, let cool slightly, and mash or puree them.

• To make soup, remove the roasted vegetables from the oven and add 4 cups of chicken or vegetable broth. Puree the mixture and serve hot.

• For a heartier dish, add 1 pound of baby new potatoes to the root vegetables before roasting.

• Add 1 pound of baby red or yellow beets to the root vegetables before roasting.

• To create a sauce for the vegetables, after roasting, place the roasting pan over 2 burners on the stove. Sprinkle 1 tablespoon of flour over the vegetables and let cook for 1 minute. Whisk in 1 cup of dry white or red wine and let simmer for a few minutes.

winter caramelized onion, walnut, and blue cheese pizza

serves 4 to 6 as a main course or 8 as an appetizer

This is a pizza for the colder months, when good tomatoes are scarce but onions are sweet and plentiful. This recipe provides enough topping for one 12-inch pizza; it can easily be doubled to make 2 pizzas.

If you're pressed for time you can always use a premade pizza dough from your local pizza shop or supermarket.

2 1/2 tablespoons olive oil

5 medium onions (about 1 1/2 pounds), very thinly sliced

3 garlic cloves, very thinly sliced

Salt and freshly ground black pepper to taste

1 tablespoon dried rosemary

1 tablespoon dried sage

1 teaspoon dried thyme

1 teaspoon unsalted butter

1 cup coarsely chopped walnuts

1/2 recipe Cornmeal and White Flour Pizza Dough (page 276)

3 tablespoons freshly grated Parmesan cheese

3 ounces Gorgonzola cheese (or your favorite blue cheese), crumbled

To caramelize the onions: Heat 1 1/2 tablespoons of the oil over low heat in a large skillet. Add the onions and garlic, and cook for about 20 to 25 minutes, stirring frequently, until the onions are soft and a pale golden brown. Season with salt and pepper, and add the rosemary, sage, and thyme; cook for 1 minute. Transfer the onions to a plate and set aside.

In the same skillet, heat 1 1/2 teaspoons of the oil and the butter over low heat. Add the walnuts and cook for 4 minutes, stirring frequently. Season lightly with salt and pepper and set aside. (The onions and walnuts can be made 1 day ahead of time; cover tightly with plastic wrap and refrigerate until ready to prepare the pizza.)

Position a rack in the middle of the oven and preheat the oven to 425°F.

Working on a lightly floured surface, roll out the dough into a 12-inch circle, and place on a cookie sheet. Brush 1 teaspoon of the oil on the dough and spread the cooked onions on top. Sprinkle the walnuts on top of the onions and top with the Parmesan cheese. Scatter the Gorgonzola over the pizza and drizzle with the remaining 1/2 teaspoon of oil and a grinding of pepper. Bake for about 15 minutes, rotating the pizza once while it bakes. The pizza is ready when the edges of the crust begin to turn golden brown and the cheese is melted and bubbling. Remove from the oven and cut into wedges.

harvest variations

- Try using pine nuts instead of walnuts.
- Use crumbled feta cheese or soft goat cheese instead of Gorgonzola.
- Spread 1 cup of sautéed baby or regular spinach on the dough to create a bottom layer for the pizza.
- Use only 2 onions and sauté them with 1 thinly sliced small leek (white part only), 2 thinly sliced shallots, and 1 chopped scallion (green and white parts).

the slow story of caramelized onions

Caramelizing onions is an act of patience. When you cook onions over a very low heat—long and slow—the natural sugars in the onions are released and naturally caramelize. The caramelization process will take place only if the onions are allowed to cook slowly – if they cook too quickly, they'll burn and become bitter.

What is the reward for all this patience? A plain old onion—or shallot, scallion, or leek—will be transformed from a pungent, often acidic vegetable into a sweet, deeply flavorful ingredient. Caramelized onions add savor and depth to salads, sandwiches, sauces, dips, stews, and pasta, and are a versatile topping for pizza, steak, chicken breast, grilled fish, and vegetarian dishes. In short, caramelized onions can add a rich, sweet onion flavor to virtually anything.

roast chicken with roasted garlic–herb butter and roasted vegetables

serves 4

Roast chicken is satisfying any time of year, but there is something particularly wonderful about this dish on a cold winter's night. What makes this recipe unique is the roasted garlic–herb butter that is tucked under the skin of the breast meat and also massaged on the outside of the bird, creating crisp skin and flavorful, moist meat.

You'll need a large roasting pan, because the chicken is surrounded by winter vegetables, making this an easy one-dish dinner. In the spring you can substitute asparagus spears and leeks (cut into $2^{1}/_{2}$-inch pieces), fresh morels, and whole baby onions. In the summer, try it with spears of zucchini and eggplant, and chopped ripe tomatoes.

for the garlic-herb butter

5 large garlic cloves

1 tablespoon olive oil

3 tablespoon unsalted butter, at room temperature

Salt and freshly ground black pepper to taste

$^{1}/_{4}$ teaspoon dried sage

$^{1}/_{4}$ teaspoon dried rosemary

$^{1}/_{4}$ teaspoon dried thyme

for the chicken and vegetables

One 3- to 4-pound roasting chicken, preferably organic or naturally raised

$^{1}/_{2}$ pound young parsnips and rutabagas or turnips (about 4 medium), peeled and cut into pieces about 2 inches long and $^{1}/_{2}$ inch wide

$^{1}/_{2}$ pound carrots (about 2 to 3 large), peeled and cut into pieces about 2 inches long and $^{1}/_{2}$ inch wide

4 medium onions, cut into quarters

$1^{1}/_{2}$ pounds fingerling or new potatoes (cut in half if large)

Salt and freshly ground black pepper to taste

$1^{1}/_{2}$ to 2 tablespoons olive oil

$1^{1}/_{2}$ cups dry red or white wine

To make the garlic-herb butter: Position a rack in the middle of the oven and preheat the oven to 350°F. Put the garlic in a small roasting pan or ovenproof skillet and pour the oil on top. Roast for 15 minutes, tossing the garlic once or twice. (If the garlic cloves are small they will be tender and ready after about 11 minutes.) Remove from the oven and let cool for about 5 minutes. Do not turn off the oven.

In a small bowl, mash the butter with the back of a spoon. Season with salt and pepper and add the sage, rosemary, and thyme and mix well. Finely chop the roasted garlic (it will become a paste, which is fine) and add it to the butter. Mix in the oil

recipe continues

from the roasting pan. (The butter can be made 1 day ahead of time and stored in the refrigerator.)

To roast the chicken and vegetables: Turn up the oven to 450°F. Rinse the chicken and cut off any excess fat near the flaps of the cavity. By wiggling your fingers under the skin, gently loosen the breast skin from the meat to create a small pocket. Distribute half of the garlic herb butter under both sides of the breast skin, massaging it into the breast meat. Rub the remaining butter over the outside of the bird, massaging it into the skin of the breast, wings, and drumsticks. Place the bird in the middle of a large roasting pan. Surround the chicken with the parsnips, carrots, onions, and potatoes and season with the salt and pepper. Drizzle the 1½ to 2 tablespoons of oil over the vegetables and potatoes and toss them with a spoon or by shaking the pan to distribute the oil and lightly coat the vegetables.

Roast the chicken on the middle rack for 25 minutes. Pour half the wine over the bird, and reduce the temperature to 375°F. Gently toss the potatoes and vegetables. Roast for another 20 minutes, and pour the remaining wine over the bird. Gently toss the vegetables again so they brown and cook evenly. Roast for another 20 to 25 minutes, or until the drumstick feels loose when you gently wiggle it, or the juices run clear, not pink, when you pierce the meat under the wing or the thickest part of the thigh. Remove the chicken and vegetables from the oven and let cool for 5 minutes before carving the chicken. Serve the meat with the potatoes and vegetables on the side and spoon any pan juices on top of the chicken.

a "rack" of potatoes

The next time you roast poultry, beef, or fish, do what we do: Use whole baby new potatoes, sliced or chunked potatoes, or medium potatoes cut in half to create a "rack" underneath a roast. The juices from the roast baste the potatoes (they will be unbelievably moist and flavorful) and the potatoes keep the roast elevated, allowing air to circulate underneath, helping to create an evenly browned exterior. It's a win-win situation—continually basted potatoes and a roast that is crisp and brown all over!

Some of our favorite combinations include new potatoes under a roasting chicken stuffed with herbs and lemon, thick slices of Yukon gold potatoes underneath a roast beef, purple or blue potatoes cut into thin wedges and placed under a leg of lamb, and whole baby red potatoes under a large fillet of salmon or whole trout.

If the meat, poultry, or fish you're roasting is small and only needs to roast for under an hour, you'll need to parboil the potatoes (before cutting them into slices or wedges) for about 10 minutes before roasting, to make sure they are thoroughly cooked by the time the roast is done.

topsy-turvy

cooking with greens from root vegetables

One of the best things about growing root vegetables (or buying them untrimmed from a farmers market) is that you can cook the greens that grow up from the roots. Tender, red-streaked leaves from beets, and spicy turnip and rutabaga greens are full of nutrients and are delicious when simply cooked— lightly steamed and tossed with a pat of butter and salt, for example, or stir-fried with other vegetables and small bits of meat and fresh ginger. Root vegetable greens go particularly well with bacon, pancetta, or prosciutto. Very young beet greens are even tender and sweet enough to be used raw in combination with lettuces for a delicious, peppery salad.

chicken stew with winter root vegetables

serves 6

If it's two degrees above zero and the night calls for something dramatically warming, this hearty stew will do the trick. Serve with Whipped Potatoes (page 187), Mashed Celery Root (page 184), or thick egg noodles.

If at all possible, for a fuller flavor, make the stew a day ahead of time and refrigerate. A layer of fat will rise to the surface, which you can simply scoop off with a large spoon before reheating and serving. This recipe calls for organic or naturally raised chicken, which tends to have less fat and a fuller flavor and is readily available at most supermarkets and butcher shops. If you don't want to cut up the chicken pieces as described in the recipe, have your butcher do it for you.

2 whole chicken breasts and 4 chicken legs
  with thigh attached
About 1 cup all-purpose flour
½ teaspoon salt
Freshly ground black pepper to taste
1 to 2 tablespoons safflower or vegetable oil
1 tablespoon olive oil
1 large leek (white part only), thinly sliced
1 large onion, thinly sliced
8 garlic cloves, 4 left whole and 4 very
  thinly sliced
2 tablespoons chopped fresh thyme,
  or 2 teaspoons dried

2 tablespoon chopped fresh rosemary,
  or 2 teaspoons dried
4 medium carrots, peeled, halved
  lengthwise, and cut into 2-inch pieces
4 parsnips, peeled, halved lengthwise, and
  cut into 2-inch pieces
2 cups dry red wine
3 cups chicken broth, preferably homemade
  (page 269)
1 bay leaf
1 cup coarsely chopped fresh parsley

Using a very sharp knife, cut each chicken breast across the bone into 3 pieces (making a total of 6 pieces), and separate each drumstick from the thigh (making a total of 8 leg pieces). You should have a total of 14 pieces of chicken.

Position a rack in the middle of the oven and preheat the oven to 350°F.

Put the flour in a resealable plastic bag or on a large plate and add the salt and pepper. Dredge the chicken pieces in the flour, coating well on all sides, making sure that there isn't too much flour clinging to the chicken. Reserve the remaining flour.

In a large ovenproof pot with a lid, heat 1 tablespoon of the safflower oil over medium-high heat. When it's quite hot (test it by adding a tiny bit of flour; it should sizzle), brown a few pieces of the chicken for 2 to 4 minutes on each side, or until the skin has a nice golden brown color. Remove the chicken and repeat with the remaining pieces, adding the additional tablespoon of oil if needed.

Use a paper towel to clean out the bottom of the pot. Place the clean pot over low heat and add the olive oil; heat for about 20 seconds. Add the leek, onion, sliced and whole garlic, and half the thyme and rosemary, and cook for 5 minutes, stirring frequently. Add the carrots and parsnips and cook for another 3 minutes. Add 1½ tablespoons of the reserved seasoned flour and stir to coat all the vegetables well; cook for 1 minute. Raise the heat to high and add the wine. Boil for 3 minutes. Add the chicken broth and boil for another 2 minutes. Add the reserved chicken pieces, reduce the heat to low, and add the remaining thyme and rosemary, the bay leaf, half the parsley, salt, and pepper, and simmer for 1 minute.

Cover the stew and remove from the heat. Place in the preheated oven and bake for 1 hour and 15 minutes. The stew should be thickened and full of flavor, and the chicken should be very tender, almost falling off the bone. Spoon off any fat that has risen to the surface. Taste for seasoning and add more salt and pepper if needed. Sprinkle with the remaining parsley before serving. (If you are making the stew ahead of time, let it cool to room temperature before refrigerating. When ready to use, remove any fat that has congealed on the top of the stew and reheat the stew over a low heat until hot and bubbling.)

osso bucco with mashed celery root

serves 4 to 6

Osso bucco is a classic Italian stew of braised veal shanks, onions, carrots, and celery in a rich tomato-and-wine-based sauce. This is an adaptation of Marcella Hazan's recipe in *The Classic Italian Cookbook*. Make the stew on a cold, wintry day, open a good bottle of wine, and wait while the kitchen fills with the scent of simmering meat, wine, and aromatic root vegetables. Serve on top of, or alongside, Mashed Celery Root (page 184). You can also serve the stew with Whipped Potatoes (page 187) or pasta or accompany with a good salad of winter greens—get ready for the warmth to spread!

1 cup flour
Salt and freshly ground black pepper to
    taste
4 pounds veal shanks, cut into 2- to
    3-inch-long pieces
About 2 tablespoons vegetable oil
1 tablespoon olive oil
1 medium onion, chopped
2 medium carrots, chopped
2 celery ribs, chopped
2 garlic cloves, very thinly sliced
2 tablespoons chopped fresh thyme,
    or 2 teaspoons dried

1 tablespoon chopped fresh rosemary,
    or 1 teaspoon dried
2 cups dry red wine
1½ cups homemade chicken (page 269) or
    beef broth, or canned broth
One 28-ounce can whole peeled Italian
    tomatoes
¼ cup chopped fresh parsley
1 bay leaf
Mashed Celery Root (page 184), Whipped
    Potatoes (page 187), or pasta, for
    serving

Put the flour on a plate and season liberally with the salt and pepper. Dredge the veal pieces in the flour, making sure to coat on all sides. Shake off any excess flour.

Position a rack in the middle of the oven and preheat the oven to 325°F.

In a large casserole with a cover or an ovenproof pot with a lid, heat 1 tablespoon of the vegetable oil over medium-high heat. When the oil is hot (test it by adding a speck of flour; it should sizzle), brown the veal shanks for about 4 minutes on one side, or until golden brown. Do not crowd the pan; work in batches, adding more oil as needed. Gently flip over the meat and brown on the other side, about 2 to 3 minutes. Brown the sides of the meat for about 1 minute. Transfer the veal shanks to a plate as they are done, and set aside. If the oil in the pan looks black or burnt, clean the pot out with paper towels to remove excess oil.

Place the pot over low heat and add the olive oil. Add the onion, carrots, celery, garlic, thyme, and rosemary and cook, stirring frequently, for 8 minutes, until the vegetables begin to turn a pale golden color. Raise the heat to high and add the wine. Bring to a boil and simmer for 2 minutes. Add the broth and the tomatoes, crushing the whole tomatoes with your hands before dropping them into the pot. Reduce the heat and simmer for 1 minute. Add the parsley, bay leaf, and browned veal pieces; season with salt and pepper, and simmer for 5 minutes.

Cover the pot and roast the osso bucco for $2\frac{1}{2}$ hours, basting the meat every 30 minutes or so. Taste for seasoning. The meat should be very tender and almost falling off the bone. Serve hot with the Mashed Celery Root, Whipped Potatoes, or pasta.

creamy scrambled eggs
with morels and chives

serves 4

You can use any type of wild or cultivated mushroom for this rich egg dish, but fresh spring morels, chives, and farm-fresh eggs are outrageously good together. This is an elegant brunch dish, best served with a variety of muffins and breads, an arugula salad, fresh-squeezed orange juice, and a bottle of icy-cold Champagne.

8 large eggs
$\frac{1}{4}$ teaspoon sea salt
Freshly ground black pepper to taste
$1\frac{1}{2}$ tablespoons unsalted butter
2 tablespoons fresh chopped chives, or
   minced scallions (green part only), plus
   whole chives for garnish

$\frac{1}{4}$ pound morels or other fresh mushrooms
   (see pages 178–179), stems trimmed,
   mushrooms left whole if small, or cut into
   thick slices if large
$\frac{1}{4}$ cup heavy cream or milk

In a medium bowl, whisk the eggs vigorously with the salt and pepper.

In a medium skillet, heat the butter over medium heat until it begins to bubble and spurt. Add the chopped chives and cook for 10 seconds. Add the morels and

cook, stirring frequently, for $1\frac{1}{2}$ minutes. Add the cream and simmer vigorously for 2 minutes, or until the cream appears thickened. Add the whisked eggs and cook, undisturbed, for 10 seconds or so. Using a fork, gently scramble the eggs, being careful not to break up the mushrooms. Cook for about 1 to 2 minutes, depending on how soft or well set you like your scrambled eggs. Transfer to a platter and garnish with the whole chives.

becomes too difficult to work with, return it briefly to the heat. Set the polenta circles aside to prepare the toppings.

To top and finish the pizzas: Position a rack in the middle of the oven and preheat the oven to 400°F. Bake the pizzas *without the toppings* for 10 minutes. Remove from the oven and lightly brush the polenta crusts with the oil. Using a spatula or pizza peel, very gently flip the crusts over. Sprinkle each polenta with some of the salt and pepper and ¼ cup of the Parmesan cheese. Bake for another 10 minutes.

Remove the pizzas from the oven and spread each one with a quarter of the topping and another ¼ cup of cheese, and bake for about 5 minutes, or until the cheese is melted and the topping is hot.

Using a spatula or a pizza peel, remove the pizzas from the oven and carefully transfer them to a serving plate. Sprinkle each one with 1 more tablespoon of the cheese and serve immediately. The pizza can be cut into wedges with a pizza cutter or served whole, to be eaten with a fork and knife.

white beans with herbs and tomatoes

serves 4

You can serve these savory beans as a side dish with grilled, roasted, or sautéed fish, poultry, or meat dishes, or use them as a topping for the polenta pizza (pages 180–181). It's also delicious spooned over mashed potatoes or couscous, or as a topping for grilled French or Italian bread.

1½ tablespoons olive oil
2 garlic cloves, very thinly sliced
1 large shallot or small onion, very thinly sliced
⅛ teaspoon sea salt, or to taste
Generous grinding of black pepper
One 19-ounce can white cannellini beans, drained and rinsed

1 tablespoon chopped fresh rosemary
1½ tablespoons very thinly sliced fresh basil
¼ cup dry white wine
1 large, ripe tomato, coarsely chopped (about ½ cup)

In a large skillet, heat the oil over medium-low heat. Add the garlic and shallot and cook, stirring frequently, for 8 minutes, until pale golden in color. Add the salt and pepper, the drained beans, rosemary, and basil and cook, stirring, for another 3 minutes. Raise the heat to medium and add the wine; simmer for 3 minutes. Add half the chopped tomato and cook for another 2 minutes. Remove from the heat and stir in the remaining tomato. Taste for seasoning. (The dish can be made several hours ahead of time; cover and refrigerate until ready to use. Reheat before serving.)

caramelized onions and spinach

serves 4 as a side dish

Serve this on top of polenta pizza (pages 180–181), or enjoy it as a simple side dish with salmon, steak, chicken, lamb chops, sausages, or as a topping for rice, pasta, or potato dishes.

1½ tablespoons olive oil
1 large onion, very thinly sliced
Salt and freshly ground black pepper
    to taste

¾ pound baby or regular spinach, any
    large stems removed, and coarsely
    chopped

In a large skillet, heat the oil over medium-low heat. Add the onion and cook, stirring frequently, for 10 minutes. The onions should be caramelized and quite sweet tasting. Add the salt and pepper and add the spinach in batches. Cook, stirring, until tender, about 5 minutes. Taste for seasoning.

harvest variations
- Add ½ cup currants, or golden raisins.
- Add 1 thinly sliced garlic clove to the skillet with the onion.
- Add 1 small ripe tomato, diced, after the spinach.
- Add ¼ teaspoon of grated nutmeg after the spinach is cooked.

mashed celery root

makes about 3½ cups; serves 6

If you've never tried celery root (also called "celeriac"), you're in for a treat. This gnarled, hairy, beige-brown root isn't much to look at, but the taste is magnificent—a subtle celery flavor infused with great earthiness; see opposite for more information on this underappreciated vegetable. It makes an excellent substitute for mashed potatoes—the celery flavor and the coarse mashed texture are superb.

Serve mashed celery root as a side dish to a rich stew or braised meat; the pale puree sets off the rich colors and flavors beautifully. Or pile sautéed scallops or shrimp on a bed of mashed celery root, allowing the rich seafood flavors to complement the aromatic puree.

Sea salt and freshly ground pepper to taste
2 large bulbs of celery root (about 3 pounds)

⅔ cup crème fraîche (see page 131) or sour cream

Bring a large pot of water to a boil. Season with a touch of sea salt.

Using a sharp knife, cut the peel off the celery root until all the skin and the thin green layer below are removed. Coarsely chop the root and add to the boiling water; cook for about 20 to 25 minutes, or until the root feels tender when tested with a small, sharp knife. Drain the celery root thoroughly.

Using a potato masher, mash the celery root. It will not be smooth, but that is fine—it is meant to be somewhat chunky. Stir in the crème fraîche and season with salt and pepper. Return the mashed celery root to the pan and warm over low heat until hot. (You can make this dish several hours ahead of time. Transfer to a small casserole and refrigerate. Before serving, warm over low heat, or in a 250°F. oven until hot, about 5 to 15 minutes.)

celery root
it may not be pretty, but it sure is delicious

Celery root, also known as "celeriac," is a lot like that nerd you went to high school with who turned out to be a great beauty. This knobby, hairy, beige-brown root, which sometimes has fingerlike roots hanging off its bottom, does not look particularly appetizing. But peel off the skin, and you find firm, cream-colored flesh bursting with the fresh flavor of celery along with parsley and a hint of nuts.

According to Elizabeth Schneider, in her book *Uncommon Fruits and Vegetables,* "Celery root, not surprisingly, is a variety of branch celery that has been cultivated for its lowers, rather than its uppers." Although the root has been grown in this country for quite some time, it is only recently that American chefs and home cooks alike have begun experimenting with it.

Celery root can be eaten raw. Grated or julienned and mixed with parsley, mayonnaise, and other seasonings, it is known as the classic French bistro dish *celeri remoulade.* Celeriac can also be cooked—mashed into a puree (see opposite), simmered in soups, sliced and baked in a gratin, or simply steamed and topped with brown butter. Always look for firm roots; once they get soft, the insides tend to turn woody.

italian-style winter squash puree

makes about 2 cups; serves 4 to 6 as a side dish

You can serve this savory puree as is, or use it as a filling for ravioli (see page 144). The dish can be made with virtually any variety of winter squash, including pumpkin. Serve with the Brined Pork Chops (page 218) or Roast Chicken with Roasted Garlic–Herb Butter (page 169).

2 pounds winter squash, such as acorn
    (see page 145), peeled and cut into
    2-inch chunks
1 tablespoon unsalted butter
2 tablespoons crème fraîche, heavy cream,
    or plain low-fat yogurt

3 tablespoons freshly grated Parmesan
    cheese
1 tablespoon chopped fresh sage,
    or 1 teaspoon dried
Salt and freshly ground black pepper
    to taste

Bring a large pot of water to a boil over high heat. Add the squash pieces and cook on medium heat, covered, for about 15 minutes, or until tender; test with a small, sharp knife. Drain the squash and return to the pan. Mash the squash with a potato masher. Stir in the butter and crème fraîche, and then add the cheese, sage, salt, and pepper.

whipped potatoes

serves 6 to 8

Imagine mashed potatoes that are lighter, fluffier, and even more appealing than usual. Cooking the potatoes and then very lightly whipping them in a standing mixer creates just the right amount of air and the perfect texture. The trick with this recipe is to be careful not to overbeat the potatoes, or they will end up with a gluey consistency.

4½ pounds potatoes (Yukon gold or your favorite variety; about 14 medium), peeled, cut in half, or in quarters if the potatoes are large

4 tablespoons (½ stick) salted butter

1 cup milk, whole or 2%

½ cup heavy cream

¼ teaspoon sea salt, or to taste

Freshly ground black pepper to taste

Bring a large pot of water to boil over high heat. Add the potatoes and cook for about 20 to 25 minutes, depending on the size, until they feel soft when pierced with a small, sharp knife. They shouldn't be falling apart, just tender. Drain the potatoes well.

Put the potatoes in the large bowl of a standing mixer fitted with a paddle. Whip the potatoes on low speed for 10 seconds. Add the butter and whip another 10 seconds. Add the milk and cream and whip until the potatoes come together in an almost smooth mass, stopping and starting the machine to avoid overbeating.

Transfer the potatoes to a large pot or casserole and add salt and pepper. (The potatoes can be made 1 day ahead of time. To reheat, place over low heat, stirring frequently, for about 10 minutes, or until hot. You can also reheat the potatoes in a preheated 350°F. oven for 15 to 20 minutes. Stir well before serving.)

a maine potato tradition

In some parts of the country, "harvest" is more than just a quaint word, or an old-fashioned concept. In mid-October across northern Maine (which some refer to as "potato country"), high schools shut down for several weeks so teenagers can help out with the potato harvest. Hard to believe that in this day and age a potato harvest would actually have the power to shut down a high school, but allowing kids to work on the harvest is a Maine tradition that's been kept alive—generation after generation. A potato picking machine costs around $30,000 and can actually bruise the potatoes, so many farmers opt to harvest their potato crop the old-fashioned way—by hand. Potato farmers are dependent on these kids since they can't find enough adults to work the harvest. The teenagers get in touch with old-fashioned values, and some even earn enough to make a down payment on a car!

parmesan potato gratin

serves 6

There are few potato dishes that provide more comfort than this creamy gratin. For added flavor and nuance, add a few tablespoons of Chive Puree (page 77) to the middle layer to infuse the dish with a subtle onion flavor and gorgeous spring green color. Use a high- or medium-starch potato, such as russet, Yukon gold, Katahdin, or Kennebec.

Serve with roast chicken, grilled meat, or on its own, accompanied by a hearty salad and a sautéed green vegetable.

1-pound chunk Parmesan cheese

1 tablespoon olive oil

4 pounds potatoes, peeled and thinly sliced (about 12 medium potatoes)

Salt and freshly ground black pepper to taste

4 tablespoons (½ stick) unsalted butter, cut into small cubes

3 tablespoons all-purpose flour

1 tablespoon minced fresh rosemary

1 tablespoon minced fresh thyme

About 4 tablespoons Chive Puree, (page 77, optional)

¾ cup whole milk

¾ cup heavy cream

Shave thin slices off the chunk of cheese with a wide vegetable peeler. Some of the slices will be thin and long and others will be smaller and crumbly. It's fine to use an assortment of shapes. When you have 2 cups of shaved cheese, set it aside.

Position a rack in the middle of the oven, and preheat the oven to 400°F. Grease the bottom of a large (14 × 9 × 2-inch) gratin dish with the oil. You can also use a large, ovenproof skillet or a large broiler pan. Arrange half the potatoes in a single layer on the bottom of the pan. Sprinkle with salt and pepper, half the butter, half the flour, and half the rosemary and thyme. Place half of the Parmesan shavings on top and drizzle with 2 tablespoons of the Chive Puree, if using. Top with the remaining potatoes, creating a neat layer of overlapping slices. Season with salt and pepper, dot with the remaining butter, and sprinkle with the remaining flour and herbs. Place the remaining cheese on top and pour the milk and cream over the whole dish. Drizzle the top with the remaining 2 tablespoons of Chive Puree, if using. (At this point the potatoes can be covered and refrigerated for up to 2 hours before baking.)

Bake the gratin for about 45 minutes. If the potatoes seem to be getting overly brown as they bake, cover loosely with foil. Reduce the heat to 300°F. and bake for another 30 to 45 minutes, or until the potatoes are tender and golden brown on top, and the cheese is melted and bubbling.

harvest variations

- For an herb-infused gratin, instead of adding the Chive Puree, substitute 1 cup of your choice of pesto (see pages 80–81) between the layers of potatoes.
- When adding the first layer of cheese shavings, add ⅓ cup of olive puree or tapenade in small dollops on top of the cheese.
- Try Gruyère, cheddar, Romano, Emmenthaler, Swiss, or a combination of these cheeses instead of the Parmesan.

roasted potatoes
with sea salt and herbs

serves 4

When you toss potatoes with olive oil, sea salt, and chopped fresh herbs and roast them in a hot oven, they turn deliciously crisp on the outside and tender and buttery on the inside. The results are so satisfying you'd think there was some secret involved, but all you need to do is get the oven hot enough and use fresh, firm potatoes and good-quality fresh herbs.

Serve the potatoes with stews, roasts, seafood, sautéed meat or poultry, grilled foods, or as a snack. They are also delicious served with Chive Puree (page 77) or Aioli (page 274). The potatoes can also be served with eggs and other breakfast dishes instead of home fries, accompanied by ketchup and hot pepper sauce.

3½ pounds high- or medium-starch potatoes (such as Idaho, russets, or Yukon gold), peeled, quartered, and then cut into wedges that are about 3 inches long and ½ inch wide

2½ tablespoons good-quality olive oil

¼ teaspoon sea salt, or to taste

Freshly ground black pepper to taste

1½ tablespoons chopped fresh thyme, or 1½ teaspoons dried

1½ tablespoons chopped fresh rosemary, or 1½ teaspoons dried

Sweet Hungarian paprika for sprinkling

Position a rack in the middle of the oven and preheat the oven to 450°F.

Put the potato wedges in a broiler pan; a large, shallow roasting pan; or a gratin dish. Add the oil, sea salt, a generous grinding of pepper, thyme, rosemary, and a generous sprinkling of paprika, and toss well to coat the potatoes with the oil and seasonings. Roast for 15 minutes. Using a spatula, gently release the potatoes and flip them over. Roast for another 15 minutes. Use the spatula to loosen the potatoes from the pan and roast another 5 to 10 minutes, or until the potatoes are crispy and golden brown along the edges and tops and they feel tender when pierced with a fork or a small, sharp knife. Serve hot.

potato primer

We love potatoes—in salads, casseroles, gratins, soups, stews, and tarts, and, even better, when simply fried, whipped, or mashed. There are few foods as deeply comforting as a potato dish—whether it's a plain old baked potato, topped with a pat of sweet butter and a sprinkling of sea salt; or a mound of creamy whipped potatoes, studded with fat cloves of roasted garlic.

Many recipes call for a specific type of potato, but is there really such a thing as the "right" potato? Ultimately, the right potato is the one you like the best—with the color, texture, shape, and taste that appeal most to you. Do you like your potatoes red, white, blue, yellow—or even purple? Round and large, oblong and medium-sized, long and narrow like a finger, or as round and tiny as a child's fist? Nowadays more and more heirloom varieties are available, and all of these choices are well worth seeking out. But different varieties are suited to different uses, and it can help to know the three basic categories of potatoes:

high-starch potatoes

Russets, Russet Arcadia, Idaho, and **Belrus** are just a few popular potatoes in this category. High-starch potatoes have a dry, delicate texture that makes them ideal for baking and frying. When making French fries, this low-moisture potato variety forms a crisp outside and light, fluffy inside. Because they are dry, high-starch potatoes will absorb milk, cream, stock, and butter well, making them a good choice for gratins and casseroles, or mashed and whipped potatoes. High-starch pota-toes do tend to fall apart when cooked in boiling water and need to be watched.

medium-starch potatoes

Potatoes like **Superior, Katahdin,** and **Kennebec,** and yellow-fleshed potatoes such as **Yukon gold, Yellow Finn, Finnish, Bintje, Long White,** and **California White** are good examples of all-purpose, medium-starch varieties. These potatoes are prized for their creamy texture and ability to retain their shape during cooking. Because medium-starch potatoes are moister than high-starch varieties, they hold up better in boiling water. Most heirloom varieties, found in many farmers markets, are medium- to low-starch. Use them for salads, chowders, home fries, roasted potatoes, and other dishes where potatoes that retain their shape are needed.

low-starch potatoes

Red potatoes (such as **Red Bliss, Red La Rouge,** and **Red Pontiac**), blue potatoes (such as **Peruvian Blue**), and white boiling potatoes are low in starch. They have thinner skins; a denser, firmer texture; and a higher moisture content than high- and medium-starch varieties. Also called a "waxy potato," this is the one to choose when a dish calls for the potato to hold its shape. Since their moisture content is so high, low-starch potatoes are not the best choice for mashing; they do hold up beautifully for potato salads, home fries, sautéing, steaming, and roasting or grilling; they also work well in chowders, soups, and stews.

new potatoes

New potatoes do not refer to a specific variety or color of potato, but rather to potatoes that are young and have been dug before they reached full maturity. Because they are young and small, they are somewhat fragile and their skins can be thin. New potatoes tend to be less starchy than older, more mature potatoes. They hold their shape after being cooked, and are elegant served whole after being roasted, steamed, fried, sautéed, or boiled.

shopping for potatoes

Look for interesting, new varieties of potatoes at farmers markets, where the potatoes will be freshly dug and won't have spent months sitting on a supermarket shelf. In general, always choose potatoes that are firm fleshed with smooth, unbroken skin. Avoid green-tinted potatoes (the color indicates that they have been improperly stored), or those with blemishes, "eyes," or sproutings. Once a potato has sprouted, the starches begin to convert to sugar, making the potato sweet and difficult to use in cooking, though not impossible. Just make sure to cut off the sprouts before cooking. Old pota-

toes tend to fall apart when cooked, breaking into many small pieces. Never buy or use potatoes that feel spongy when squeezed.

storage

The best place to store potatoes is a root cellar—a cool, dry space that is between 45 and 50 degrees, but obviously we don't all have the luxury of having one. However, you can set up conditions similar to those found in an old-fashioned root cellar: Remove the potatoes from a plastic bag and store them in a well-ventilated basket or storage bin, away from light, frost, heat, and moisture. (Gardeners are always told to harvest potatoes on dry days, when there is little, or no, moisture in the soil.) They are best stored low to the ground, where it tends to be cooler.

sweet potato fries with aioli

serves 6

Although, botanically speaking, sweet potatoes are not related to regular potatoes, they can be cooked in identical ways. Turns out that sweet potatoes make unbelievably good fries, particularly when served with this garlicky mayonnaise.

For a fun, bistrolike presentation, make newspaper cones from several sheets, staple the sides closed, and pile the hot sweet potato fries inside.

2 pounds sweet potatoes, peeled or
   unpeeled, and scrubbed
2 cups vegetable shortening, such as Crisco

Sea salt and freshly ground black pepper
   to taste
Aioli (Garlic Mayonnaise, page 274)

Cut about 1 inch off the ends of each potato. Cut the potatoes into sticks that are ½ inch wide and 3 to 4 inches long—like thick-cut French fries. (If you want to cut the potatoes ahead of time, put them in a large bowl and cover with cold water. Before frying, drain the potatoes and dry them well with paper towels.)

Put the shortening in a large, cast-iron or heavy-bottom skillet over high heat. Heat the oil to about 350°F. on a deep-fry or candy thermometer. To test if the oil is hot enough, drop a small piece of sweet potato into the hot oil; it should sizzle and

bubble. Working in small batches to avoid crowding the pan, drop a handful of sweet potatoes carefully into the oil—be careful, since the fat will splatter. Cook the potatoes, fully submerged, for about 3 minutes, turning occasionally with a slotted spoon. The fries are done when the outsides have browned, and the insides are tender. (To test, remove one fry, drain on a paper towel, and cut through with a small, sharp knife.) If the oil begins to get too hot and fries are browning too quickly, reduce the heat to medium.

Remove the fries with a slotted spoon and drain immediately on paper towels or a clean brown grocery bag. Sprinkle with salt and pepper. Repeat with the remaining potatoes. Serve immediately with the Aioli.

morel and pea sauté

serves 4

Morels look like brown gnomes, or a child's drawing of the shape of a little tree. They have a spongy texture and an earthy scent and flavor that blends beautifully with fresh peas and garlic. Serve this alongside grilled or roasted dishes, or as a main course with crusty bread, followed by a light green salad. This sauté also makes a great topping for polenta, couscous, pasta, or rice.

1 tablespoon olive oil
2 garlic cloves, minced
½ pound fresh morels (see page 179), stems trimmed, left whole if small or cut into thick slices if large

½ pound fresh snap peas, ends trimmed
Sea salt and freshly ground black pepper to taste
3 tablespoons heavy cream

In a large skillet, heat the oil over medium heat. Add the garlic and cook, stirring frequently, for 2 minutes. Add the morels and cook for 3 minutes, stirring occasionally. Add the peas and cook for 2 minutes. Season with the salt and pepper and add the cream. Raise the heat to high and cook for 2 minutes, or until the cream begins to thicken and the peas are just tender, but still a bit crunchy.

buttermilk onion rings

serves 4

When you have a craving for onion rings (the real thing and not the frozen kind), it's not something you can easily ignore. Here is the recipe to use; these rings are among the best we've tasted anywhere. The oil temperature must be hot (when you drop a speck of flour into the hot oil, it should sizzle up immediately), but not be so hot that the onions burn. Try these with sweet Vidalia-style onions, just-dug garden onions, red Bermuda onions, or plain old "onion onions."

For a special presentation, serve the onion rings with an assortment of dipping sauces—hot pepper sauces, ketchup, Chive Puree (page 77), Lemon Thyme–Pistachio Pesto (page 80), Coriander-Cashew Pesto (page 81), Tartar Sauce (page 275), Aioli (page 274), or a simple bowl of really good sea salt (see page 137).

2 large onions

2 cups buttermilk

Salt and freshly ground black pepper
    to taste

Dash of hot pepper sauce

1 1/2 cups all-purpose flour

About 4 cups good-quality vegetable
    shortening, such as Crisco; or canola or
    vegetable oil

Peel the onions and separate them into rings. Be sure to keep the inner sections of the onion, even though they are not technically rings.

Whisk together the buttermilk, salt, pepper, and hot pepper sauce in a large bowl. Add the onions and marinate for at least 15 minutes, and up to several hours.

Put the flour in a bowl or a resealable plastic bag and season liberally with salt and pepper. Working in batches, remove the onion rings from the buttermilk and dredge lightly in the seasoned flour.

Preheat the oven to 200°F.

In a large, heavy skillet (cast iron is ideal), heat the oil. (You can also use a wok.) It should reach about 350°F. on a candy or deep-fry thermometer, or test the oil with a speck of flour. Working in small batches, drop the coated onion rings into the hot oil, a few pieces at a time (if you crowd the pan, the oil temperature will drop and the onions will be greasy and absorb too much oil). Cook for about 1 1/2 minutes on each side, or until golden brown and crispy. Drain on several sheets of paper towel (or a brown grocery bag), sprinkle with salt, and place in an ovenproof bowl or plate. Place the cooked onions in the oven to keep warm while you fry the next batch. Onion rings aren't meant to sit around—serve them as soon as possible with the dipping sauce(s) of your choice.

maple baked beans

serves 8 to 10

Beans-in-the-hole, an old New England culinary tradition, are literally beans cooked underground—the landlubber's version of a clambake. It takes hours of preparation, days of cooking, and centuries of folk wisdom to prepare this traditional New England festival dish.

This easy variation on the recipe does not require digging a hole, but the results are very satisfying. The beans are soaked overnight, mixed with a sweet and savory maple-laced sauce, and baked, long and slow, in the oven for 6 to 12 hours. We like to prepare the beans the night before, and let them bake in the oven all night while we sleep.

Serve the beans with baked ham, potato salad and coleslaw, warm biscuits, and plenty of ice-cold beer or cider.

1 pound kidney beans, or a variety of
    beans, such as navy, Great Northern,
    Jacob's Cattle, or cannellini
1 large onion, cut into eighths
1 bay leaf
6 peppercorns
1/2 teaspoon salt, or to taste
3/4 cup medium amber maple syrup (see
    page 200 for more on maple syrup)

1/2 cup light brown sugar
1/2 cup ketchup
1 tablespoon Chinese chile paste or hot
    pepper sauce to taste
1 1/2 teaspoons powdered ginger
5 ounces salt pork or thick, country-style
    bacon, cut into about 6 cubes

Soak the beans in a large bowl of cold water overnight. Drain and rinse the beans, and drain again. Alternately you can use this quicker technique: Put the beans in a pot and cover them well with water. Bring the water to a boil and boil for a minute or two. Turn heat off, cover pot, and steep for 1 hour, then drain. The beans are now ready for cooking.

Put the beans in a large pot and cover with 2 quarts of water, the onion, bay leaf, peppercorns, and salt and bring to a boil. Reduce to a low simmer, cover, and cook for about 50 minutes, or until tender. A good test is to scoop up several beans in a spoon and blow on them—if the skin starts to peel off, they are done. Drain the beans, *making sure to reserve the bean liquid.*

Position a rack in the middle of the oven and preheat the oven to 225°F.

In a small saucepan, whisk together the maple syrup, brown sugar, ketchup, chile paste, and ginger with 1 1/2 cups of the reserved bean liquid. Bring to a simmer over medium heat and cook for about 6 minutes, or until slightly thickened.

Transfer the beans to a medium to large casserole or ovenproof bean pot. Push half the salt pork cubes down into the beans and scatter the remaining half on top. Pour the sweet, warm maple sauce on top.

Bake the beans for a minimum of 6 hours and up to 12 hours, checking to make sure they have not dried out. If the beans appear dry, add about $1/2$ cup of the reserved bean liquid. Remove the lid for the last 30 to 45 minutes, to crisp up the salt pork on top and further reduce the bean broth down to a thick, sweet essence. You can always place the beans under the broiler for 5 minutes or so to crisp up the pork and give the beans a golden brown "crust." Serve piping hot, straight from the casserole.

maple syrup
sugar of the trees

The calendar says it's the first day of spring, but wet, heavy snow is spitting from the gray sky. Cabin fever is a cliché by now and the calendar's announcement feels like a cruel joke. For New Englanders, March and early April is a rough time of year. The rest of the country celebrates spring while we still feel stuck in winter's grip. But there is a sweet note to the season that no New Englander can deny—it's maple sugaring time.

For the maple sap to run, there must be temperate, sunny days followed by cold, frosty nights—precisely the conditions here in spring. Across the New England landscape, maples are usually tapped with plastic pipes and spigots, but occasionally with old-fashioned metal buckets hanging from the trees. The plink-plunk sound of sweet sap dripping into the bucket signals the changing season, and a sweet treat to come. Maple syruping involves patience and long hours. It takes between thirty and forty gallons of sap to create one gallon of thick, sweet syrup. The sap needs to be closely watched as it boils down to avoid burning.

Is it worth the effort? The difference between the generic syrup sold in plastic jugs at the supermarket and the delicately sweet, golden-hued syrup harvested on maple farms in New England, eastern Canada, and parts of the upper Midwest is like that of jug wine and fine, well-aged Burgundy.

buying maple syrup

Most maple syrup is sold in plastic jugs. The plastic doesn't affect the flavor of the syrup, but it obviously makes it impossible to see its color and thickness. When you feel like splurging and are going to serve the syrup with something really special, look for varieties sold in glass jars so that you can judge the contents. Look for a relatively thick, clear syrup (not cloudy), with a burnt amber color.

The grading system for maple syrup is as follows:
Light Amber or **Fancy** is the first-run, most delicate syrup. It literally melts in your mouth. This is our choice for drizzling over pancakes, waffles, French toast, muffins, or fresh fruit and yogurt.

Medium Amber is the most popular and most commonly sold syrup. It has a rich maple flavor, but isn't heavy or overwhelming. It can be used for cooking as well as drizzling over food.

Dark Amber is the syrup harvested toward the end of the season, when the concentration of sugar in the sap is lower and more sap and more boiling are required to make syrup. This is the darkest and heaviest syrup, and is primarily used for cooking.

great ways to cook with maple syrup

Some people go through life believing that the possibilities for eating and cooking with maple syrup end when breakfast is over. But there are lots of ways to take advantage of this natural sweetener:

• Roast baby carrots at 400°F. for about 15 minutes, drizzle them with a few tablespoons of maple syrup and roast for another 10 minutes, until tender and caramelized.

• Sauté a thick slab of smoked ham in a skillet with a light drizzling of syrup and a touch of butter, and cook for about 8 minutes, until a thick, gooey glaze forms. Or drizzle a tablespoon over thick slab bacon and broil until crisp.

• Pour maple syrup over ice cream, pound cake, or butter cookies.

• Make maple syrup butter by mixing 1 stick of unsalted butter, at room temperature, with 3 to 4 tablespoons of maple syrup, and serve with toast, muffins, scones, pancakes, or waffles.

• Spoon maple syrup over grapefruit sections or salads, stir into vinaigrettes, and mash into baked or mashed sweet potatoes.

• For a quick dessert, cut a banana in half lengthwise, sauté in a hot skillet with butter for 5 minutes, drizzle liberally with syrup, and cook for 2 minutes.

maple and chile bbq sauce

makes about 1 cup

This dark, rich sauce gets its flavor from the balance of sweet and spicy ingredients. Use a medium amber maple syrup and taste how well it blends with garlic, ginger, soy sauce, balsamic vinegar, chile paste, and ketchup. Serve with grilled ribs, chicken, burgers (instead of plain old ketchup), or steak.

1 tablespoon vegetable oil
1 tablespoon minced fresh ginger
1 garlic clove, minced
About 1/2 to 1 teaspoon Chinese chile paste, or hot pepper sauce
2 tablespoons soy sauce

2 tablespoons balsamic vinegar
1/2 cup light or medium amber maple syrup
1 cup ketchup
Sea salt and freshly ground black pepper to taste

In a medium saucepan, heat the oil over medium heat. Add the ginger and garlic and cook for about 3 minutes, or until they just begin to turn golden brown. Stir in the chile paste and cook for 5 seconds. Add the soy sauce and vinegar and then stir in the maple syrup and ketchup, blending well to create a smooth sauce. Add salt and pepper and simmer over very low heat for about 8 minutes, or until thickened. Let cool. (The sauce can be made about 3 days ahead of time. If you want sauce on hand for several months, you can make a large batch, pour the sauce into a sterilized mason jar, and process for 20 minutes in a boiling water bath.)

rosemary-infused honey

This simple technique for infusing honey with fresh rosemary transforms even ordinary supermarket honey into something really memorable. But the better the quality of the honey you start with, the more interesting the final infused honey will be.

You can use virtually any type of fresh herb you like, or a combination. Keep the herbs on the stem so it will be easy to remove them when you are done with the infusion. Some ideas for combinations include lavender-rosemary, thyme–lemon thyme, coriander-mint, lemon verbena–mint, and parsley-sage.

Herb-infused honey gives a wonderful flavor to a pot of hot or iced tea along with some fresh herb leaves. Use it to flavor a cake or pudding, stir it into vinaigrettes, or spread it on chicken, pork, or duck for a sweet, herb-flavored glaze. We like to spread it on breakfast toast or a baguette, with thin slices of sharp cheddar and fresh figs.

6 ounces good-quality honey

About 6 sprigs fresh rosemary on the stem, or other fresh herbs of your choice

Pour the honey into a small jar (a canning jar is ideal), and add the herbs. Place the jar in a small pot of simmering water so that the water comes only halfway up the sides of the jar. Let the water simmer (but not boil) for about 10 minutes over medium-low heat. Carefully remove the jar from the pot with a pot holder or tongs and let the honey cool for 30 minutes to infuse. Remove the herbs, cover, and keep the honey in a dark, cool spot. It will keep for several weeks.

fruits of the earth

the sun in

mid-August can get awfully hot, so we

head out early in the morning when there's still a slight breeze. We put on our jeans, t-shirts, socks, and old shoes and hike through the berry patch carrying plastic buckets. One of us crouches down low to pick the blueberries off the bushes, while the other works up higher, plucking raspberries and oversized, juicy blackberries from the vines. In New England the season for fruit is embarrassingly short, but perhaps that's what makes us appreciate it so much more. Our berries seem sweeter and plumper than those we've tried in other, more fruit-famous areas of the country. Is it our imagination, or do our fruit-filled pies, jams, jellies, tarts, and cakes really taste better?

Come fall, the trees swell with apples and pears—crisp, juicy, and full of unexpectedly complex flavors. We get to work, canning applesauce and pear butter; making pies, cobblers, and crisps; freezing whatever fruit we're lucky enough to have left over. We know the time will come soon when we will have to rely on fruit from our southern and western neighbors, fruit that never tastes quite the same after it's been shipped on a truck across the country.

figs stuffed with herbed goat cheese with balsamic glaze

serves 8

These cheese-stuffed figs make an elegant appetizer or hors d'oeuvre. You can make this even more special by wrapping them in a thin piece of prosciutto. The dish can be prepared several hours ahead of time, making this ideal party fare.

for the goat cheese
1/2 cup walnut halves
5 ounces soft goat cheese, at room
    temperature
1 tablespoon minced fresh basil
1 tablespoon minced fresh chives
1 tablespoon minced fresh parsley
1 tablespoon minced fresh thyme
Salt and freshly ground black pepper
    to taste
2 tablespoons heavy cream

for the figs and balsamic glaze
6 fresh ripe figs (see page 222)
1/4 pound very thinly sliced prosciutto
    (optional)
1/2 cup good-quality balsamic vinegar
1 cup nasturtiums or other edible flowers,
    for garnish (optional)

To prepare the goat cheese: Preheat the oven to 400°F. Place the nuts on a cookie sheet and bake for about 8 minutes, or until lightly toasted and fragrant. Remove from oven and let cool; then finely chop.

In a medium bowl, mix the nuts with the goat cheese, herbs, salt, pepper, and cream until smooth.

To stuff the figs and make the glaze: Trim the ends off each fig and cut it into quarters. (You should have a total of 24 small wedges.) Use about 1 heaping table-spoon of herbed cheese to sandwich together 2 fig pieces. If using the prosciutto, take a slice of the meat and fold it over lengthwise. Place the stuffed fig in the middle and roll the prosciutto around the fig. Repeat with the remaining fig pieces. Refrigerate until ready to serve.

Meanwhile, heat the vinegar in a small saucepan over medium-high heat until reduced by half, about 8 to 10 minutes. The vinegar should be thick and syrupy enough to coat a spoon. Don't let it get too thick, or it will burn. (The recipe can be made about 6 hours ahead of time up to this point.)

To serve, place the figs on a serving plate and drizzle with the vinegar glaze. Surround with nasturtiums or other edible flowers.

strawberry "sandwiches"

makes 16 to 24 "sandwiches," serves 8 to 10

This is a whimsical idea, a kind of savory, new-wave version of chocolate-dipped strawberries. Prosciutto and baby spinach or watercress leaves are sandwiched between ripe, fresh strawberry halves. To finish them off, the berry "sandwiches" are drizzled with a reduced balsamic vinegar glaze, which complements both the berries' sweetness and the savory filling.

Serve these at a tea party, with cocktails, or on top of a salad.

½ cup good-quality balsamic vinegar
About 16 medium to large ripe
    strawberries, or 24 small to medium,
    stemmed
¼ pound imported prosciutto, very thinly
    sliced

1 cup packed baby spinach, watercress, or
    baby arugula, washed and thoroughly
    dried
Freshly ground black pepper to taste

Pour the vinegar into a small saucepan and place over medium heat. Cook for about 10 minutes, watching it like a hawk, until the vinegar is quite reduced and becomes a black glaze, thick enough to coat a spoon. Remove from the heat and set aside.

Cut the berries in half lengthwise. Fold a slice of prosciutto in half crosswise and then in thirds and place on half of a berry. Place 2 to 3 leaves of the spinach on top of the prosciutto and sprinkle lightly with pepper. Top with the other berry half. Repeat with the remaining berries and place them on an attractive serving platter. Drizzle the balsamic glaze over the berries, creating a squiggly design.

spicy greens salad with sautéed pear wedges, blue cheese, and sun-dried cranberry vinaigrette

serves 4 to 6

This salad uses a variety of winter fruit to wake up even the most jaded palate. The dish can be made several hours ahead of time, but don't dress the salad until just before you're ready to serve it. This makes a great first course for Thanksgiving or any holiday dinner. Serve with Garlic Croûtes (page 271) or toast triangles.

for the vinaigrette
Salt and freshly ground black pepper
    to taste
2½ tablespoons red wine vinegar
¼ cup olive oil
2 to 3 tablespoons dried cranberries, left
    whole or coarsely chopped

for the salad
1 large Bosc pear, peeled or unpeeled

1½ teaspoons olive oil
½ tablespoon unsalted butter
Salt and freshly ground black pepper
    to taste
¼ cup pine nuts, unsalted cashews, slivered
    almonds, or walnut halves
½ pound baby arugula, baby spinach, or
    watercress (about 6 packed cups), larger
    stems removed
¼ cup crumbled blue cheese

To make the vinaigrette: Mix the salt, pepper, and vinegar in a small bowl. Whisk in the oil to make a smooth mixture. Gently stir in the cranberries and set aside. (The vinaigrette can be made several hours ahead of time; cover and refrigerate.)

To make the salad: Cut the pear into 8 wedges, removing the core. In a large skillet, heat the oil and butter over medium heat. Add the pear wedges, flesh side down, and sauté for 4 minutes. Sprinkle with the salt and pepper. Gently flip the pear wedges over and cook for another 4 minutes on the other side; the pears will turn a golden brown and should be just tender. Remove and drain on a paper towel.

Meanwhile, heat the oil and butter remaining in the pan over medium-low heat. Add the nuts and cook for about 2 to 3 minutes, stirring, until they are golden brown. Remove from the heat.

Put the greens in the bottom of a salad bowl or on a medium-size serving platter. Arrange the pears around the outside of the greens. Sprinkle the salad with the blue cheese and sautéed nuts. (The salad is best served while the pears and nuts are still a bit warm, but you can make everything ahead of time up to this point.) Drizzle the vinaigrette over the salad just before serving.

winter salad of mixed greens, persimmons, and pomegranate with fresh ginger vinaigrette

serves 4 to 6

The sweet, juicy flavor of persimmon mixed with slightly acidic, sweet pomegranates creates a winning salad when tossed with a refreshing, ginger-spiked vinaigrette. Look for persimmons that feel firm but not rock hard, and pomegranates that feel heavy in your hand.

for the vinaigrette

1 tablespoon Dijon mustard
1 1/2 tablespoons minced or grated fresh ginger
Salt and freshly ground black pepper to taste
1/4 cup red wine vinegar
1/2 cup olive oil

for the salad

1 pomegranate (see page 225)
2 firm Fuyu persimmons (see opposite)
1 pound mesclun greens; or 2 medium heads lettuce, large leaves torn into bite-size pieces
1 cup Garlic Croûtes (page 271, optional)

To make the vinaigrette: In the bottom of a large salad bowl, mix the mustard, ginger, salt, and pepper. Add the vinegar and then the oil, whisking to create a smooth vinaigrette.

To make the salad: Cut the pomegranate in half. Using a small, sharp knife, or your fingers, remove the seeds from the pomegranate and set aside. Discard the pomegranate skin. Use the knife to remove the skin and the core of the persimmon. Cut the persimmon flesh into small, 1/2-inch cubes.

Put the greens in the salad bowl on top of the vinaigrette. Top with the persimmons and the pomegranate seeds, and the croûtes or croutons, if using. Do not toss the salad until ready to serve. (The salad can be made about 2 hours ahead of time. Store, covered, in the refrigerator. Toss with the vinaigrette just before serving.)

persimmons

Winter fruit is scarce and variety is limited in Maine, so when a close friend from northern California sent a box of bright orange, round Fuyu persimmons in mid-December with a note to enjoy them right away, while they were still firm and juicy, we jumped at the chance and started to eat.

A cross between a crisp, juicy apple and a subtle, perfumed pear, the Fuyu persimmon (see Resources on page 279) has a gorgeous pale orange flesh that goes equally well with sweet or savory foods. We ate them raw; as a topping for yogurt, granola, and cereal; alongside creamy goat cheeses; tossed into green salads (see page 212); and pureed into smoothies with vanilla yogurt—and we never grew tried of their unique, fresh flavor.

Our favorite way to eat Fuyu persimmons is wrapped in a paper-thin slice of salty prosciutto. Trim the fat from the prosciutto and wrap a thin slice of fruit in the pink ham, sprinkle lightly with pepper, and get ready for some serious flavor. Winter never tasted so good.

Another persimmon to look for is the Hachiya, or Japanese persimmon, a larger and rounder variety with a reddish-orange skin. Unlike Fuyu persimmons, the Hachiya should be soft when ripe, with a smooth texture and a full, sweet, and almost tangy, astringent flavor. Both varieties of persimmon, which are full of vitamin A and some C, can be used in muffins and other baked goods, and in fruit salads.

roasted cherry and arugula salad
with parmesan shavings

serves 2 as a main course or 4 as a salad course

Roasted cherries are a revelation. The sweet juices become even more intensified, and the cherries take on added depth of flavor. In this salad, roasted cherries are tossed with peppery arugula leaves and thin shavings of Parmesan cheese. To pit the cherries, remove the stem and, using your fingers or a small, sharp knife, make a tiny slit in the side of the cherry and push the pit out. Or you could use a cherry pitter.

You can also serve roasted cherries with any roasted or grilled meat or seafood (it is particularly delicious paired with grilled salmon), with a cheese platter, or as a garnish to holiday game.

Note: To shave the Parmesan cheese, use a wide vegetable peeler or the long, wide opening of a cheese grater and work from a wedge of Parmesan. The shavings should be as thin and as long as you can make them.

About 18 red or yellow cherries (about
    $^1/_2$ pound), pitted
3 tablespoons plus 1 teaspoon olive oil
$^1/_2$ pound arugula, stems trimmed, or
    watercress

$^1/_2$ cup Parmesan shavings (see Note)
1 tablespoon balsamic vinegar
Salt and freshly ground black pepper
    to taste

Position a rack in the middle of the oven and preheat the oven to 400°F. Put the pitted cherries in a small, ovenproof skillet or roasting pan and drizzle with 1 teaspoon of the oil. Roast for 12 to 14 minutes, depending on the size of the cherries. They are done when they appear to be soft and are almost beginning to lose their shape. Remove from the oven.

Put the arugula in a salad bowl. Scatter with the Parmesan shavings and top with the warm cherries. Pour on the remaining 3 tablespoons of oil and the vinegar, season with the salt and pepper, and gently toss. Serve immediately.

harvest variation
Replace the cherries with roasted peach or nectarine slices.

chicken salad with blood oranges, candied walnuts, and baby spinach

serves 3 to 4

Use a deli-roasted chicken or leftover meat from a poached, roasted, or broiled chicken to make this vibrant winter salad. You can easily substitute tangerines or regular oranges for the blood oranges, but you'll miss the vivid, reddish-pink color and distinctively sweet flavor. Serve with hot crusty bread, muffins, or biscuits.

¼ cup Homemade Mayonnaise (page 273), or store-bought
1 tablespoon grated or minced fresh ginger
¼ cup blood orange juice (from 1 large orange; see page 263), or regular orange juice
½ teaspoon salt, plus extra for seasoning
Freshly ground black pepper to taste
2 cups cooked chicken, cut into thin strips

1 blood orange, or regular navel orange
1 teaspoon unsalted butter
⅔ cup walnut halves
1 tablespoon good-quality honey
About 2 cups baby spinach, spinach, arugula, or a mixture of your favorite greens, larger stems removed
1 tablespoon olive oil
½ tablespoon balsamic vinegar

In a medium bowl, mix the mayonnaise, ginger, and orange juice, and season with salt and pepper to taste. Gently mix in the chicken strips.

Peel the blood orange and separate it into segments; cut each segment in thirds, removing the seeds. Gently fold half the orange segments into the chicken salad; set the remaining orange segments aside.

To toast the walnuts: Heat the butter in a small skillet over medium heat. Add the walnuts, ½ teaspoon of salt, and a generous grinding of black pepper and cook for 3 minutes, stirring frequently. Add the honey, stir well to coat the nuts, and cook for 1 more minute.

Place the spinach on a medium-size serving plate. Place the chicken salad in the middle of the greens and scatter the reserved orange sections over the chicken salad and the greens. Scatter the walnuts all over the salad and drizzle the oil and vinegar over the greens. Serve cold or at room temperature.

harvest variations
- Use cooked duck or turkey instead of chicken.
- Use almonds, pine nuts, pistachios, or pecans instead of walnuts.
- Substitute grapefruit, tangerines, pitted cherries, or halved Concord grapes (seeded) or seedless green grapes for the blood oranges.

roast pork with an apple-herb stuffing and cider-applesauce

serves 6

Ask your butcher for a boneless pork roast with a slit down the length of the roast, cut three-quarters of the way through the middle (but still attached) so there is a large pocket for the stuffing. (Be sure to have kitchen string on hand to truss the roast.) The pocket is filled with a savory apple-and-breadcrumb stuffing, and the roast is surrounded by apple chunks and cloves of garlic, splashed with apple cider, and placed in a hot oven. The high heat causes the apples to cook down into a delicious, naturally chunky applesauce.

Serve with Parmesan Potato Gratin (page 188) and apple or hard cider.

for the stuffing

½ tablespoon olive oil

½ tablespoon unsalted butter

1 small onion, finely chopped

2 garlic cloves, minced

Salt and freshly ground black pepper
   to taste

1 tablespoon minced fresh chives

1 tablespoon minced fresh parsley

½ tablespoon minced fresh sage

½ tablespoon minced fresh thyme

1 large, tart apple, peeled and chopped
   into ½-inch pieces

¾ cup homemade breadcrumbs (page
   270), or store-bought

⅓ cup apple cider

for the roast

One 4-pound boneless pork roast, with a
   slit cut lengthwise, three-fourths of the
   way through the middle but not all the
   way through

Salt and freshly ground black pepper
   to taste

1½ tablespoons minced fresh sage

1½ tablespoons minced fresh rosemary

9 garlic cloves, 8 left whole and 1 thinly
   sliced

3 tart apples, peeled, cored, and cut into
   6 wedges each

1½ cups apple cider

To make the stuffing: In a large skillet, heat the oil and butter over low heat. Add the onion and garlic, season with salt and pepper and cook, stirring, for 5 minutes, until pale gold. Stir in the chives, parsley, sage, and thyme and cook for 1 minute. Add the chopped apple and cook for 4 minutes. The apples will *just* be getting soft. Remove from the heat and stir in the breadcrumbs and cider and season with salt and pepper. (The stuffing can be made several hours ahead of time; cover and refrigerate.)

To cook the roast: Position a rack in the middle of the oven and preheat the oven to 450°F. Open the meat up and season both sides with salt and pepper. Sprinkle a quarter of the sage and a quarter of the rosemary on each side. Spread the stuffing along the bottom half of the meat, making sure to spread it out in an even layer. Cut five 18-inch lengths of kitchen string. Lift the pork up, take one piece of the kitchen string, and tie it tightly around the roast to hold the stuffing in. Repeat with the remaining strings, tying a knot every 3 inches or so. Place the meat, with the fat side up, in a large roasting or broiler pan.

Use a sharp knife to score several large X's in the fat side of the roast. Insert the thinly sliced garlic into the X's and tuck several slices under the string. Place the whole garlic cloves and the apple wedges around the roast, and pour the cider over all. Sprinkle the roast and apples with salt and pepper, and the remaining half of the sage and rosemary.

Roast the pork for 15 minutes. Reduce the oven temperature to 400°F. and roast for about 1 hour more, basting the meat once or twice. When done, a meat thermometer stuck in the middle of the roast will register 150 to 155°F. and the stuffing will be hot. Some stuffing may ooze out of the roast, but it will still be delicious and can be served in a separate bowl. Let the roast sit for 5 to 10 minutes before removing the strings and thinly slicing. Spoon the fresh, warm applesauce over the meat to serve.

brined pork chops with roasted mashed apple-pear sauce

One day last winter we spotted some thick, fabulous looking, all-natural pork chops at the butcher. In recent years pork has become quite lean (almost 50 percent leaner than it was a few decades ago) and because of this, pork chops are often dry, lacking in flavor, and, in general, disappointing. We decided to try a brine mixture of salted water flavored with crushed chile peppers, garlic, and coriander seeds; the result was incredibly juicy and flavorful chops. To get the same results, plan on letting the chops soak for at least 3 hours and up to 24.

Serve with the Roasted Mashed Apple-Pear Sauce (page 223), and/or the Fresh Mango Winter Salsa (page 261).

¼ cup kosher salt

2 tablespoons sugar

4 garlic cloves

Pinch of table salt

2 tablespoons coriander seeds

½ teaspoon red chile flakes

8 boneless or bone-in pork chops, about 1 inch thick (about 3½ pounds)

1 to 2 tablespoons olive oil

In a large bowl or large resealable freezer bag, mix 8 cups of water, the salt, and the sugar. Using a mortar and pestle or a small wooden bowl and spoon, crush the garlic cloves with the table salt. Add the coriander seeds and red chile and crush until the mixture is a thick mash. Add the mash to the saltwater and stir well. Add the pork chops, cover or seal, and brine for at least 3 hours and up to 24.

Preheat the oven to 425°F.

Remove the pork chops from the brine. Dry the pork chops thoroughly with paper towels. Using one or two large skillets, heat 1 tablespoon of the oil over medium-high heat. Working in batches (or in two skillets), brown half the chops for 3 minutes on each side, until they turn a golden brown color. Transfer to a medium-size roasting pan. Repeat with the remaining chops. Roast the pork chops for 13 minutes, or until the internal temperature of a chop reaches 155°F. (if they are thicker than 1 inch, they will take closer to 20 minutes). Serve immediately.

roast leg of lamb with fresh figs and shallots

serves 4

This recipe takes advantage of the natural affinity between figs and lamb. The meaty flavor of lamb seems to bring out the savory essence of fresh figs. The majority of American figs come from California and are harvested throughout the summer and fall. Because they are so fragile, figs are often shipped unripe. Seek out truly ripe figs—ones that hold their shape but are slightly soft to the touch (not mushy or falling apart).

Try to make this dish in the late summer or early fall, when fresh figs are available. But you can make the dish the rest of the year with dried figs marinated in red wine and balsamic vinegar to soften and flavor them. Note: If using dried figs, cut the figs into quarters. Put the figs in a medium bowl and cover with $1/2$ cup red wine and 1 tablespoon balsamic vinegar. Marinate for about 15 minutes to 1 hour. The figs will soak up the wine and take on its flavor, and the figs' often tough texture will soften.

One 5-pound leg of lamb, bone-in, trimmed of excess fat

14 garlic cloves, 12 left whole and 2 very thinly sliced

$1/3$ cup balsamic vinegar, plus 2 more tablespoons if using fresh figs

$1/4$ cup soy sauce

1 cup dry red wine

1 tablespoon olive oil

2 tablespoons grated or minced fresh ginger

2 tablespoons minced fresh rosemary

Salt and freshly ground black pepper to taste

24 shallots, left whole, or 16 small onions

$1/3$ cup good-quality honey, preferably herb-flavored (see page 202)

12 fresh figs, or 12 dried figs (see Note), ends trimmed

Place the lamb in a roasting pan, fat side up. Make several small slits in the skin with a small, sharp knife. Insert the thin slivers of garlic into the slits. Place the whole garlic cloves around the roast, and into any crevices you find on the meat. Pour $1/3$ cup of the balsamic vinegar, and the soy sauce, wine, and oil over the meat and sprinkle the ginger, rosemary, salt, and pepper on top. Cover, refrigerate, and marinate at least 1 hour, and up to 24.

Position a rack in the middle of the oven and preheat the oven to 450°F. If using marinated dried figs, tuck them under the roast. The meat juices will drip on the figs, making them unbelievably flavorful. If using fresh figs, cut them in half and place in a small bowl, cover with the remaining 2 tablespoons of vinegar, and let sit for 20 minutes. Scatter the shallots around the lamb. Roast the lamb, uncovered, for 20 minutes.

Remove the lamb from the oven and baste. Using a spoon or a pastry brush, spoon the honey onto the lamb. Place the fresh figs onto the honey, pressing very lightly to make them stick. Roast for another 45 minutes to 1 hour and 20 minutes more (depending on the thickness of the roast), or until the internal temperature of the lamb is 125°F. for rare and 135°F. for well done. The lamb will continue to cook when removed from the oven, so be careful not to overcook it.

Let the meat rest, loosely covered with aluminum foil, for about 5 to 10 minutes before carving. Pour the pan juices into a small saucepan, removing any excess fat floating on the top. Bring to a boil over high heat. Reduce the temperature to low and simmer for 5 minutes to reduce and concentrate the flavors.

Serve the lamb in slices, topped with the reduced pan juices, figs, and shallots.

adam, eve, pass that fig!

Long live the fig! What other fruit has such history (Adam and Eve, the Garden of Eden, the most talked about fruit in the Bible)? How many other fruits have been considered sacred for so long, a symbol of peace and prosperity?

There are pages and pages of fascinating facts about this sacred fruit. Consider, for example, some of the many powers the fig is thought to possess: Figs can help you stop smoking (due to their high alkalinity), stop drinking coffee (they're considered a stimulant), aid digestion, treat skin pigmentations, and naturally "tan" your skin. Also, according to the California Fig Advisory, "although we consider it a fruit, the fig is actually a flower that is inverted into itself. The seeds are drupes, or the real fruit." And let's not forget the health benefits: Our friend the fig is high in fiber, iron, calcium, and potassium. And, as if all that were not enough, figs contain no fat, sodium, or cholesterol!

Until recently, most Americans knew only the meaty, sweet flavor and chewy texture of figs through Fig Newton cookies—a mass-marketed cookie filled with dried figs. But that cookie doesn't give you the slightest idea of the flavor possibilities of a fresh fig.

Unlike peaches and pears, berries and apricots, the flavor of a fig is subtle. It doesn't scream "sweetness," but rather creeps up on you with a subtle sweetness and appealingly tender flesh. Cut open a fig and you are confronted with a pink blush, tiny seeds, and a rich, meaty inside. The entire fruit is edible, soft, silky, and almost erotic. It is one of the few fruits that is just as comfortable in savory dishes as it is in sweet ones—figs go equally well in tarts, pies, puddings, jams and jellies, as well as salads and stews; roasted along with chicken, lamb (see page 220), or pork; and as a topping for seafood or vegetable dishes.

roasted mashed apple-pear sauce

makes about 4 cups

Wouldn't it be nice to make applesauce by simply chopping some fruit, tossing it with some sugar and butter, and then roasting it for a while? Turns out it really is that simple. Unlike regular applesauce, which requires peeling and seeding apples and then simmering them, this roasting method results in a sauce with a slightly smoky flavor and a wonderfully thick texture.

There are all kinds of variations you can try with this basic roasting technique. This version, made with autumn apples and pears, is particularly good served with the Brined Pork Chops on page 218, or the Roast Chicken with Roasted Garlic–Herb Butter and Roasted Vegetables on page 169.

You can make the sauce a day ahead of time and reheat it over a very low temperature, or serve it cold or at room temperature.

8 McIntosh or tart apples, peeled, cored, and quartered

4 almost ripe Bosc pears, peeled, cored, and quartered

3 tablespoons unsalted butter, cut into small cubes

¼ cup sugar

Pinch of salt

Position a rack in the middle of the oven and preheat the oven to 400°F.

Toss the apples and pears with the butter, sugar, and salt in a large roasting pan. Cover tightly with a lid or aluminum foil. Roast for 25 minutes, tossing the fruit once or twice during cooking. Uncover the pan and roast for another 5 to 10 minutes, or until the fruit feels quite tender when tested with a small, sharp knife.

Remove the pan from the oven and, using a potato masher, mash the fruit until thick and chunky. The applesauce will keep in a covered jar in the refrigerator for several days.

harvest variations
Add the following ingredients before roasting:
- 1 tablespoon chopped fresh ginger
- ¼ teaspoon ground ginger, cinnamon, nutmeg, allspice, or cardamom
- 1 tablespoon chopped fresh rosemary, sage, and/or thyme
- Maple syrup or brown sugar instead of white sugar
- ½ cup cranberries
- ½ cup seeded Concord grapes
- 2 ripe quince (peeled, cored, and chopped)
- Instead of apples, 3 to 4 cups pitted cherries

roasted carrots with fresh pomegranate glaze

serves 4 as a side dish

Sweet winter carrots are roasted with the juice of a pomegranate, transforming one of our most overlooked vegetables into something exotic and mysterious. The sweet pink glaze on top of the orange carrots is as fabulous to look at as it is to eat.

1 large, ripe pomegranate, scrubbed clean (see opposite)

1 pound small, garden-fresh carrots, peeled and cut into 2-inch chunks or sticks

1 teaspoon olive oil

Salt and freshly ground black pepper to taste

Preheat the oven to 400°F.

To make the pomegranate juice, cut the pomegranate in half. Using an electric or manual juicer, push the juice out of half of the pomegranate, releasing the seeds and all the juice. Strain the juice over a small strainer; you should have about ⅓ cup. Reserve the remaining pomegranate half.

Put the carrot chunks in a small roasting pan or ovenproof skillet. Add the oil, season with salt and pepper, and toss well to coat. Roast for 20 minutes and then gently toss the carrots, flipping them over. Add the pomegranate juice, toss well, and roast for another 15 to 25 minutes, depending on the thickness of your carrots, or until the carrots feel tender when tested with a small, sharp knife, and the juice has reduced and glazed the carrots.

While the carrots are roasting, scoop out the seeds from the remaining pomegranate half with a small spoon or your fingers. When the carrots are done, sprinkle the pomegranate seeds on top for a crunchy texture.

the powerful pomegranate

We love pomegranates. The ruby red color, the exotic, jewel-like seeds, the sweet, tangy, sour flavor. On Kathy's first trip to Turkey, she was walking through a small park outside Istanbul on a hot day. She discovered a man standing by a small cart with a juicer making ice-cold drinks from a gorgeous pile of fruit—melons, lemons, blood oranges. His most popular drink was a spectacular pinkish-red, something she had never seen before. It turned out to be fresh-squeezed pomegranate juice, and it was one of the most refreshing and energizing juices imaginable.

Traditionally, pomegranates are seen as symbols of harvest and seasonal change. They figure prominently in the story of Persephone, a classic Greek myth. Recent health reports indicate that pomegranates not only taste great and add an amazing vibrant pink color to foods, but have a high level of potassium and a good amount of vitamin C, and are said to help fight cancer and other diseases.

Look for pomegranates that feel heavy in your hand, with a brilliant color and no blemishes. Cut one open and you'll find lots of little seeds separated by a white membrane; avoid eating the membrane as it is quite bitter. The sweet and sour flavor of pomegranate seeds makes them a delicious snack, and they can also be used as a garnish for roasts, salads, or sauces.

To make fresh pomegranate juice, choose a pomegranate that feels heavy, indicating it is fresh and full of juice. (See the recipe opposite for directions.) A medium-large ripe pomegranate should yield about 1/3 to 2/3 cup of fresh juice. Drizzle fresh pomegranate juice over fruit salads, use it to add color and sweet flavor to vinaigrettes, to deglaze the pan when sautéing shrimp (see page 107), fish, or chicken, or as a glaze for roasted lamb. It also adds an excellent tart-sweet flavor to chicken, lamb, or vegetable stew.

peach and mango muffins

makes about 18 regular-sized muffins or 10 big muffins

Serve these muffins warm, straight from the pan, with sweet butter and hot coffee. This is a great recipe for using overripe fruit.

½ cup (1 stick) unsalted butter, softened, plus about 1½ tablespoons for greasing the pans

1 very ripe mango

2 cups plus 2 tablespoons sugar or vanilla sugar (see page 277)

1½ cups milk, whole or 2%

2 eggs

About 3 cups flour

5 teaspoons baking powder

2 ripe peaches, or nectarines, preferably local, peeled (see page 239) and cut into ½-inch dice

Position a rack in the middle of the oven and preheat the oven to 400°F.

Lightly grease 18 regular-sized muffin cups or 10 oversized muffin cups with the 1½ tablespoons of butter.

To cut the mango: Hold the mango upright on a cutting board and, using a large, sharp knife, cut just over ⅓ of the fruit off each side of the mango, so you have 2 large pieces of mango without the irregular shaped pit. Use a small sharp knife to cut a tic-tac-toe pattern into the fruit of each slice without piercing the skin. The parallel cuts should be about ½ inch apart. Push the mango skin to turn the slices inside out and make the tic-tac-toe cubes pop out into little squares. Cut the squares off, away from the peel. You should have about 2 cups of mango cubes.

In the bowl of an electric mixer, beat the ½ cup butter until soft and smooth. Add 2 cups of the sugar and blend until light and fluffy, about 4 to 5 minutes. Blend in the milk and the eggs and beat well.

Sift 3 cups of the flour and the baking powder over the mixture and gently fold in the mango and diced peaches. (If you have very juicy fruit, the batter may appear thin; add an additional ¼ cup flour as needed.) Pour the batter into the muffin pans, filling each cup about three-fourths full, and bake for 5 minutes. Sprinkle the top of the muffins with the 2 remaining tablespoons of sugar and bake until very lightly gold on top, another 10 to 12 minutes for regular-size muffins, or about 22 minutes for oversized muffins. Let cool for 5 minutes in the pan. Use a table knife to loosen the muffins from the pan, and serve warm.

harvest variation
Substitute 4 cups mixed fresh berries for the mango and peaches.

cranberry-lemon bars

makes 16 squares

Be sure to make these thin, delicate bars in the fall, when cranberries are fresh and plentiful. The bars—a shortbreadlike pastry topped with a bright cranberry puree and a pungent lemon filling—can be made a full day ahead of time.

You will need an 11 × 8-inch rectangular tart pan with a removable bottom, or a regular 9 × 14-inch baking pan; if you use the 9 × 14-inch pan, the bars will be much thinner.

for the cranberry puree
2¹/₂ cups (8 ounces) fresh cranberries
¹/₂ cup sugar

for the crust
1¹/₂ cups all-purpose flour
¹/₄ cup plus 2 tablespoons confectioners' sugar
³/₄ cup (1¹/₂ sticks) unsalted butter, softened and cut into cubes

for the lemon filling
2 large eggs
³/₄ cup plus 2 tablespoons sugar
¹/₂ teaspoon baking powder
Pinch of salt
2 tablespoons grated lemon zest
2¹/₂ tablespoons fresh lemon juice

Confectioners' sugar, for topping

To make the cranberry puree: Combine the cranberries and ¹/₂ cup of water in a small saucepan and bring to a boil over medium heat. Stir and cook until the berries burst and the mixture reduces to about ³/₄ cup, about 8 to 10 minutes. Remove from the heat and stir in the sugar. Strain the mixture through a sieve into a bowl; you should have around ³/₄ cup. (The puree can be made 1 day ahead of time; cover and refrigerate until ready to use.)

Position a rack in the middle of the oven and preheat the oven to 350°F.

To make the crust: Mix the flour and the confectioners' sugar in a medium bowl. Add the butter and, using your hands or a pastry blender, mix well until the butter breaks down into small pea shapes. Press the crust evenly into the tart pan with your hands (it will be very dry and crumbly), building a ¹/₂-inch edge up the sides. Bake for 15 minutes and remove the crust from the oven.

While the crust is baking, make the lemon filling: Using an electric mixer, beat the eggs and sugar for about 3 minutes, or until they are light in color. Add the baking powder, salt, lemon zest, and lemon juice and beat for another 2 to 3 minutes, or until the mixture is light and frothy.

Use a spoon or soft spatula to spread the cranberry puree on the bottom of the hot crust, creating a thin layer. Pour on the lemon mixture and place the tart (in its pan) on a cookie sheet. Bake 30 to 35 minutes. If the top of the pastry begins to turn brown, very loosely place an aluminum foil "tent" over it, being careful not to let the foil touch the tart, or it may stick to the surface. Bake until a toothpick inserted in the center comes out clean. Let cool to room temperature in the tart pan. To remove the sides of the pan, gently lift the bottom of the tart up and out of the pan with a narrow spatula. Cut into 16 squares; transfer the squares to a serving plate. Sift the confectioners' sugar on top before serving.

cranberries
tart and true americans

Grown in eastern Massachusetts, cranberries are a uniquely American food. The Pilgrims ate them during their first winter here and they got their name because of their resemblance to a sand crane's profile—crane berry. First farmed commercially in Dennis, Massachusetts, in 1816, cranberries are loaded with vitamin C and antioxidants. The berry harvest begins in late September and continues through early November. Cranberries can be frozen, directly in the bag, and stored for up to six to eight months.

Because they are so tart, cranberries need to be balanced with something sweet—other fruits, maple syrup, honey, and a touch of white or brown sugar all work well. In addition to the well-known sauce, cranberries can be used to balance the richness of roast duck or goose, or added to breads, cakes, and muffins.

apple crumble

serves 4

This is the dessert we like to make in the fall when we don't have the time or energy for a full-blown pie. A variety of fresh fall apples are mixed with spices, brown sugar, and cranberry juice and then covered with a crumbly, granola-flecked topping. The addition of cranberry juice creates an exceptionally juicy, flavorful crumble. For an extra burst of tartness, add 1 cup of raw cranberries to the apples before baking.

You can assemble the crumble several hours ahead of time and pop it into the oven about 45 minutes before you want to serve it. Serve with whipped cream, ice cream, or the Lemon Spice Cream on page 248.

for the apples
Unsalted butter, for greasing the gratin dish
6 apples (a combination of Macoun, Baldwins, McIntosh, Pink Lady, or other fall varieties), about 1 1/2 to 2 pounds
1/3 cup light brown sugar
1/2 teaspoon ground cinnamon
1/4 teaspoon ground allspice
1/2 cup unsweetened cranberry juice
Scant 1/8 teaspoon vanilla extract

for the topping
1 cup all-purpose flour
1/2 cup light brown sugar
Dash of cinnamon
Dash of allspice
1/2 cup (1 stick) unsalted butter, cut into small cubes
1 cup good-quality granola with nuts

Butter the bottom and sides of an 8-inch gratin dish or Pyrex pie plate.

To prepare the apples: Peel the apples, core them, and cut each one into 12 slices about 1/4 inch thick. Toss the apple slices with the brown sugar, cinnamon, allspice, cranberry juice, and vanilla, and pour the fruit and any juices into the bottom of the greased pan.

Position a rack in the middle of the oven and preheat the oven to 350°F.

To make the topping: Mix the flour, brown sugar, cinnamon, and allspice in a bowl. Add the butter and, using your hands or a pastry blender, blend it into the sugar and flour mixture until it resembles coarse breadcrumbs. Stir in the granola. Pour the topping on top of the apple slices and, using your hands, pat the topping down over the fruit so that it resembles a crust and covers all the apples. (The dish can be assembled up to this point, covered, and refrigerated for up to 6 hours before baking.)

Bake the crumble for 45 minutes, or until the top is golden brown, the apples are tender, and the juices begin to bubble up through the top crust. Serve warm with any of the suggested toppings.

harvest variations

Instead of apples, substitute the following:

- 4 to 5 cups assorted summer berries
- 3 apples and 3 pears, peeled and thinly sliced
- 3 ripe peaches and 3 ripe nectarines, peeled and thinly sliced
- A variety of 6 ripe pears, peeled and thinly sliced
- 2 cups of ripe strawberries and 2 cups of chopped fresh rhubarb
- 12 to 14 ripe, quartered figs

pear and apple clafoutis

This French-inspired dessert combines winter fruit—pears and apples—with a simple, vanilla-scented egg batter. The result is a cross between a custard and a pudding, plump with sweet fruit.

You can make the clafoutis several hours ahead of time and then, just before serving, sprinkle it with confectioners' sugar and broil it until the top is caramelized and golden brown. The clafoutis is satisfying enough to serve on its own, but it's also delicious topped with vanilla-flavored whipped cream or ice cream.

1 tablespoon unsalted butter
2 tart apples, peeled, cored, and cut into
 8 to 10 thin wedges each
3 just-ripe pears, peeled, cored, and cut
 into 8 to 10 thin wedges each
1/2 cup plus 2 tablespoons Vanilla Sugar
 (page 277), or plain sugar
2 large eggs

1/4 cup heavy cream
1/4 cup milk, whole or 2%
1/4 teaspoon vanilla extract, or 1/2 teaspoon
 if not using Vanilla Sugar
Pinch of salt
About 2 tablespoons confectioners' sugar
 (optional)

Position a rack in the middle of the oven and preheat the oven to 400°F. In a large flame-proof gratin dish or ovenproof skillet, heat the butter over medium-low heat until melted. Add the fruit wedges and cook for 2 minutes. Stir well and sprinkle 2 tablespoons of the Vanilla Sugar on top. Cook, stirring, for another 4 minutes. Remove from the heat.

Using an electric mixer, beat the eggs until frothy in a large bowl. Add the remaining 1/2 cup of sugar and beat for 1 more minute. Add the cream, milk, vanilla extract, and salt, and beat for another minute. Pour the mixture over the fruit. Place the dish in the oven and immediately lower the heat to 350°F. Bake for 35 to 50 minutes, or until the clafoutis looks set and a toothpick inserted in the center comes out clean. Let cool to room temperature.

You can serve the clafoutis as is, or preheat the broiler to caramelize the top with sugar. When the clafoutis has cooled to room temperature, place the confectioners' sugar in a small sifter and sift evenly over the top of the clafoutis. Place under the boiler, about 1 inch from the heat. Broil until the sugar is golden brown and caramelized, about 3 to 5 minutes. Serve at room temperature with whipped cream or ice cream.

harvest variations

Instead of apples and pears, substitute any of the following:

- 2 pounds of pitted cherries (The French believe that cherry pits actually add flavor to a clafoutis, and therefore they don't pit their cherries. The choice is yours.)
- 4 cups of mixed summer berries
- 2 cups of fresh currants and 2 cups of gooseberries
- 4 cups of an assortment of peeled and thinly sliced ripe nectarines, apricots, plums, and peaches
- 4 cups of seeded Concord or seedless green grapes
- 4 cups of fresh pineapple slices or chunks

poached pears in orange-ginger-champagne syrup

serves 6

It was New Year's Day and friends were coming to dinner. After all the holiday festivities, it was too much to think about baking a cake or serving anything rich for dessert. A basket of ripe winter Bosc pears sat on the counter alongside a half-drunk bottle of Champagne from the previous evening's party. Why, of course: pears poached in Champagne, flavored with aromatic winter oranges and slivers of fresh ginger.

3 cups Champagne, white or red wine, or water

1 cup Vanilla Sugar (page 277) or plain sugar

6 large Bosc pears

2 tablespoons julienned fresh ginger

2 tablespoons julienned orange zest (the zest from 1 large orange; see page 251 for more about zest)

To make the syrup: In a pot that is large enough to hold all the pears on their sides, mix the Champagne, 1 cup of water, and sugar together. Bring to a boil over high heat. Reduce the heat to medium, stir well to dissolve the sugar, and simmer for about 10 minutes.

Meanwhile, peel the pears, leaving the stems attached. Use a small, sharp knife to remove the core from the bottom of the pear. Work the knife up into the fruit, and scoop out the core. Cut off a very thin slice from the bottom of the pear so that it will stand up straight.

Add the ginger and orange zest to the syrup and gently place the pears in the pot; the pears should be lying down on their side. Reduce the heat to low, cover, and simmer gently for 30 to 45 minutes, depending on the size of the pears, flipping the pears from side to side every 10 minutes or so. To test a pear, gently insert a small, sharp knife into the thickest part of the fruit. It should feel soft and yielding and come out of the pear without resistance. Remove the pears with a slotted spoon to a serving bowl.

Very carefully taste the syrup in the pan; it will be hot. It should be sweet and full of rich pear, ginger, and orange flavors. Reduce the syrup over medium-high heat for about 5 to 10 minutes to thicken and further reduce and concentrate the flavors. It should be almost thick enough to coat a spoon. Pour the hot syrup with the julienne strips of ginger and orange over the pears and let cool. Refrigerate until ready to serve. (The pears can be made up to 8 hours ahead of time.)

broiled apricots with lavender honey and crème fraîche

serves 6

This is just the sort of dessert we look for in summer—something fresh, simple, and stunning that takes less than 15 minutes. Fresh apricots are drizzled with a lavender-scented honey, broiled until soft and caramelized, and then served hot with a dollop of crème fraîche. Serve the apricots hot from the oven or at room temperature with an assortment of cookies or chocolates, and tiny cups of strong coffee.

6 ripe apricots

About 8 teaspoons lavender-infused honey
    (see page 202), or store-bought
    lavender honey

6 teaspoons crème fraîche (see page 131)

Preheat the broiler, placing a rack about 5 inches from the heat.

Cut the apricots in half and remove the pits. Place the apricot halves in a small roasting or broiler pan, or an ovenproof skillet. Spoon $\frac{1}{2}$ to $\frac{3}{4}$ teaspoon of honey into the "cavity" of each apricot half. Broil for about 7 to 9 minutes; the apricots are ready when the honey has caramelized and the fruit is tender. They should be turning golden brown on top, and starting to soften. Remove the apricot halves from the broiler and place on a serving plate with a dollop of crème fraîche on top of each fruit half. (The dish can be made several hours ahead of time.) Serve hot or at room temperature.

harvest variations

- Use white peaches, regular peaches, plums, or nectarines instead of apricots. Large peaches will take closer to 9 minutes to cook and caramelize properly.
- Scatter tiny edible violets or other edible flowers on top of the apricots when serving.
- Use an herb or fruit-flavored honey instead of lavender. Try rosemary, lemon balm, blueberry, or raspberry. See page 202 for directions on infusing your own honey with a variety of flavors.
- Coarsely chop almonds, pine nuts, pistachios, or walnuts and scatter on top of the apricots and the crème fraîche.
- Instead of broiling, place the fruit on a hot grill (wood, charcoal, or gas) and grill until just tender.
- Scatter finely chopped fresh mint, lemon verbena, lemon thyme, or scented basil on top of the cooked fruit, and serve it as a savory dish, alongside roasted or grilled meats, or as part of a salad course.

desserts 237

plum-peach crostata

serves 6

A crostata is a rustic pie made from a single round of buttery dough that is filled with fruit. The edges of the dough are folded over the fruit (creating a crust), and the crostata is baked until tender and golden.

The dough needs to chill for at least 2 hours, so plan your time accordingly.

for the dough
2 cups all-purpose flour
Pinch of salt
3/4 cup (1 1/2 sticks) unsalted butter, well chilled, and cut into small cubes
About 1/4 cup ice water

for the filling
2 ripe plums (about 1/2 pound)
3 large ripe peaches (about 1 to 1 1/2 pounds)
1/4 cup plus 1 tablespoon packed light brown sugar
1/8 teaspoon vanilla extract
1 tablespoon all-purpose flour

About 1 cup whipped cream, for serving
Fresh mint sprigs, for garnish

To make the dough: Blend the flour and salt in a food processor. Add the butter and pulse the machine about 15 times, or until the mixture resembles coarse cornmeal. Blend in just enough ice water to make the dough pull away from the sides of the bowl. Wrap the dough in foil and refrigerate for at least 2 hours, or overnight.

To make the filling: Peel the plums and peaches (see page 239 for instructions), and cut into scant 1/2-inch slices. Add the fruit slices to a bowl and gently toss with 1/4 cup of the sugar, the vanilla, and flour.

Position a rack in the middle of the oven and preheat the oven to 450°F.

Remove chilled dough 30 minutes before rolling it out. Working on a floured surface, roll out the dough into a large circle, about 12 to 14 inches in diameter. Place on an ungreased cookie sheet. Place the fruit filling in the middle of the dough, leaving a border of 1 1/2 to 2 inches. Drape the edges of dough over the filling and press down lightly to crimp them. The dough won't cover the filling completely. Sprinkle the top with the remaining tablespoon of sugar. Bake for about 25 to 30 minutes, or until the dough is golden brown and the filling tender and bubbling. Serve hot or at room temperature with whipped cream and garnish with mint.

harvest variations

Instead of peaches, substitute one of the following:

- 5 large, ripe nectarines, peeled and thickly sliced
- 5 tart apples, peeled and thickly sliced, along with 1 cup of raisins or golden currants
- 3 cups of mixed summer berries with 1 tablespoon grated lemon zest
- 5 ripe pears, peeled and thickly sliced, along with ½ teaspoon ground ginger
- 6 ripe plums, peeled and thickly sliced, mixed with 2 tablespoons of chopped crystallized ginger

peeling stone fruits

Peeling stone fruit—peaches, nectarines, apricots, and plums—can be a tricky business. If you try to peel them the way you would an apple or pear, you lose a lot of precious juices and some of the flesh, since the peel on stone fruit clings to the flesh. But there is a quick way to peel the skin right off a peach, nectarine, plum, or apricot:

Bring a pot of water to boil. Add the stone fruit, just a few at a time, and let cook for about 10 seconds to 1 minute, depending on how large and ripe the fruit is. Small, very ripe peaches will only take 10 seconds or so, while larger, harder, unripe fruit takes closer to a minute. Remove the fruit with a slotted spoon and immediately place into a bowl of ice-cold water. (The cold water causes the skin to "shrink" away, and it's a breeze to peel it right off.) Peel the skin off using your fingers or a small, sharp knife. Cut the fruit in half and remove the pit. You can then slice, chop, or dice the peeled fruit as needed.

maple crepes with summer berries

makes about 12 to 15 crepes; serves 4 to 6

This is a truly special dish for breakfast, brunch, or dessert. Hot crepes are lined with jam or jelly and fresh berries, rolled up, and then drizzled with warm maple syrup and more fresh berries.

The crepe batter needs to sit for at least 30 minutes, or up to 6 hours.

1 cup milk, whole or 2%
3 large eggs
1 cup all-purpose flour
2 tablespoons unsalted butter, melted, plus extra melted butter for greasing the pan
About 1/2 cup plus 6 tablespoons light or medium amber maple syrup (see page 200)

Pinch of salt
About 1 cup jam, jelly, or preserves (raspberry, strawberry, or blueberry)
About 2 cups assorted fresh berries (strawberries, raspberries, blackberries, blueberries and/or gooseberries)

Mix the milk, ¼ cup of water, and the eggs in a bowl and blend with a hand-held mixer on medium speed for about 1 minute. Sift the flour on top and gently mix on low speed until just combined. The batter may have some small lumps. Add the melted butter, 6 tablespoons of the maple syrup, and the salt and mix on high for about 30 seconds. Let the crepe batter sit for at least 30 minutes, and up to 6 hours, covered and refrigerated.

Very lightly grease a good, heavy 8-inch nonstick skillet or crepe pan over low heat. (The best way to grease the pan is using a pastry brush so there is only a very light coating.) Add about ¼ cup of batter to the hot pan, immediately swirling the batter around the bottom of the pan so it creates a thin, even pancake. Cook the crepe for about 20 to 40 seconds, loosening the bottom of the crepe with a spatula. Gently flip the crepe and cook for another 45 seconds. Use the spatula to loosen the crepe and transfer to a plate. (Try not to be discouraged if the first few crepes don't come out perfectly. They will get better.) You can make several crepes ahead of time, layer them on a plate, and keep them warm in a 250°F. oven, or simply reheat them in a warm pan, one at a time, just before serving.

Pour the remaining ½ cup of syrup in a small saucepan and warm over low heat.

To serve, place each warm crepe on a plate and spread about 1 tablespoon of the jam on top. Fold the crepe in half, scatter a handful of berries on top, and fold in half again. You can also spread the jam on the crepes, scatter the berries, and roll the crepes up into large cigar shapes. Serve any remaining berries on top or on the side, along with the warm maple syrup.

harvest variations
Instead of berries, substitute one of the following:
- 2 cups of peeled and thinly sliced peaches, nectarines, and/or plums
- 2 cups of fresh figs (about 6 to 8, depending on the size), cut into quarters, or fig jam
- 2 cups of cubed fresh mango
- 1 cup of peeled, chopped apple, ½ cup of red and green grapes, and ½ cup of thinly sliced banana
- 2 cups of thinly sliced pears and apples (about 1 to 2 large)

mixed berry and peach cake

serves 8

This is the simplest of cakes, a quick and easy batter mixed with an assortment of fresh berries (we use raspberries, blackberries, blueberries, and a few strawberries). The entire cake takes just over an hour to make. Serve with whipped cream, vanilla ice cream, or a simple sprinkling of confectioners' sugar and tall glasses of iced tea, garnished with sprigs of fresh lemon verbena or mint.

$1/2$ cup (1 stick) unsalted butter, plus extra for greasing the pan

$1 1/2$ cups cake flour, plus extra for flouring the pan

1 cup sugar

1 teaspoon vanilla extract

2 large eggs

$1 1/2$ teaspoons baking soda

3 ripe peaches, peeled and cut into thin slices (see page 239 for more on peeling stone fruit)

4 cups mixed fresh berries

Confectioners' sugar, whipped cream, or ice cream, for serving

Position a rack in the middle of the oven and preheat the oven to 350°F.

Butter and flour a 10-inch springform pan with a removable bottom. Shake out any excess flour.

With an electric mixer, cream the $1/2$ cup butter and the sugar in a large bowl until light and fluffy, about 10 minutes on medium speed. Add the vanilla and beat for 1 minute. Add the eggs, one at a time, beating to fully incorporate each one. Add the $1 1/2$ cups flour and the baking soda and very gently mix until just incorporated.

Gently fold the peeled peach slices and 3 cups of the berries into the batter. Pour into the prepared pan (the batter will be quite thick). Place on a cookie sheet and bake for 50 to 60 minutes, or until a toothpick set in the center comes out clean. Let cool until room temperature, and then remove the sides of the cake pan. If the cake sticks, simply run a flat knife around the edges to loosen the cake. Place the confectioners' sugar in a small sieve or sifter and sprinkle on top of the cake, and scatter the remaining 1 cup of berries on top.

chocolate-dipped berries

Dipping fresh, ripe berries into chocolate is one of the simplest, most deliciously quick desserts we can think of. Present an assortment of berries dipped in a variety of chocolates on a platter. Imagine raspberries dipped in dark chocolate, strawberries in bittersweet chocolate, blackberries in milk chocolate, and blueberries in white chocolate.

Chocolate bar(s) of your choice, cut into small chunks (about 6 ounces chocolate for each 1 ½ cups fruit)

Fresh berries, at room temperature

Put the chocolate in the top of a double boiler set over barely simmering water (or place it in a bowl set over a pot of water). Too much heat, or direct heat, will cause the chocolate to clump, and it won't melt properly. Stir the chocolate with a spatula until it's melted (the temperature should be between 90 and 95°F. on a candy thermometer).

Gently wash and *thoroughly* dry the berries. If you're working with particularly small or delicate ones, place them on a thin bamboo skewer to help dip them in the chocolate.

Remove the chocolate from the heat and dip about two-thirds of each berry into the chocolate. Place on wax paper and let cool until the chocolate hardens around the berry. Refrigerate any berries you are not serving right away.

fresh mint leaves stuffed with gingered mascarpone and raspberries

serves 8

Imagine a dainty green leaf, stuffed with a creamy filling, flecked with bits of crystallized ginger, and topped off with a juicy raspberry. These mint leaves are, for lack of a better word, adorable. They are a perfect palate cleanser, served between courses at a multicourse meal, at a tea party, or with summer cocktails. We like them best for dessert with a plate of really fine chocolates. Mascarpone is a thick, soft, Italian-style cheese that is available in specialty food shops.

$\frac{1}{2}$ cup mascarpone cheese

$1\frac{1}{2}$ teaspoons minced crystallized ginger, plus 1 tablespoon cut into very thin strips

1 tablespoon confectioners' sugar

16 fresh mint leaves, at least 1 inch long

About 1 cup fresh raspberries

In a small bowl, mix the mascarpone, minced ginger, and sugar until smooth. Using a spoon or a small rubber spatula, spread about 1 heaping teaspoon of the cheese mixture onto each mint leaf. Pinch the leaf *slightly* so that it forms an oval "bowl." Place a thin strip of crystallized ginger on top and a raspberry next to the ginger. Repeat with the remaining mint leaves. Place any remaining raspberries in the center of a serving plate and surround with the stuffed mint leaves. Serve within an hour.

meringue cake with whipped cream and summer berries

serves 8

While this is one of those desserts that looks like it took hours to put together, these meringues actually take very little time to prepare. What makes this cake so extraordinary is the contrast between the crisp and crunchy outside and the chewy, soft interior of the meringue. Use a variety of berries for color, texture, and flavor.

Try not to make the cake on a humid day. The moisture in the air makes it difficult for the meringue to hold together and stay crisp. You will need superfine sugar to make it. Superfine sugar is not the same as confectioners' sugar. It is a specially sifted sugar, often used for iced tea and baking, and is available in most grocery stores. For a quick substitution, add regular granulated sugar to a food processor and blend for a few minutes, until the sugar crystals break down to a fine consistency.

This recipe is an adaptation of one by baker Elinor Klivens.

for the meringue layers
Butter and confectioners' sugar, for
  preparing the pans
8 large egg whites, at room temperature
1/2 teaspoon cream of tartar
2 cups superfine sugar
2 tablespoons cornstarch, sifted
2 teaspoons fresh lemon juice
2 teaspoons vanilla extract

for the filling
2 cups heavy (whipping) cream, chilled
1/3 cup granulated or confectioners' sugar
1 1/2 teaspoons vanilla extract
About 3 cups mixed berries (raspberries,
  blackberries, blueberries, strawberries,
  gooseberries, or any combination)
About 1 cup grated coconut, toasted on a
  baking sheet at 350°F. for 10 minutes
  (optional)

To make the layers: Preheat the oven to 250°F. Line two baking sheets with parchment paper. Use a tiny bit of butter to attach the bottom of the paper to the baking sheets. Butter the paper lightly and dust with confectioners' sugar. Trace the outline of a 9-inch pie plate, creating a 9-inch circle, on each sheet of parchment. Set aside.

In the bowl of a standing mixer, use a whisk attachment to beat the egg whites on low speed until frothy. Increase the speed to medium-high and beat until soft peaks form. Lower the speed to medium and add the cream of tartar. Slowly add the superfine sugar and beat until soft peaks form, about 5 minutes. Add the sifted cornstarch and then the lemon juice and vanilla and beat until incorporated.

Using a spoon or a rubber spatula, carefully spread the meringue mixture over

recipe continues

the marked circles. You don't need to be overly precise. The idea is this: You want one circle to act as the base of the cake, so use your rubber spatula to smooth out the meringue into the circle to create a flat, even base. The second circle of meringue should have a slight rim and a depressed center (which will later be filled with the whipped cream and fruit). It will act as the top, show-off layer of the cake. Use the rubber spatula to create an indentation in the center, pushing the meringue mixture out away from the center toward the sides. Bake both layers for 1 hour and 30 minutes, or until the meringues feel crisp on the outside. Let cool on the baking sheet, and very carefully remove with a large rubber spatula. (The meringue can be made 1 day ahead of time and stored in a dry spot or a tin; it can also be frozen for up to 1 month.)

To make the filling: Just before you are ready to serve the cake, with an electric mixer, whip the cream in a large bowl until soft peaks form. Add the sugar and vanilla and whip until *barely stiff* peaks form.

Place the flat layer of the meringue on a large serving plate. Add less than half of the whipped cream and, using a rubber spatula, spread the cream over the meringue, making sure not to spread it too close to the edges. Scatter $1\frac{1}{2}$ cups of the berries on top, pressing them slightly into the cream. Carefully place the top layer of the meringue over the cream and fruit with the depressed center facing up. Fill the center of the meringue with the remaining whipped cream and arrange the remaining berries on top, scattering the different types of berries to create a colorful fruit topping. Sprinkle the toasted coconut on top of the fruit, if using. (The cake should not be assembled with the cream and fruit more than 20 minutes before serving, or it will soften. Refrigerate if not serving immediately.) Use a large (fairly sharp) cake knife to cut the cake.

the wild, wild blues

In Downeast and the southwestern corner of Maine, there are thousands of acres of tiny, tart wild blueberries growing. Maine is ideal for these indigenous berries due to its naturally acidic, rich glacial soil. Unlike cultivated blueberries, which tend to grow on high bushes and are larger and less tart, these lowbush berries have a hint of . . . well, wildness, mixed with a subtle sweetness, making them an excellent choice for pies, jams, jellies, tarts, cakes, breads, and eating out of hand.

Wild Maine blueberries are said to have a higher level of antioxidants than any other fruit or vegetable—higher than kale, spinach, or garlic! They are harvested in August and can be found fresh in mid to late summer and frozen and canned year-round.

blueberry pie with lemon spice cream

serves 8

The inspiration for this wonderful fruit pie came from Jessica Thomson, our talented intern who helped test so many of the recipes in this book. A rich crust is filled with fresh blueberries and spiked with lemon juice and lemon zest, making it one of the juiciest, most flavorful fruit pies we've ever tasted. Plan on making the crust and letting it chill at least 1 hour before you're ready to assemble the pie. The pie needs to chill at least another 30 minutes before baking, so plan your time accordingly.

The Lemon Spice Cream is a delicious topping for any fruit pie. Try it with the Apple Crumble on page 230, or the Plum-Peach Crostata on page 238. It also pairs well with a mixture of fresh summer berries.

for the crust
2½ cups all-purpose flour
½ cup sugar
1½ teaspoons salt
1 cup (2 sticks) unsalted butter, chilled and
    cut into small pieces
2 tablespoons vegetable shortening
1 large egg, beaten
1 tablespoon grated lemon zest
1 to 3 tablespoons ice water

for the fruit filling
1 tablespoon unsalted butter
2 tablespoons all-purpose flour
5 cups wild or cultivated fresh blueberries
½ cup plain sugar or Vanilla Sugar
    (page 277)

1 tablespoon grated lemon zest
1 tablespoon fresh lemon juice
Pinch of salt
¼ teaspoon ground cinnamon
¼ teaspoon freshly grated or ground
    nutmeg

1 large egg, beaten (optional)

for the lemon spice cream
1 cup cold heavy cream
1 tablespoon grated lemon zest
1 tablespoon confectioners' sugar
2 teaspoons vanilla extract
½ teaspoon freshly grated or ground
    nutmeg
½ teaspoon ground cinnamon

To prepare the crust: Mix the flour, sugar, and salt in a large bowl. Add the butter and shortening and, using a pastry blender or your hands, break up the butter and work it into the flour mixture until it resembles coarse breadcrumbs. Mix the beaten egg and lemon zest into the flour mixture thoroughly. Mix in 1 tablespoon of the ice water, and gradually add more, if needed, until the dough begins to come together and there is no excess flour in the bottom of the bowl. Divide the dough in half, shape each half into a round, flat disc, and wrap it in a large piece of plastic wrap.

Chill for at least 1 hour, and up to 48. Remove dough 30 minutes before rolling out.

To prepare the filling: Melt the butter over low heat in a medium saucepan. Sprinkle in the flour and stir to combine, about 1 minute. Add half of the berries and all the sugar and cook, stirring, for 8 to 10 minutes, or until the sugar is dissolved and the mixture has boiled and thickened. Add the remaining berries, the lemon zest, lemon juice, salt, cinnamon, and nutmeg and stir well to combine. Raise the heat to medium, cook for 1 minute, and remove from the heat. Let the filling cool to room temperature. (The recipe can be made several hours ahead of time up to this point. Cover and refrigerate until ready to assemble the pie.)

Position a rack in the middle of the oven and preheat the oven to 375°F.

Sprinkle a clean work surface with flour. Roll one of the dough circles into a circle about 11 inches in diameter. Transfer the dough to a 9-inch pie plate, allowing the edges to fall over the sides of the pie plate. Spoon the cooled blueberry mixture into the bottom crust. Roll out the other piece of dough to a circle about 11 inches in diameter. Using a pizza cutter or a small, sharp knife, cut strips about $1/2$ inch wide out of the dough. Place the strips on top of the fruit filling, creating a crisscross lattice pattern. Trim off any excess crust and crimp the edges of the lattice together with those of the bottom crust, creating a decorative pattern. Place the pie in the refrigerator for at least 30 minutes and up to 4 hours.

Place the pie on a cookie sheet and brush the pastry with the beaten egg, if desired. (It will make the crust shiny.) Bake for 50 to 60 minutes, or until the crust is golden brown and the filling is bubbling. If the pie begins to brown too fast, cover loosely with a sheet of aluminum foil. Let the pie cool slightly before cutting.

To make the Lemon Spice Cream: Pour the cream into a mixing bowl and, using chilled beaters, beat the cream with an electric mixer on medium speed until it forms soft peaks. Add the lemon zest, sugar, and vanilla and beat for 10 seconds. Add the nutmeg and cinnamon and beat for another 10 seconds. Serve cold with the warm pie.

harvest variations
Instead of using 5 cups of blueberries, substitute one of the suggestions below:

- 3 cups of fresh blueberries and 2 cups of peeled, thinly sliced peaches, nectarines, and plums (see page 239)
- 5 cups of assorted fresh berries—raspberries, blueberries, blackberries, strawberries, and gooseberries

blueberry-lemon–sour cream coffee cake

see photograph on page 205

serves 12

Light, fluffy, and exceedingly moist, this coffee cake is layered with fresh blueberries, chopped walnuts, cinnamon, and a grating of lemon zest. The recipe is an adaptation of the sour cream coffee cake that appears in Nick Malgieri's fabulous book *Perfect Cakes.* Serve the cake for breakfast, brunch, tea time, or dessert.

Butter and flour, for greasing the pan

for the blueberry filling
1 1/2 cups fresh blueberries
1/2 cup coarsely chopped walnuts
2 tablespoons plain sugar or Vanilla Sugar
 (page 277)
1 1/2 teaspoons grated lemon zest
1 teaspoon ground cinnamon

for the topping
1/2 cup coarsely chopped walnuts
1/4 cup plain sugar or Vanilla Sugar
1 teaspoon ground cinnamon

for the cake batter
2 cups all-purpose flour
1 teaspoon baking powder
1/2 teaspoon baking soda
1 cup (2 sticks) unsalted butter, at room
 temperature
1 1/2 cups plain sugar
2 large eggs
1 cup sour cream
1/2 tablespoon grated lemon zest

Position a rack in the middle of the oven and preheat the oven to 350°F. Grease a 12-cup tube pan with butter, flour it lightly, and set aside.

To make the blueberry filling: Mix the blueberries, walnuts, sugar, lemon zest, and cinnamon in a small bowl, and set aside.

To make the topping: Mix the walnuts, sugar, and cinnamon in another small bowl and set aside.

To mix the cake: In a medium bowl, sift together the flour, baking powder, and baking soda and set aside. In the bowl of a standing mixer, use a paddle attachment to cream the butter and sugar until pale yellow, soft, and fluffy, about 5 minutes at medium speed. Using a spatula, scrape down the sides of the bowl. Add the eggs, one at a time, beating well after each addition. Reduce the mixer speed to low and add half the flour mixture. Beat until well incorporated. Add half the sour cream and all the lemon zest and beat well. Add the remaining flour and then the remaining sour cream, using the spatula to scrape down the sides and make sure the batter is smooth and fully incorporated.

Spoon half the batter into the prepared pan, smoothing it down with a spatula. Sprinkle with the blueberry filling. Top with the remaining batter, using your spatula to smooth it slightly. Don't worry if the batter seems thick and difficult to work with; the cake will turn out just fine! Sprinkle the walnut-and-sugar topping on top. Bake the cake for 55 minutes to 1 hour, or until a toothpick inserted in the center comes out clean.

Remove the cake and let cool for 30 minutes. Using a flat table knife, release the cake from the pan by running the blade around the outside of the cake and along the inside, near the tube, to help loosen it. Invert the cake onto a serving plate and remove the pan. Reinvert the cake so the side with the topping is facing up. The cake will keep, tightly wrapped in plastic, at room temperature for several days, or it can be wrapped and frozen for several months.

a zest for zest

We love the power of zest. When you grate the outer rind of a citrus fruit (not the bitter white pith), it releases aromatic essential oils that add a citrus flavor and gorgeous fragrance to foods. Zest is also said to have more vitamin C than any other part of the fruit.

When using the zest of a fruit, always wash the outside of the fruit to remove any waxy coating or chemicals that the fruit may have been sprayed with. Organic fruit is an even better choice. To grate citrus zest, you can use the small holes of a regular grater. But we've found that the ultimate tool for grating citrus zest is a Microplane (see Resources on page 282). This fabulously simple tool, which has been used for years by carpenters and wood workers (they call it a wood rasp), has the ability to grate the citrus zest into tiny particles without digging into the white, bitter-tasting inner pith. In addition, the zest doesn't get stuck in the grater.

We like to add the zest from lemons, limes, oranges, grapefruits, and kumquats to all kinds of foods—from fruit salads, cakes (see page 250), and puddings to salad dressings, sauces, and stews. Try grating tangerine zest into a chicken stew, or lime zest into a vinaigrette with a touch of fresh grated ginger. Add kumquat zest to a fruit salad, or sprinkle Meyer lemon zest onto a chicken or shrimp salad. Add orange, lemon, and grapefruit zest to a lemon sorbet, and the flavors will explode.

berry, berry good

Every summer, we look forward to watching the berry bushes fill with fat, juicy fruit. When ripe and fresh they are the perfect dessert—requiring nothing more than a dusting of sugar, a dollop of whipped cream or crème fraîche, or a bowl of yogurt and granola. The best berry is the one you pop in your mouth, still warm from the sun, while you collect others for the evening's dessert.

Aside from their natural sweetness and ability to work well in just about any dessert, berries are low in calories and contain almost no fat, cholesterol, or sodium. They are high in vitamin C, fiber, folic acid, and antioxidants—making them high on the list of good-for-you foods. Here are some favorites:

blueberries should be plump. The silver white frost found on the berry is called the "bloom" and is a sign of freshness. Look for firm berries that are of a uniform blue color. Wild blueberries are smaller and more tart than the cultivated variety. They are fragile and need to be eaten or frozen the same day they are picked.

blackberry bushes are things to be careful of—all thorny and prickly and apt to attack you as you remove the luscious, large, fat, juicy, black-and-blue-colored berries from its vines. The name "blackberry" actually refers to a whole range of bush berries, including loganberries, boysenberries, marionberries, and ollalieberries.

raspberries are delicate and refined. One of the great treats of summer is a bowl filled high with just-picked raspberries, topped with heavy cream. The color of a raspberry ranges from reddish-pink to golden yellow to a darker reddish-blue.

strawberries, when fully ripe, are among the juiciest fruits you'll ever find. When the first sweet, red berries ripen in New England toward the end of June, we have been known to eat far too many. We use them to make pancakes, jams and jellies, sorbet and ice cream, and, of course, pies and cakes. We love to dip them in sour cream and brown sugar. Seek out evenly colored red berries that look firm and fresh. Look for the *fraise des bois,* a tiny, wild strawberry that has the subtle scent and flavor of roses.

gooseberries, though less well known, are becoming increasingly popular in this country; see Resources for information on buying plants so you can grow your own. They have long been adored throughout Britain for their tart, sour flavor and make excellent jams and jellies.

shopping for berries

Look for berries from May, when strawberry season begins, through October, when the later varieties of raspberries and blackberries can be found. All berries are fragile and highly perishable. Be careful not to overhandle them, or they will bruise. They can be refrigerated, or kept in a cool, dark spot out of direct sunlight. Raspberries and blackberries will keep for 2 to 3 days, while strawberries and blueberries stay fresh for up to 5 days. Avoid buying berries whose colors have leeched out and stained the paper or basket they are resting in. Don't wash the berries until you are ready to eat or cook with them; then, gently rinse in cold water and dry immediately, gently patting them dry with paper towels. Berries can be successfully frozen. Place freshly harvested berries on a cookie sheet and place in the freezer. When they are partially frozen, put them in an airtight plastic container or bag, and they won't clump together. Berries can be frozen for up to 8 months.

watermelon-raspberry ice

serves 6

This ice is one of the most refreshing desserts imaginable. It's like a cross between a sorbet, a slush, and a frozen ice—and you don't need any equipment other than a freezer and a metal or glass dish.

⅔ cup sugar

2 cups cut-up seeded watermelon (cut into chunks)

2 cups fresh raspberries

Combine 1 cup of water and the sugar in a medium saucepan and bring to a boil, stirring frequently. Cook for 2 minutes after the sugar syrup comes to a boil, stirring to fully dissolve the sugar.

Put the watermelon and berries in a blender or food processor and blend. Add the hot syrup and blend until almost smooth. Transfer the mixture to a shallow glass or metal dish (about 13 × 9 inches) and place in the freezer, uncovered, for 1½ hours, or until almost solid. Remove from the freezer and, using a fork, break up the frozen fruit into a somewhat smooth mixture and freeze for another hour. Break up the ice with a fork and serve in parfait or wine glasses.

harvest variations
- Substitute fresh blueberries, strawberries, and/or blackberries for the raspberries.
- Substitute an equal amount of seeded cantaloupe, honeydew, or any other ripe melon for the watermelon.
- Substitute 2 cups of pitted cherries for the raspberries.
- Try a three-melon slush: Combine 1 cup of watermelon chunks, 1 cup of honeydew chunks, and 2 cups of cantaloupe chunks.

strawberry glazed pie

serves 6

There are few ways to showcase the season's first ripe berries better than atop this gorgeous pie. A pie crust is prebaked (you can always cheat and use a store-bought 9-inch crust) and then the most gorgeous fresh berries are piled into the golden brown shell. The remaining berries are made into a glaze, so this is the perfect place for those bruised and not-so-perfect specimens. If you want to get patriotic (or create the perfect dessert for a Fourth of July celebration), pile ripe blueberries or blackberries in between the strawberries and top with whipped cream.

The dough for the crust needs to chill for at least 1 hour, or overnight, and the finished pie needs to be refrigerated for several hours, so plan your time accordingly.

for the crust
(or substitute a 9-inch storebought pie crust)
2 cups all-purpose flour
Pinch of salt
1 cup (2 sticks) unsalted butter, chilled and
    cut into small cubes
About 1/3 cup ice water

for the strawberry filling and glaze
2 quarts ripe, fresh strawberries, hulled
About 1 to 1 1/2 cups sugar, depending on
    the sweetness of the berries
3 1/2 teaspoons cornstarch
1 tablespoon unsalted butter

for the whipped cream
1 cup heavy cream
2 tablespoons sugar
1 teaspoon vanilla extract

To make the crust: Blend the flour and salt in the bowl of a food processor. Add the butter and pulse about 15 times, until the mixture resembles coarse breadcrumbs. With the motor running, add half the water and let the dough come together. Mix in just enough of the remaining water to make the dough begin to release from the sides of the bowl. Alternately, mix the flour and salt in a medium bowl. Add the butter and, using a pastry blender or two flat kitchen knives, work the butter into the flour until it resembles coarse breadcrumbs. Add enough water to make the dough begin to come together. Place the dough on a sheet of aluminum foil, wrap into a disc shape, and refrigerate for at least 2 hours, or overnight. Remove dough 30 minutes before rolling out.

When ready to bake, position a rack in the middle of the oven and preheat the oven to 400°F. Roll out the dough on a lightly floured surface to a circle about 10 to 12 inches in diameter. Place in a 9-inch pie plate and trim and crimp the edges.

Using a fork, prick the crust all over the bottom and up the sides. This will help prevent the dough from puffing up and allows air to circulate underneath. Bake for about 20 to 25 minutes, or until the crust is golden brown and feels firm to the touch. Remove from the oven and let cool. (The crust can be made 1 day ahead of time; gently cover and refrigerate until ready to fill the pie.)

When the crust is cool, fill the pie: Choose the best-looking strawberries (about half of the total quantity) and fit them into the crust like pieces to a puzzle, with the stem end down and the pointy side up. You may need to cut a few berries in half or into thin slices to fit them into the crust, forming an almost solid berry layer. Set aside.

To make the glaze: Put the remaining berries in a large skillet over low heat. Add $\frac{1}{2}$ cup of water and, using a potato masher, coarsely mash the berries. Add 1 cup of the sugar (if your berries are exceptionally sweet, you need to add only $\frac{3}{4}$ cup), raise the heat to high, and bring to a boil. Reduce the heat to low and simmer for 3 minutes. Put the cornstarch in a small bowl and mix in some of the hot strawberry "mash," stirring to create a smooth, thick paste. Return the mash to the pan and simmer for about 5 minutes, until the mixture is slightly thickened. Add the butter and stir until it melts. Remove the pan from the heat and taste for sweetness; if the berries are not very fresh or ripe, add the additional sugar.

Pour the strawberry mixture into a fine-mesh sieve set over a large bowl. Stir the mixture until a thick strawberry glaze is released through the sieve. Pour the glaze into a small saucepan and place over medium heat for 5 minutes, until reduced and somewhat thickened. Pour about half of the glaze over the berries, making sure each berry is coated. Be careful not to add too much glaze, or it will spill over the pastry. Pour the leftover glaze into a small bowl, cover, and refrigerate; enjoy it on top of toast and pancakes, or drizzled over ice cream. Refrigerate the pie for several hours.

When ready to serve, make the whipped cream: Whip the cream with an electric mixer in a medium bowl until soft peaks form. Add the sugar and vanilla and beat until almost stiff. Place a few dollops of the cream along the edges of the pie and serve the remaining whipped cream on the side.

rhubarb and strawberry pie

serves 6

Most cooks make the mistake of trying to balance rhubarb's tartness with an over-abundance of sugar. But the sour flavor is a big part of rhubarb's appeal, so in this pie the rhubarb is only lightly sweetened with a bit of sugar and vanilla and the natural sweetness of spring strawberries. Serve the pie warm or at room temperature with whipped cream, vanilla ice cream, or ginger ice cream.

The pastry needs to chill for at least 2 hours, or overnight.

for the crust
2 cups all-purpose flour
2 tablespoons sugar
Pinch of salt
¾ cup (1½ sticks) unsalted butter, chilled
   and cut into small cubes
About ⅓ cup ice water

for the filling
1 to 3 stalks rhubarb (about 1½ pounds
   untrimmed), depending on the size, cut
   into small, ¼-inch-thick pieces (2 cups)
½ cup plus 1 tablespoon sugar
½ teaspoon vanilla extract
2 cups thinly sliced ripe, fresh strawberries
2 tablespoons all-purpose flour

To make the crust: Add the flour, sugar, and salt to the bowl of a food processor and pulse for 2 seconds. Add the butter and pulse the machine about 15 times, or until the mixture has the consistency of coarse cornmeal. With the motor running, gradually add water to the pastry, continuing to pulse, until it begins to come together and pull away from the sides of the bowl. Alternately, mix the flour, sugar, and salt in a bowl. Add the butter and, using two table knives or a pastry blender, blend the butter into the flour until it resembles coarse cornmeal. Blend in enough water to make the dough just begin to hold together. Remove the pastry (it still may appear crumbly), and wrap into a disc shape in aluminum foil. Place in the refrigerator for at least 2 hours, or overnight. Remove dough 30 minutes before rolling out.

When ready to bake, assemble the filling: Put the rhubarb in a large bowl and sprinkle with ½ cup of the sugar. Mix well. Let "marinate" or soften for about 15 minutes. Gently mix in the vanilla, strawberries, and flour.

When ready to bake, position a rack in the middle of the oven and preheat the oven to 400°F. Roll out the pastry on a lightly floured work surface to a circle about 12 inches in diameter. Transfer the dough to a 9-inch pie plate and let the excess hang over the sides. Trim off the excess dough, leaving a ¾-inch border, and roll the dough into a ball. Roll out the excess dough and cut it into long, thin lattice strips about ½ inch wide. Press the dough down along the edges of the pan to create neat edges. Pile the fruit into the pie crust. Place the lattice strips on top of the fruit, making a crisscross pattern. Sprinkle the top with the remaining 1 tablespoon of sugar.

Place the pie on a cookie sheet and bake for 30 minutes. The crust should begin to turn golden. Reduce the heat to 350°F. and bake for another 25 to 30 minutes, or until the crust is golden brown and the fruit filling is bubbling and soft. Let cool for about 5 minutes to allow the juices to settle. Serve warm or at room temperature, with any juices from the bottom of the pie plate spooned over the pie.

flourless chocolate cake with orange chocolate ganache

serves 8 to 10

Jessica Thomson, our fearless intern, created the recipe for this moist, flourless chocolate cake laced with orange. Surround the cake with small triangles of oranges, tangerines, and/or blood oranges and serve with tiny shots of Cointreau or Grand Marnier and hot espresso.

Note: Dutch-processed cocoa is nonalkalized. If you use regular cocoa powder (which is alkalized), substitute $1/2$ teaspoon baking soda for the 1 teaspoon of baking powder.

The cake is delicious served freshly baked, but after it sits for a day in the refrigerator, it takes on a thicker, almost fudgelike texture.

for the cake
Butter and flour, for greasing the pan
4 ounces semisweet chocolate, chopped into small pieces
$1/2$ cup (1 stick) unsalted butter, cut into small pieces
5 large eggs, at room temperature
1 cup sugar
$1/2$ cup Dutch-processed cocoa powder (see Note)
1 teaspoon baking powder
1 tablespoon orange liqueur, such as Grand Marnier
1 teaspoon vanilla extract

Pinch of salt
1 teaspoon packed grated orange zest

for the ganache
4 ounces semisweet chocolate, chopped into small pieces
$1/2$ cup heavy cream
1 tablespoon orange liqueur, such as Grand Marnier

1 orange, blood orange, or tangerine for garnish
Confectioners' sugar, for dusting

To make the cake: Position a rack in the middle of the oven and preheat the oven to 375°F. Generously grease a $9^{1/2}$-inch springform pan with butter. Cut a round piece of parchment paper to fit the bottom of the pan and line the pan with the paper. Grease the parchment and sides of the pan, and lightly coat the entire pan with flour, tapping out any excess flour from the sides and bottom. Set aside.

Melt the chocolate for the cake in the top of a double boiler set over barely simmering water. (You can also melt the chocolate in a bowl set over a pot of barely simmering water.) Remove from the heat and stir in the butter until the mixture is smooth. Set aside to cool.

recipe continues

With an electric mixer on medium speed, beat the eggs in a large bowl until thick and foamy, about 1 minute. Add the sugar in a slow, steady stream, continuing to beat until the mixture has increased in volume, thickened, and is a pale, yellow color (about 8 to 10 minutes). Sift the cocoa powder and baking powder over the batter and fold in gently with a rubber spatula until almost combined. Set aside briefly.

Add the orange liqueur, vanilla, salt, and orange zest to the melted chocolate mixture and fold them in. Put about 1 cup of the egg-and-sugar batter into the melted chocolate mixture, stirring to lighten and cool the chocolate mixture. Pour the chocolate mixture into the bowl with the remaining batter, gently and carefully folding all ingredients together until just combined. Pour the batter into the prepared cake pan.

Bake the cake for 20 to 25 minutes, or until a skewer inserted into the center of the cake comes out clean (the cake may begin to shrink away from the sides of the pan). Let the cake cool for about 5 minutes in the pan, and then remove the sides of the springform pan. Let cool completely on a cooling rack.

If there are any crusty, dark pieces along the top of the cake, use a small, sharp, serrated knife and, keeping the knife level with the cake, cut off the darkened pieces. Place a large cake plate over the cake and very carefully flip the cake over onto the plate. Remove the bottom of the pan and peel off the parchment paper. Carefully flip the cake back onto the cooling rack. Place a sheet of aluminum foil under the cooling rack (it will help catch the drips when you spread the ganache on).

To make the ganache: Melt the chocolate in the top of a double boiler set over barely simmering water, stirring until smooth. Add the cream and stir until smooth. Mix in the liqueur. Remove the mixture from the heat and let sit until cooled slightly, about 10 minutes.

Pour half the ganache over the cake and, using a straight or offset spatula, gently spread it over the top of the cake until smooth. Let the ganache drip down the sides. Pour the remaining ganache over the cake and smooth the top with the spatula. Let the cake sit at room temperature until the ganache is totally dry. Using a spatula or a pizza paddle, carefully transfer the cake to a serving plate. (If making ahead, lightly cover the cake with wax paper and refrigerate until 1 hour before serving.)

Peel the orange and separate into sections. Cut each section into small pieces or triangles and place them around the cake. (You can also add a few orange triangles around the rim of the cake.) Sift the cake with powdered sugar *just* before serving.

fresh mango winter salsa

makes about 2½ cups

The fresh, tropical flavors of this salsa simply defy winter. The salsa can be made several hours ahead of time. It's delicious served with the Shrimp, Corn, and Ginger Pancakes (page 92), tacos, tortillas, or simply a bowl of good taco chips.

2 ripe mangos, peeled and chopped into ½-inch cubes

1 small sweet red pepper, diced

1 tablespoon grated or finely chopped fresh ginger

2 tablespoons chopped scallions (white and green parts)

2 tablespoons finely chopped fresh cilantro

3 tablespoons lemon, Meyer lemon, or fresh lime juice (see page 262)

1 tablespoon olive oil

Pinch salt, or to taste

Dash hot pepper sauce

In a medium bowl, gently mix all the ingredients together. Taste for seasoning and add more salt or hot pepper sauce as needed. The salsa can be made several hours ahead of time; cover and refrigerate as needed.

lemons and oranges and grapefruit...
oh my!

In order to survive the doldrums of long, cold Maine winters, we rely heavily on citrus fruits. A bowl of bright oranges, pale yellow grapefruit, sweet and sour kumquats, orangey Meyer lemons, and bright green limes can wake up our senses on even the coldest, most miserable days.

lemons

Prized for its acidity, the lemon is the most common citrus fruit for cooking. Filled with vitamin C, lemons can be used for their juice and their aromatic rinds.

Meyer lemons are a lemon lover's friend. They look almost identical to regular lemons, but one taste, and you'll realize you've discovered a citrus fruit worth knowing. Named after scientist Frank N. Meyer, a Meyer lemon tastes like a cross between a tart lemon and a sweet orange. Its skin is a rich yellow color (unlike many commercially grown regular lemons, Meyer lemons do not have their skin dyed the "perfect" shade of lemon yellow). They tend to grow on small farms and were used primarily as ornamental trees until the early 1980s, when chefs began discovering their extraordinary taste. What makes a Meyer lemon even more unique is that the entire fruit is edible. The skin (which in a regular lemon tends to be tough and coated with preservatives) is tender and sweet, and can be used to flavor cakes, tarts, drinks, and salads. The Meyer lemon can be substituted for regular lemons; you may find you can use less of it because of its concentrated sweetness.

To take the edge off a sore throat or to soothe cold winter bones, add the juice and chopped-up rind of a Meyer lemon to 1 cup of boiling water and stir in 1 tablespoon of good honey. A dash of good rum only makes it better. Look for Meyer lemons during the winter months in specialty food shops (see Resources on page 279) and choose firm, plump fruit, without soft spots.

limes

Grown throughout Florida year-round, limes are prized for their distinctively sour, pleasingly acidic taste. A great source of vitamin C, limes can be used instead of the more common lemon to add an exotic twist to everyday foods. Try adding lime juice to sautéed fish fillets instead of lemon, and watch how interesting a basic dish becomes. Add a touch of fresh lime juice and grated zest to a rich chicken or seafood stew and taste how other flavors jump forward. Add lime to mayonnaise and spread on a chicken or a roasted vegetable sandwich, or add it to fresh salsa and vinaigrettes.

Key limes (also known as Mexican limes) were brought to America from Asia in the sixteenth century and are grown in many parts of Florida. The domestic crop is dwindling, however, so many of the Key limes we find in the States are imported. Round- to oval-shaped fruit, Key limes are smaller and a paler green (closer to yellowish-green) than regular limes. They are popular because of their distinctive aroma; thin, bitter green rind; and juicy, tender flavor. Traditionally used in Key lime pie, Key lime juice can also be used to flavor drinks, pastries, whipped cream, stews, and any seafood dish.

oranges

There are two major species of oranges: **sweet oranges** (*Citrus sinensis*) and **sour** or **bitter oranges** (*Citrus aurantium*). Although oranges are available year-round, their growing season in this country runs from December to May.

Sweet oranges are the most popular type of orange, due to their rich, sweet, and slightly acidic orange flavor; they are also a great source of vitamins C and A. There are dozens of varieties, including the familiar **navel oranges** (small and seedless); tender, juicy **Jaffa oranges** and **Valencia oranges** (favored for juice and eating), and lesser-known species with wonderful names, such as **Jincheng, Parson Brown,** and **Shamouti.**

Blood oranges, which have been popular throughout the Mediterranean for centuries, have become increasingly available in this country and are available from December to May. Pigmented with anthocyanin, their flesh has a unique, deeply reddish color ranging from a rich burgundy to pale maroon. The rind may be pitted or smooth and generally has a gorgeous red blush. Many cooks compare the flavor of blood oranges to overripe berries, especially raspberries.

Sour oranges are highly acidic and are used more for cooking than eating raw. The peel gives Grand Marnier its characteristic flavor. Sour oranges are also prized for making bitter marmalades.

tangerines

Tangerines, available from December to April, can be eaten or used for juice. The reddish-orange peel and tart, plumlike taste wakes up the flavor of many winter foods. Try pairing them with pungent cheeses and mix the segments with bitter greens in salads.

mandarin oranges

Mandarin oranges (or **clementines**), available from October through March, are a cross between a Mediterranean mandarin and a sour orange.

Introduced in Florida in 1909 and later in California, they are a medium-size fruit with few seeds and a deep orange color. They separate into segments easily, and some find they taste like apricot nectar. Mandarin oranges and tangerines are interchangeable in recipes.

kumquats

Kumquats, which are available from October to May, are oval, and look like miniature orange footballs. Although many people make the mistake of using kumquats only as a garnish (they are frequently scattered around holiday birds for a festive look), they can be eaten whole, and explode in your mouth with a sweet and sour flavor. Thinly sliced and seeded (the seeds are very bitter and should be avoided), they make excellent jam, and can be roasted whole and served with duck or as an accompaniment to cheese.

grapefruit

Grapefruit, a cross between a sweet orange and a pummelo, are available from November through May. There are two basic types of grapefruit: **white-fleshed** and **pink.** The color of the flesh ranges from deep red burgundy to pale yellow, depending on the type of grapefruit, and the rind can be orange-tinged or bright yellow. Look for grapefruit that feels heavy in your hand; this is a sign that the fruit has a high juice content. Grapefruit is thought of as diet food because of its low calorie content and sweet juice; it's also a great source of vitamins C and A, and has quite a bit of calcium. Grapefruits can add an interesting, tart flavor to food when substituted for oranges. They can be cut in half, sprinkled with brown sugar and a splash of dry sherry, and broiled until the sugar caramelizes; or tossed in a salad with avocado and banana slices.

pummelos

Pummelos, the largest of all citrus fruit, are the botanical ancestor of the grapefruit. They are slightly pear shaped, greenish to yellow-pink in color, and have a thick skin. The flesh color ranges from white to deep pink.

gingered cranberry sauce
with pineapple and pecans

makes about 10 cups

Cranberry sauce, the classic accompaniment to Thanksgiving turkey, also doubles as a sweet sauce for ice cream, pound cake, angel food cake, or cookies. Try spreading it on your morning muffin or toast, or on top of pancakes and waffles. The sauce is also the key ingredient in the ultimate sandwich: thick slices of white or wheat toast spread with a good spoonful of this sauce, slices of leftover turkey, leftover holiday stuffing, and several leaves of crisp lettuce.

2 cups sugar

7 cups (1 1/2 pounds) fresh cranberries

1 cup orange juice, preferably fresh-squeezed

6 tablespoons julienned orange zest (see page 251 for more about zest)

1/3 cup pure maple syrup

3 tablespoons minced fresh ginger

1 medium pineapple, peeled, cored, and diced

1 1/2 cups chopped pecans

Mix the sugar with 6 cups of water in a large saucepan and bring to a boil over high heat. Boil for 5 minutes. Reduce the heat to medium and simmer for 15 to 20 minutes, or until the sugar syrup is somewhat reduced and turns a pale vanilla color. Add the cranberries and simmer until they begin to pop, about 5 minutes. Add the orange juice, orange zest, maple syrup, ginger, and pineapple and simmer over medium heat for about 15 minutes, or until the sauce is somewhat thickened. If the sauce still seems thin, reduce it over medium heat for another 10 to 15 minutes. It will thicken when you add the nuts and the sauce cools, but this is not a super-thick sauce.

Remove from the heat and cool several minutes. Stir in the nuts and let cool to room temperature. Store in a clean glass jar in the refrigerator for up to 7 days, or freeze for up to 6 months.

rhubarb

spring's first treat

There is often still snow on the ground when the first greenish-pink leaves of the rhubarb plant begin to sprout and unfurl through the spring earth. In New England it is the first fruit of the season, a harbinger of good things to come.

An odd-looking plant, with its pinkish-red, over-sized, celery-like stalks, rhubarb is often misunderstood. Like some people we know, it's exceedingly sour and needs to be balanced with something sweet. But the whole point of rhubarb is its pleasingly tart, tangy, almost berrylike flavor.

A member of the Polygonaceae family, rhubarb is easy to grow; in fact, it's practically a weed, multiplying each year by sending out new shoots. Always pick rhubarb when it is still young, since it bolts to seed quickly, sending a wild-looking group of seed pods shooting up from the top of the plant that indicate that rhubarb season is pretty much over.

Cook with rhubarb stalks that are not too fat (those tend to be pithy or woody); longer, thinner stalks are best. There are two basic varieties: *hothouse-grown rhubarb* tends to be a lighter pink color with yellowish leaves and a milder flavor, while *field-grown rhubarb* has darker red stalks and green leaves. Always look for stalks that are crisp and firm, moist looking, and brightly colored. Rhubarb leaves are quite toxic and should always be removed and discarded.

When cooked, rhubarb can leech out much of its color, but not its taste. It's a great companion to strawberries (see pages 256 and 267) and, because it contains a great deal of water, it doesn't need to be cooked with much liquid. Rhubarb is excellent in crisps and cobblers, chutney, muffins, jams, and jellies, or for adding a tart counterpoint to rich meats, such as duck or game.

gingered rhubarb-strawberry sauce

makes 3 cups

Everyone knows what good companions rhubarb and strawberry are, but ginger is the surprise in this sweet sauce. Ginger seems to bring out the exotic, earthy quality in rhubarb, and this sauce is a great way to showcase the combination. It's an ideal topping for vanilla ice cream, but you can also eat it for breakfast with muffins or toast, or serve it as a dessert compote with a drizzle of heavy cream and a few fresh strawberries scattered on top.

1½ pounds rhubarb, rinsed, and cut into 1-inch pieces, about 2 cups

1 cup fresh strawberries, stemmed and cut in half

2 tablespoons packed freshly grated ginger

1 cup sugar

Mix the rhubarb, strawberries, ginger, sugar, and ¾ cup of water in a large pot and bring to a boil over high heat. Reduce the heat to low, cover, and cook for 10 minutes. Remove the cover and cook for another 15 to 20 minutes, or until the sauce is thick enough to coat the back of a spoon. Raise the heat to medium-high and boil gently until thickened. (The sauce can be made up to 2 days ahead of time and stored, covered, in the refrigerator.) Serve at room temperature or chilled.

harvest
basics

basic chicken broth

serves 8

This is probably the most versatile broth you'll ever make. It is delicious served as is, or it can be used as the base of many soups, stews, and sauces. When a recipe calls for homemade chicken broth or stock, this is what you want to use.

Use the cooked chicken in salads, tortillas, burritos, or sandwiches.

One 3 1/2-pound chicken, preferably
   organic or naturally raised
4 large carrots, cut into 1-inch pieces
4 celery stalks, cut into 1-inch pieces
1/2 cup minced fresh parsley

1 bay leaf
6 peppercorns
1/2 teaspoon salt, or to taste
3 to 4 sprigs fresh thyme, or 1 teaspoon
   dried

Put the chicken in a large soup pot and *barely* cover with cold water. Add the carrots, celery, parsley, bay leaf, peppercorns, salt, and thyme and bring to a boil over high heat. Reduce the heat to low, cover, and simmer for 1 hour. Uncover the pot and reduce the broth for another 30 minutes.

The chicken should be tender and almost falling off the bone. The broth should be very flavorful. If the broth still tastes weak, remove the chicken with a slotted spoon and set aside in a large bowl. Reduce the broth over medium-high heat for about 5 to 10 minutes, or until full flavored. Season with more salt if needed.

The broth can be refrigerated, covered, for 4 to 5 days, or frozen up to 4 months.

chicken broth
doctoring the canned stuff

All too often there's no time to cook a pot of homemade chicken broth, and we find ourselves grabbing a can or carton of chicken broth instead. Here are a few simple tricks for making store-bought broth taste more like it came right out of your kitchen:

• Simmer canned chicken broth with 1 bay leaf, 1 peeled onion, 4 peppercorns, 1 sprig of fresh parsley, and 1 celery stalk for 10 minutes; strain before using.

• When adding canned chicken broth to Asian-flavored dishes, heat the canned broth with a knob of peeled, fresh ginger and a few sprigs of fresh cilantro for 10 minutes; strain the broth before using.

• Add a handful of fresh or dried herbs to the broth to wake up the flavors—we like parsley, basil, tarragon, rosemary, and chives. Match the herbs to the other flavors you're using in the rest of the dish.

breadcrumbs

Commercially made breadcrumbs are often mixed with artificial flavorings and additives to help them last longer. But if you keep a bag of leftover bread around (the heel of a baguette or Italian loaf, or several slices from an almost-stale loaf of white, wheat, or dark rye), you can make fresh breadcrumbs in less than a minute.

Like so many other things, the better the quality of bread you start with, the better your breadcrumbs will be. Always make sure there is no sign of mold or discoloration on your bread.

Break up the bread into small pieces. Put in the bowl of a food processor or blender and whirl until the bread reaches the desired texture. Some cooks prefer breadcrumbs with a coarser texture, others like their breadcrumbs very fine. Store in an airtight container in a cool, dark spot.

harvest variations
- For an herb-flavored mixture, add 2 to 3 teaspoons of dried herbs to 1 cup of finished breadcrumbs and mix well.
- For cheese-flavored crumbs, add ¼ cup of grated Parmesan or another sharp cheese to 1 cup of finished breadcrumbs and keep refrigerated.
- For a slightly spicy bite, add a dash of red chile flakes to the finished breadcrumbs.

garlic croûtes

serves 8

A large, garlicky version of croutons, these toasts can be served on top of soups, stews, or chowders, or alongside roasts, salads, and fish dishes. They can also be served, instead of chips and crackers, with dips, salsa, or a cheese course. They're particularly good with the New England–Style Fish Stew on page 93.

8 thin slices French or Italian bread, cut about 2½ inches long and almost ½ inch thick

¼ cup minced garlic
¼ cup olive oil

Preheat the oven to 350°F. Place the bread on a cookie sheet and bake for 5 minutes. In a small bowl, mix the garlic and oil. Flip the bread over and spread or brush the garlic oil evenly over all 8 slices. Bake for about 5 to 10 minutes more, or until the toasts are golden brown. Remove from the oven and let cool. The croûtes can be made 1 day ahead of time; wrap tightly and store at room temperature.

herb butter

makes 1 cup

This is a great way to take advantage of a garden or a farmers market overflowing with fresh herbs. You can use virtually any combination of culinary herbs. The Herb Butter will keep in the refrigerator for several days, or you can wrap it and freeze it for several months. To serve it alongside other dishes, simply whip it with a fork and serve in a small ramekin or bowl.

½ cup (1 stick) unsalted butter, at room temperature

⅓ cup minced fresh herbs (see suggested combinations below)

Salt and freshly ground black pepper to taste

Put the butter in a medium-size bowl and stir with a wooden spoon to soften it. Stir in the herbs, salt, and pepper, making sure the herbs are fully incorporated into the butter. Put the butter in the middle of a sheet of plastic wrap and cover with one side of the plastic wrap. Roll the butter into a long log or fat cigar shape, wrap it completely, and place in the refrigerator or freezer until ready to use. Serve the rolled-up log or cut off slices as needed.

harvest variations

Blend in ⅓ cup of any of the following combinations of fresh herbs:

- Parsley, chives, and scallion
- Tarragon, lemon thyme, and scallion
- Basil, summer savory, and lemon verbena
- Lemon thyme, thyme, and chives
- Sage, rosemary, and thyme
- Lemon thyme, basil, and lemon verbena
- Lavender and lemon thyme
- Chives, garlic chives, and thyme
- Cilantro and lemon verbena
- Mint and lemon thyme
- Chervil and parsley

homemade mayonnaise

makes 1 cup

There are times when homemade mayonnaise can really make a difference. The garlic-flavored Aioli on page 274 is delicious made with bottled mayonnaise, but try it with this simple, homemade version and it becomes a sauce friends and family will swoon over. Add homemade mayonnaise to sandwiches and sauces, stir it into a vinaigrette for a creamy texture, or use it as a base for Tartar Sauce (page 275), or a dip. You can make the mayonnaise using only olive oil, but it will have a very rich flavor. For a mellower version, half olive and half vegetable oil works best.

2 egg yolks, at room temperature
1 teaspoon Dijon mustard
1 tablespoon fresh lemon juice
1 teaspoon white wine vinegar

Salt and freshly ground black pepper
  to taste
1/2 cup extra virgin olive oil
1/2 cup canola oil

Put the egg yolks, mustard, lemon juice, vinegar, salt, and pepper in the bowl of a food processor or blender and puree briefly until thick and pale yellow. With the machine running, slowly add the olive oil, 1 teaspoon at a time, letting the mixture emulsify after each addition. As the sauce begins to thicken, add the canola oil in a slow, steady stream, scraping down the side of the blender or food processor as needed. Taste for seasoning. The sauce will keep, covered and refrigerated, for about 3 to 4 days.

harvest variations

- Stir in about 3 tablespoons of your choice of minced fresh herbs (tarragon, basil, rosemary, chives, parsley, fennel, chervil, sage) to create an herby green mayonnaise.
- Substitute lime or orange juice for the lemon juice and add 1 1/2 teaspoons of grated lime or orange zest for a citrus-flavored mayonnaise.
- For a nutty-flavored mayonnaise, use 3/4 cup of olive oil and 1/4 cup of walnut or hazelnut oil.
- Add 1 roasted red pepper for a pink, sweet pepper–flavored mayonnaise.
- For an anchovy-flavored mayonnaise, add 1 to 2 minced anchovy fillets with 1 teaspoon of the anchovy oil.
- Add 1 1/2 teaspoons of green or black olive puree or paste for an earthier mayonnaise.
- For a smoky, spicy mayonnaise, add 2 tablespoons of chopped canned chipotle peppers.

aioli
(garlic mayonnaise)

makes 1 cup

Garlic lovers will have a field day with this sauce. A handful of garlic cloves are pounded with sea salt and then mixed with mayonnaise, lemon juice, and pepper. This heady sauce is superb served with Sweet Potato Fries (page 194), soups, stews, and fish dishes, or slathered on a roast beef or cheese sandwich. The Aioli will last, covered and refrigerated, for several days.

1 tablespoon sea salt, or more to taste
3 to 6 whole garlic cloves (depending on
   your love of garlic)

1 cup Homemade Mayonnaise (page 273)
   or store-bought
2 tablespoons fresh lemon juice
Freshly ground black pepper to taste

Combine the salt and garlic cloves in a mortar, or a small wooden bowl. Using a pestle or the back of a wooden spoon, mash the garlic into the salt to form a paste—the garlic should look creamy and chunky. A small food processor can also be used.

In a small serving bowl, gently mix the garlic puree, mayonnaise, and lemon juice. Add the pepper and more salt, if needed.

harvest variations

- You can also make a mellower, less assertive sauce by roasting the garlic cloves in a 350°F. oven for about 10 minutes, or until tender; mince the roasted garlic before adding to the mayonnaise.
- Mash ¼ cup of finely chopped roasted red pepper with the garlic puree for a sweet, pink garlic sauce.

lemon-ginger mayonnaise

makes ½ cup

Serve this full-flavored sauce with the Shrimp, Corn, and Ginger Pancakes on page 92, with sautéed or fried fish, or spread on a chicken, roast beef, or vegetable sandwich. It also makes an excellent dipping sauce for steamed artichokes or asparagus.

½ cup Homemade Mayonnaise (page 273) or store-bought
2 tablespoons minced fresh ginger

2 tablespoons fresh lemon or Meyer lemon juice (see page 262)
Freshly ground black pepper to taste

In a small bowl, mix the mayonnaise, ginger, lemon juice, and pepper. (The mayonnaise can be made 1 to 2 hours ahead of time; cover and refrigerate.)

tartar sauce

makes about 1 cup

A tart, pungent sauce that wakes up the flavors of fried fish, sautéed fish, chicken filets, or sandwiches.

1 cup Homemade Mayonnaise (page 273), or store-bought
2 scallions (white and green parts), very thinly sliced
3 tablespoons minced fresh parsley
3 tablespoons fresh lemon juice
3 tablespoons chopped gherkin or cornichon pickles

2 tablespoons caperberries, stemmed and coarsely chopped; or 3 tablespoons capers, drained
Salt and freshly ground black pepper to taste
Dash of hot pepper sauce

Put the mayonnaise in a serving bowl. Stir in the remaining ingredients, and taste for seasoning, adding more salt, pepper, hot pepper sauce, or lemon juice as needed.

cornmeal and white flour pizza dough

makes enough dough for two 12-inch pizzas

This is an excellent, versatile pizza dough with the added texture and flavor of cornmeal. The dough needs to rise for several hours, so plan your time accordingly.

1 envelope yeast (2½ teaspoons)

1 cup warm water

Pinch of sugar

½ cup coarse cornmeal

2 to 2½ tablespoons olive oil

3 cups all-purpose flour

1½ teaspoons kosher or sea salt

In a large bowl, mix the yeast with the water and sugar and let sit in a warm spot for 5 minutes, or until the yeast begins to bubble and foam. (The water used to dissolve the yeast should be neither cold nor boiling hot; it should feel warm to the touch.) If it doesn't foam, the yeast is probably dead and should be discarded. Start again with a new, fresh packet of yeast.

Add the cornmeal and 1½ tablespoons of the oil and stir well. Gradually sift the flour and salt into the mixture and stir until the dough forms a loose ball.

Working on a lightly floured surface, knead the dough until it feels soft and elastic, about 5 minutes. Shape the dough into a ball and place it in a large bowl. Drizzle the dough with about ½ to 1 tablespoon of the remaining oil and gently toss it around so the dough is coated with oil on all sides. Cover the bowl with a clean tea towel or plastic wrap and place in a warm, draft-free spot for about 2 hours. The dough should double in bulk. Punch down the risen dough and knead it again for just a few minutes. Reshape into a ball and return to the bowl. Cover and let rise another 40 minutes to an hour, or until the dough has risen again.

Punch down the dough and divide it in half. See pages 180 and 181 for rolling out and final baking directions.

vanilla sugar

makes 4 cups

Burying a vanilla bean inside a jar of sugar yields a vanilla-infused treat that comes in handy in a wide variety of dishes: Stir a teaspoon or two into a mug of cocoa, coffee, or tea; use it for sweetening and flavoring cakes, puddings, and pies; or simply sprinkle it over fresh berries.

About 4 cups sugar   **1 vanilla bean, cut in half lengthwise**

Pour the sugar into a jar and bury both halves of the vanilla bean in the sugar. Cover and let it work its magic. Replace the sugar as you use it. The vanilla bean should stay fresh and infuse the sugar for quite some time—at least a few months.

resources

The whole idea behind this book is to seek out local, seasonal, freshly harvested foods. However, there are times when we can't find seasonal foods in our neighborhood— soft-shell crabs, Fuyu persimmons, organic grapefruit or kumquats, organic pork, California olive oil, or just-harvested peaches and nectarines. When our local butcher, vegetable stand, fruit orchards, bakeries, or specialty food stores don't have what we need, we like to turn to these places— they are all committed to providing fresh, seasonally harvested food.

Stonewall Kitchen
Stonewall Lane
York, ME 03909
800-207-JAMS (5267) or 207-351-2713
www.stonewallkitchen.com

At Stonewall Kitchen we tap in to the best harvest products Maine and the country have to offer, with our award-winning sweet and savory jams, Maine Sea Salt, olive oil, vinegars, maple syrup, honey, salad dressings, barbecue sauces, cedar planks for barbecuing, baking kits, and much more.

produce

Diamond Organics
P.O. Box 2159
Freedom, CA 95019
888-ORGANIC (674-2642)
www.diamondorganics.com

Diamond Organics is a one-stop organic grocery, with everything from fresh figs, cranberries, and Green Zebra tomatoes to green and red lentils and dried beans. You'll also find top sirloin, strip, and rib eye steaks from Organic Valley, as well as organic butter and eggs.

Earthy Delights
1161 East Lark Road, Suite 260
DeWitt, MI 48820
800-367-4709 or 517-668-2402
www.earthy.com

Earthy Delights specializes in wild mushrooms and other wild spring foods, such as ramps and fiddlehead ferns. The morel season usually starts around April 1, and cultivated mushrooms, including Baby Blue Oyster, Trumpet Royale, Clamshell, enoki, and Cinnamon Cap, are available year-round.

Frog Hollow Farm
P.O. Box 872
Brentwood, CA 94513
888-779-4511
www.froghollow.com

Frog Hollow Farm sells Cal-Red peaches, Warren and Asian pears, nectarines, cherries, and apricots. All fruit is organically grown and tree-ripened.

Marché aux Delices
P.O. Box 1164
New York, NY 10028
888-547-5471
www.auxdelices.com

Since all of Marché aux Delices's mushrooms are wild, availability changes on a daily basis; the Internet is the best way to buy. Marché aux Delices offers porcini, chanterelle, morel, and hedgehog mushrooms, as well as seasonal produce such as ramps and fiddleheads.

Melissa's (World Variety Produce)
P.O. Box 21127
Los Angeles, CA 90021
800-588-0151
www.melissas.com

Named after its founder's daughter, Melissa's is the largest distributor of specialty produce in the country, selling everything from Washington's Rainier cherries and Shinseiki Asian pears to Californian Pixie tangerines and Italian Volcano oranges. Melissa's also sells mangos, nectarines, plums, and apricots.

Red Jacket Orchards
957 Canandaigua Road
Geneva, NY 14456
800-828-9410 or 315-781-2749
www.redjacketorchards.com

Red Jacket Orchards is well known for their tree-ripened apricots from the Finger Lakes region of upstate New York. Their summer harvest also includes sweet and sour cherries, strawberries, raspberries, and plums.

South Tex Organics
P.O. Box 172
Mission, TX 78573
888-895-0108
www.stxorganics.com

Owners Dennis and Lynda Holbrook say their organic Rio Star grapefruit are so popular, they can't keep up with the demand! They also have 100 percent USDA Certified Organic Texas Temptation and South Tex Special grapefruit, Natural Chico oranges, and Meyer lemons, all picked to order.

Starr Organic Produce
P.O. Box 551745
Fort Lauderdale, FL 33355
888-262-1242
www.starrorganic.com

Starr Organic Produce harvests Kent, Keitt, Tommy Atkins, and Hadin mangos in the summer, while winter brings Honey tangerines, Mineola tangelos, and temple and Valencia oranges, just to name a few. Avocados and papaya are also available in season.

Wood Prairie Farm
49 Kinney Road
Bridgewater, ME 04735
800-829-9765
www.woodprairie.com

Wood Prairie Farm grows an astounding selection of Certified Organic red, white, blue, and fingerling potatoes. You'll find more familiar varieties, such as Yukon gold, Butte, and All Blue potatoes, and some exotic varieties, such as Elba, Island Sunshine, and Cranberry Red. They also sell beets, heirloom carrots, parsnips, onions, shallots, and a small selection of seeds.

meat

Niman Ranch
1025 East 12th Street
Oakland, CA 94606
510-808-0330
www.nimanranch.com

Niman Ranch's pork, beef, and lamb are raised naturally under humane husbandry principles. No growth hormones are used. Beef tenderloin, short ribs, osso bucco, and more than a dozen cuts of steak are always shipped fresh, never frozen. Niman Ranch also sells racks and legs of lamb.

Sunnyside Farm Market
P.O. Box 478
Washington, VA 22747
540-675-3636
www.sunnysidefarmmarket.com

Sunnyside Farm raises 100 percent USDA Certified Organic Virginia Kobe beef. The farm breeds cows that are half Japanese Kobe and half American Angus with purebred Kobe bulls to achieve the flavor characteristics and tenderness that make Japanese Kobe beef world famous. Flank, skirt, sirloin, rib eye, and New York strip steaks are all available. They also sell organic eggs, berries, apples, cherries, peaches, and heirloom vegetables.

cheese

Formaggio Kitchen
244 Huron Avenue
Cambridge, MA 02138
888-212-3224 or 617-354-4750
www.formaggiokitchen.com

Ishan Gurdal built a cave in 1995 to age his own cheeses, and remains at the forefront of the cheese industry today. He always finds exceptionally interesting cheeses—try Mrs. Appleby's full, rich Cheshire from Shropshire, England; sharp, deeply veined Bleu Picon from Cantabria, Spain; or silky Epoisses de Bourgogne from Burgundy, France. Formaggio is an excellent source for good Italian Parmigiano-Reggiano.

fish

Browne Trading Company
Merrill's Wharf
269 Commercial Street
Portland, ME 04101
800-944-7848 or 207-766-2402
www.Browne-Trading.com

Browne Trading Company provides the nation's best restaurants with imported and American caviar, fresh fish and shellfish, and smoked fish. Their reputation for freshness and quality is exceptional.

Citarella
2135 Broadway
New York, NY 10023
212-874-0383, ext. 1
www.citarella.com

Citarella's reputation as one of the best markets in New York stems from its array of fresh fish and shellfish, purchased from New York's Fulton Fish Market and shipped straight to your door. Halibut, tuna, swordfish, and salmon steaks, as well as lobster, stone crab, soft-shell crab, oysters, and clams are all shipped overnight. Citarella also sells caviar and high-quality beef.

FinestKind Fish Market
855 U.S. Route 1
York, ME 03909
800-288-8154 or 207-363-5000
www.finestkindlobster.com

No fresh lobster in Nebraska? Owner Michael Goflin personally picks fresh fish and shellfish from each day's catch to send anywhere in the U.S. Day boat scallops, diver scallops (in season), steamers, mussels, halibut, salmon, cod, and sole are just a few of FinestKind's diverse offerings. FinestKind will ship complete clam bakes.

Linton's Seafood, Inc.
4500 Crisfield Highway
Crisfield, MD 21817
877-LINTONS (546-8667)
www.lintonsseafood.com

Linton's ships Chesapeake Bay soft-shell crabs from mid-April to mid-September each year. Depending on the season, fresh or frozen crabs come immaculately cleaned and ready to cook. Shrimp, clams, oysters, and scallops are also available year-round.

Moore's Stone Crab
800 Broadway Street
Longboat Key, FL 34228
888-968-CRAB (2722) or 941-383-1748
http://home.earthlink.net/~mooresrest/

Moore's Stone Crab has specialized in fresh stone crab since 1967. They ship fresh claws anywhere in the country between October 15 and May 15.

staples

DaVero Olive Oil
Toscana-Sonoma, Inc.
1195 Westside Road
Healdsburg, CA 95448

707-431-8000 or 877-7DA-VERO (732-8376)
www.davero.com

DaVero's artisanal Dry Creek Estate extra virgin olive oil comes from Tuscan olive trees that have been transplanted to Sonoma County, California. All of their olive oils, including a peppery Meyer lemon variety, add brightness and flavor as only fresh olive oil can do.

Dean & Deluca
Catalog Center
2526 East 36th Street North Circle
Wichita, KS 67219
800-221-7714
www.deandeluca.com

Dean & Deluca is a time-tested favorite for meats, smoked and cured fish, caviar, olive oils, vinegars, an amazing array of cheeses from around the world, imported Arborio rice for risotto, high-quality dried pastas, and sea salts from France, Italy, and Hawaii.

Deep Mountain Maple
P.O. Box 68
West Glover, VT 05875
802-525-4162
www.deepmountainmaple.com

Deep Mountain Maple has produced syrup in Vermont's Northeast Kingdom for almost twenty years. Deep Mountain is Certified Organic, and sells Fancy, Grade A Medium Amber, Grade A Dark Amber, and Grade B syrups. For true maple syrup lovers, Deep Mountain sells a thirty-gallon drum!

Grain & Salt Society
273 Fairway Drive
Asheville, NC 28805
800-867-7258
www.celtic-seasalt.com

The Grain & Salt Society sells hand-harvested Celtic Sea Salt from France. Their catalog also includes organic grains (including basmati rice and rolled oats); organic dried lentils; garbanzo, pinto, and navy beans; and rice and soba noodles.

Penzeys Spices
P.O. Box 924
Brookfield, WI 53008
800-741-7787
www.penzeys.com

Penzeys' spice collection includes a large variety of black and white peppercorns, saffron, and dried herbs, plus baking necessities such as cinnamon, cardamom, vanilla, and crystallized ginger.

Willow Creek Olive Ranch
8530 Vineyard Drive
Paso Robles, CA 93446
805-227-0186
www.willowcreekoliveranch.com

Willow Creek's extra virgin olive oil is sold under the name Pasolivo. A blend of olives are pressed onsite within twenty-four hours of being hand picked. Each year's olive oil has a unique taste, but Pasolivo typically has a deep green color and peppery flavor. The oil is unfiltered.

tools

Sur La Table
1765 Sixth Avenue South
Seattle, WA 98134-1608
800-243-0852
www.surlatable.com

Sur La Table's catalog is a great resource for appliances and kitchen goods. Their stock includes cedar planks, standing mixers, and Microplane graters.

plant seeds

Johnny's Selected Seeds
955 Benton Avenue
Winslow, ME 04901-2601
207-861-3901
www.johnnyseeds.com

Johnny's has been our most trusted Maine seed source for the past twenty-five years. Their variety of herbs and vegetables, both heirloom and organic seeds, is impressive. With Jersey Knight asparagus, Mirage shallots, Zefa Fino fennel, four watercress varieties, and six leek varieties, Johnny's is a great starting point for a unique kitchen garden.

Miller Nurseries
5060 West Lake Road
Canandaigua, NY 14424-8904
800-836-9630
www.millernurseries.com

Miller Nurseries specializes in fruit and nut trees, grape vines, and berry plants. Apple, cherry, peach, pear, plum, and nectarine tree stock are shipped to you at the beginning of each growing season. In addition to blackberries, strawberries, and raspberries, Miller grows cranberry, gooseberry, elderberry, and currant plants.

Seed Savers Exchange
3076 North Winn Road
Decorah, Iowa 52101
563-382-5990
www.seedsavers.org

SSE is a member-driven nonprofit company that encourages the planting and harvesting of heirloom vegetables, fruits, and grains. Shopping through their catalog is an adventure—you'll find twelve varieties of organic garlic; Burpee's Golden, Chiogga, and Cylindra beets; and heirloom tomatoes of every color (Brandywine, Beam's Yellow Pear, Aunt Ruby's German Green, Crnkovic Yugoslavian Pink, Cherokee Purple, and Black Krim are just a few).

Seeds of Change
P.O. Box 15700
Santa Fe, NM 87592-1500
888-762-7333
www.seedsofchange.com

Seeds of Change offers 100 percent USDA Certified Organic seeds, including greens such as sorrel, mizuna mustard, arugula, radicchio, and endive. The catalog has an entire page of organic basil seeds! They also offer an online discount.

ethnic

Oriental Pantry
423 Great Road (Route 2A)
Acton, MA 01720
978-264-4576
www.orientalpantry.com

Oriental Pantry's online collection of Asian goods rivals that of any well-stocked Chinatown grocer. You'll find staples such as sesame oil, rice vinegar, soy sauce, shoyu, and hot Chinese chile oil, in addition to bean thread noodles, rice sticks, and panko breadcrumbs. They also carry equipment like bamboo dumpling steamers.

bibliography

Charles, Rebecca. *Lobster Rolls & Blueberry Pie*. New York: HarperCollins, 2003.

Davidson, Alan. *Fruit*. New York: Simon & Schuster, 1991.

Finamore, Roy, with Molly Stevens. *One Potato Two Potato*. New York: Houghton Mifflin, 2001.

Forley, Diane. *The Anatomy of a Dish*. New York: Artisan, 2002.

Gunst, Kathy. *Roasting*. New York: Macmillan, 1995.

Gunst, Kathy, and Robert Cornfield. *Lundy's*. New York: HarperCollins, 1998.

Hazan, Marcella. *Classic Italian Cookbook*. New York: Alfred A. Knopf, 1978.

Hesser, Amanda. *The Cook and the Gardener*. New York: W.W. Norton, 1999.

Krasner, Deborah. *The Flavors of Olive Oil*. New York: Simon & Schuster, 2002.

Leibenstein, Margaret. *The Edible Mushroom*. New York: Ballantine Books, 1986.

Malgieri, Nick. *Perfect Cakes*. New York: HarperCollins, 2002.

Mariani, John. *The Dictionary of American Food and Drink*. New York: Ticknor & Fields, 1983.

Marshall, Lydie. *A Passion for Potatoes*. New York: HarperCollins, 1992.

Raichlen, Steven. *A Celebration of the Seasons*. New York: Poseidon Press, 1988.

Rodgers, Judy. *The Zuni Café Cookbook*. New York: W.W. Norton and Co., 2002.

Schneider, Elizabeth. *Uncommon Fruits & Vegetables*. New York: Harper & Row, 1986.

Schneider, Sally. *A New Way to Cook*. New York: Artisan, 2001.

Seymour, Miranda. *A Brief History of Thyme and Other Herbs*. New York: Grove Press, 2002.

Wells, Patricia. *At Home in Provence*. New York: Scribners, 1996.

Wolke, Robert. *What Einstein Told His Cook*. New York: W.W. Norton, 2002.

index